CASE STUDIES IN REGULATION
Revolution and Reform

CASE STUDIES IN REGULATION
Revolution and Reform

Editors

Leonard W. Weiss
University of Wisconsin, Madison

Michael W. Klass
Glassman-Oliver
Economic Consultants, Inc.

Little, Brown and Company
Boston   Toronto

Library of Congress Catalog Card No. 80–85350

ISBN 0–316–928933

9 8 7 6 5 4 3 2

ALP

Published simultaneously in Canada
by Little, Brown & Company (Canada) Limited

Printed in the United States of America

Preface

This book grows out of a study conducted for the Senate Governmental Affairs Committee in 1976 and 1977. We went to Washington that summer with the hope and expectation that something would come out of our efforts — that we would play a role in the regulatory reform movement then under way. We left a year later convinced that nothing much would happen.

Our effort did produce two volumes on regulation (Senate Committee on Governmental Affairs, *Study on Regulation,* Vol. VI, *Framework for Regulation* and *Appendix to Volume VI,* 1978). The second of these contained a series of case studies in federal regulation done mainly by the authors of the studies in this book.

All of them were, and are, leaders in their respective fields. Their studies were excellent. But they were published a year too late — many of the reforms had been made by the time the book came out — and the volume was soon out of print.

By then it was clear that something had happened after all. The revolution that occurred in federal regulation between 1977 and 1980 received surprisingly little general attention. We are convinced that it was of major importance. The present volume is meant to evaluate past regulation in the affected fields and to describe and analyze the reforms that finally occurred.

This book is ideally suited for use in courses on regulation, industrial organization, government and business, or public control of business. One of the editors used it successfully in an introductory survey course. The papers are shorter than those in the original study, and they are, of course, updated to cover the regulatory changes that took place between 1978 and 1980. They are written at a level accessible to an intelligent lay person. We hope they will help to keep alive the movement of the last few years.

Leonard W. Weiss
Michael W. Klass

Contents

CASE STUDIES IN REGULATION
Revolution and Reform

Introduction: The Regulatory Reform Movement

Leonard W. Weiss
University of Wisconsin, Madison

This book has as its topic a remarkable series of events that occurred in the United States during the 1970s and that appeared to reach a climax in 1978–1980. The subject, of course, was regulation. The change came to be known as the "regulatory reform" movement and there were many participants: businessmen who found themselves pestered with a flood of reports to file, businessmen who felt that regulations were raising their costs of production or weakening their competitive positions, economists who thought that regulation often reduced competition and increased costs, and political scientists and lawyers who thought that the regulatory agencies were often captured by those they were meant to regulate.

Three successive presidents — Nixon, Ford, and Carter — took active roles in the regulatory reform movement, each sending numerous proposed bills on the topic to Congress. After 1973 regulatory reform became one of the few policies that they felt confident would slow inflation. Regulatory reform also seemed consistent with their emphasis on competitive free enterprise and smaller government, two other goals that were very hard to attain in most areas of government policy. In the mid-1970s, despite the wide range of support for the movement, regulatory reform seemed a forlorn hope, but by the end of the decade quite a lot had been accomplished.

1

THE SCOPE OF REGULATION

Table 1 lists the major regulatory agencies and their dates of establishment, jurisdictions, and 1980 budgets. They are broken into two groups. The first comprises those agencies devoted to "economic regulation." They almost always control entry into the regulated field, and they commonly control prices and service as well. The second category includes those agencies devoted to "environmental, safety, and health regulation" — what is often referred to as the "new regulation" (though some of it goes back to 1906) because it grew rapidly in the 1960s and 1970s. One can see by their budgets that the new regulation involves a much greater administrative effort than the traditional economic regulation. The EPA alone spends almost as much on administration as *all* the federal economic regulatory agencies put together. There is some logic to this. Economic regulation deals with small segments of the economy, such as railroads and trucks, but the EPA regulates all industries.

THE ECONOMISTS AND REGULATORY REFORM

Some economists became leading actors as the regulatory reform drama unfolded. A well-known economist (and an enthusiastic performer of Gilbert and Sullivan), A. E. Kahn of Cornell University wrote a classic study of regulation in 1971. Then, as chairman of the New York Public Service Commission, he led in applying economic principles to state regulation. Next, as Carter's chairman of the CAB, he worked a revolution in the airlines. Finally, as the nation's chief "inflation fighter," he was the power behind the scenes in reforming regulation in many fields.

Or consider Darius Gaskins, a professor from the University of California. Gaskins went to the Department of Interior to run a study that finally led to the prohibition of joint ventures among the largest oil companies in bidding for offshore oil leases. He next became the director of the Bureau of Economics at the Federal Trade Commission. Kahn brought him to the Civil Aeronautics Board to head the agency's Office of Economic Analysis during 1977 and 1978. Next came a brief stay at the Department of Energy. At the start of 1980 he became Chairman of the Interstate Commerce Commission, where he has led a systematic effort to lessen the limitations on competition in trucking and railroad traffic. By now this energetic economist-regulator has become a man to watch as the regulatory reform movement proceeds.

Many other economists played important roles in regulatory reform, though few of them can match Kahn's and Gaskins's spectacular trips through the Washington bureaucracies.

The first course in public utilities came with the first modern public utility commission — both in Wisconsin in 1907. Like the Wisconsin Public Service Commission, the course was widely copied and became a standard part of many university offerings in the 1920s and 1930s. Most of the literature produced in the field was aimed at better regulation; it especially criticized judicial restrictions on the regulators. Few scholars in the field seriously contemplated deregulation of any of the conventionally regulated industries. The major exception was in the area of trucking. Within a year of the legislation assigning responsibility for interstate motor carriers to the ICC, economists were in print criticizing the move for its clearly anticompetitive effects in an inherently competitive industry.

Most of the economic criticism of regulation, however, developed after World War II. Criticism of the anticompetitive characteristics of ICC regulation of freight carriage was widespread in the postwar period. The critics claimed that the main effects of ICC regulation were to prevent price competition among carriers, to shift freight to high-cost carriers, to impose high costs on the railroads by resisting abandonment of uneconomical branch lines, and to discourage cost-saving innovations. By the late 1970s the bulk of American economists had come to the conclusion that ICC regulation was oriented toward protection of the carriers and that, far from reducing costs to shippers, it almost certainly increased them by perhaps billions of dollars a year.

The postwar years also saw the development of an equally large literature criticizing the CAB's policies toward airlines. Its complete prohibition of entry of new trunk airlines from 1938 to 1978 despite a several-thousand-percent increase of traffic was widely attacked. The intrastate airlines in California and Texas that had much lower fares than airlines subject to CAB regulation were studied and publicized. And the tendency for higher fares to result in more departures on competitive routes and hence to a great deal of excess capacity was analyzed and became a part of most discussions of the airlines.

The FCC's regulation of broadcasting and especially of cable TV was widely criticized. Economists have argued that by assigning too small a band to VHF (very high frequency) TV and by emphasizing localism in allocating frequencies, the agency left us with room for only three viable commercial networks. Moreover, they argue that by restricting importation of distant signals by cable companies the FCC slowed the spread of cable in larger markets and, again, left viewers with a great deal less choice than they might have had otherwise. For instance, in Japan most viewers have access to four commercial networks and two public networks.

Table 1. The Major Regulatory Agencies, Their Jurisdictions, and Their 1980 Budgets

Agency	Date Established	Jurisdiction	1980 Budget (Millions of Dollars)[a]
ECONOMIC REGULATION			
Interstate Commerce Commission (ICC)	1887	Interstate railroads (1887) Interstate trucks (1935) Interstate water carriers (1940) Interstate telephone (1910–1934) Interstate oil pipelines (1906–1977)	80.0
State Regulatory Commissions	35 states 1907–1920; 50 states by 1973	Local electricity (46 states in 1973) Local gas (47 states in 1973) Local telephone (48 states in 1973)	148.0 [b]
Federal Communications Commission (FCC)	1934	Interstate telephone (1934)[c] Broadcasting (1934)[d] Cable television (1968)	77.2
Federal Power Commission (FPC) and Federal Energy Regulatory Commission (FERC)	1935 ⎫ 1977 ⎬	Interstate wholesale electricity (1935) Interstate natural gas pipelines (1938) Field price of natural gas sold in interstate commerce (1954) Oil pipelines (1977) Intrastate gas and gas pipelines (1978)	72.3
Civil Aeronautics Board (CAB)	1938	Interstate airlines (1938)[e]	29.7
Federal Maritime Commission (FMC)	1936	Ocean shipping (1936)[f]	11.7
Federal Energy Administration (FEA) Changed to Economic Regulatory Administration (ERA)	1973 ⎫ 1977 ⎬	Petroleum prices and allocations (1973)	155.4

Agency	Date Established	Jurisdiction	1980 Budget (Millions of Dollars)[a]
ENVIRONMENTAL, SAFETY, AND HEALTH REGULATION			
Food and Drug Administration (FDA)	1906	Safety of food, drugs (1906), and cosmetics (1938), effectiveness of drugs (1962)	324.2
Animal and Plant Health Inspection Service	1907	Meat and poultry packing plants (1907)	258.6
Federal Trade Commission (FTC)	1914	False and misleading advertising (mainly after 1938)	31.0 [g]
Securities and Exchange Commission (SEC)	1934	Public security issues and security exchanges (1934) Public utility holding companies (1935)	72.9
CAB	1938	Airline safety (1938) (flight standards program only)	227.9
Federal Aviation Administration (FAA)	1958		
Atomic Energy Commission (AEC)	1947 ⎫	Licensing of nuclear power plants (1947)	368.2
Nuclear Regulatory Commission (NRC)	1975 ⎭		
National Highway Traffic Safety Administration (NHTSA, pronounced Neetsa)	1970	Automobile safety (1970), automobile fuel economy (1975)[h]	58.9
Environmental Protection Agency (EPA)	1963–1972 [i]	Air, water, and noise pollution[j]	420.0
Occupational Safety and Health Administration (OSHA)	1971	Industrial safety and health (1971)	187.2
Mine Enforcement Safety Administration (MESA)	1973 ⎫	Safety and health in mining, especially coal mines (1973)	144.1
Mine Safety and Health Administration	1978 ⎭		
Consumer Product Safety Commission	1972	Safety of consumer products (1972)	40.2

Table sources and notes at foot of next page.

With respect to natural gas, many economists claimed that by limiting price increases on old gas (gas developed and committed to interstate commerce before a specified date), the FPC and the FERC after it have maintained retail gas prices far below marginal costs and given the consumers inadequate incentive to conserve. Moreover, even the prices of new gas (gas not previously committed to interstate commerce) were kept below equilibrium levels, though the prices of successive periods of new gas were raised regularly. In view of the costs of other fuels during the 1970s, this policy offered too little incentive to explore and provided strong incentives to withhold newly discovered gas in anticipation of higher prices later.

The American oil price controls after 1973 and especially after 1975 were criticized for similar reasons. Again, oil was priced in several tiers with much of it kept below world prices. These various prices were converted into oil-product prices by means of an extremely complicated procedure that lent itself to errors and fraud. Retail prices were below world levels, thereby encouraging high levels of consumption. Newly developed domestic oil yielded producers less than imported oil was bringing. Many economists felt that government price policies were encouraging the country's rapid shift to imported oil.

The Securities and Exchange Commission did not regulate prices itself, but it did permit the security exchanges to fix brokers' fees. In the 1970s this practice became the subject of extensive study by academic and government specialists in finance. They generally found little justification for stock market fixing of brokerage fees.

In spite of the increasing concern about the costly and anticompetitive effects of regulation, we increased the scope of regulation greatly during the 1970s. Most of this increase occurred in environmental, safety, and health regulation areas (though our tortuous oil regulation began in 1973 as well). In this book, the Environmental Protection Agency and the Occupational Safety and Health Administration rep-

---

Sources: The Budget of the United States, 1981, and FPC, *Federal and State Commission Jurisdiction and Regulation of Electric, Gas and Telephone Utilities, 1973.*

a Excludes subsidies, research and training programs.

b Based on 1971 budgets (total of $78.9 million) multiplied by 1.874 to allow for inflation based on average gross weekly earnings for all private, nonagricultural employees. This assumes no growth in state commissions' staffs 1971–1980.

c Regulated by ICC from 1910.

d Regulated by Federal Radio Commission from 1927.

e Partially regulated by the ICC and the Post Office from 1934.

f Partially regulated from 1916.

g Consumer protection only. Excludes antitrust.

h Excludes grants and research.

i Various environmental laws were enforced by several agencies 1963–1972. Combined into EPA in 1972.

j Excludes grants.

resent such areas of increasing regulation. The new agencies, especially EPA and OSHA, are widely criticized for imposing costly rules that bring about few if any benefits. Running EPA is very expensive in itself, but the costs to industries and municipalities of complying with EPA orders have been estimated to be in the billions of dollars per year. OSHA has a smaller budget, but its impact on industrial costs is not small, and benefits have been hard to identify. It seems unlikely that agencies such as EPA and OSHA will go away soon, but many economists feel that those agencies' procedures and rules could be greatly improved.

Finally, straightforward prices and rate-of-return regulation of the type applied to local electric, gas, and telephone utilities by state commissions have been the subject of a great deal of study since World War II. Much of this study was quite abstract, and most of it was economists talking to economists. They "solved" quite a few theoretical problems of regulation, but the solutions seldom got to the commissions.

Then came the Arab oil embargo, which led to rapidly rising electric and gas prices, and the public suddenly became very interested in utility regulation. To make matters worse, the cost of new plant and equipment for the electric utilities soared after having fallen or remained fairly stable in the 1950s and 1960s. The economists proposed a solution — to base utility rates on marginal costs — and this time a lot of the utilities and state commissions listened.

REGULATORY REFORM
IN PRACTICE

Altogether, regulation became a hot topic among economists after World War II. For quite a while their impact on regulatory practice seemed slight, but in the late 1970s their criticisms began to have an effect.

One of the first changes took place on the stock market. After careful study both Congress and the SEC took steps to prevent the exchanges from fixing brokerage fees. The SEC ordered an end to the practice as of May 1, 1975. There were substantial changes in fees and some change in the structure and practices of the brokerage industry, but the disaster that the industry predicted did not occur.

The next major change came in the airline industry. In 1975 Senator Kennedy held extensive hearings on the CAB, publicizing the many criticisms that had been aimed at it. Early in the 96th Congress (January 1977) a bill was introduced that would generally deregulate airlines over a period of several years. Most of the airlines opposed it vigorously.

At the same time, however, two well-known economists were appointed to the CAB — A. E. Kahn (as chairman) and E. E. Bailey. Under Kahn's leadership the airlines were given much more freedom in pricing and much easier access to routes they had not previously served. The results were spectacular. Fares for tourists fell drastically (though fares for business travel did not). The planes filled up, and airline profits soared. By the time the Cannon-Kennedy bill came to a vote in the autumn of 1978 hardly anyone was opposed to it, and the bill passed with large majorities.

In the case of cable TV, regulatory reform may come entirely from the inside. In July 1980 the FCC issued an order eliminating most of its regulation of cable TV, though aspects of the industry are still regulated at the state or local levels.

The toughest nut to crack was surface freight transportation. Regulatory reform came harder there because the carriers were less likely to improve their profitability the way the airlines did. However, on January 1, 1980, Darius Gaskins became chairman of the ICC and a second economist (M. Alexis) became one of its six members. By mid-1980 it seemed certain that major reform would come from inside the commission. Apparently the trucking industry became convinced that it would receive better treatment from Congress than from the ICC; in any event, a new trucking bill sailed through Congress and became law in June 1980. The legislation did not end truck regulation, but it left individual truckers with much more freedom in pricing, made entry much easier, and eliminated a number of costly restrictions the ICC had imposed.

The regulation of gas and oil were two of the leading issues before the 95th Congress (1977–1978) and, in the case of oil, of the 96th Congress (1979–1980) as well. The gas legislation in 1978 resulted in the transfer of regulatory responsibility from the FPC to the FERC, regulation of intrastate as well as interstate gas production by the FERC, and complete deregulation of *new* gas as of 1985.

The Carter administration proposed that oil prices be allowed to rise to levels that reflected world oil prices to encourage conservation but that taxes be imposed on oil that had been selling at less than world levels to eliminate the "windfall profit" that would otherwise accrue. From 1976 to 1980 Congress and the President wrangled about taxes on oil producers. In April 1980 Congress finally passed a set of "windfall profits taxes" designed to capture for the government some, but not all, of the gains from higher crude oil prices. The President released so much oil per month from controls aiming to decontrol all oil by October 1, 1981. When Reagan became President he ended all oil controls, but only 15% of our oil was still controlled by then.

The "new regulation" by such agencies as the EPA and OSHA concerning the environment, safety, and health was clearly not likely to go the way of airline regulation. In fact during the 1970s Congress strengthened regulation in these areas. Few scholars advocated deregulation in these fields, but many advocated that in evaluating new regulations more weight be given to costs.

Even here, however, there was some movement toward more economic regulation. The EPA has adopted a policy whereby firms in areas with high pollution levels (such as Los Angeles) can install new plant and equipment that might create more pollution if they produce greater reductions elsewhere within the area. For instance, a firm planning to build an oil terminal can do so if it can find ways to reduce pollution from laundries and street paving by more than the new pollution the terminal will cause. This means that polluters clean up where it is easiest to do so, a result that is economically preferable to the situation where EPA orders a particular type of cleanup in an industry regardless of how costly it is or how readily available cheaper alternative cleanup possibilities might be.

There has been some movement at OSHA, too. The agency has de-emphasized its pettifogging, accident-oriented equipment standards (for instance, elaborate rules that specify the material and design specifications for ladders), where workers' compensation already covered those injured and, for large firms, imposed insurance charges that reflected their accident experience. OSHA has shifted emphasis to serious accident records, regardless of equipment specifications, and to industrial diseases where workers' compensation generally does not apply. For instance, byssinosis is a disease that affects a quarter of the workers in cotton (but not synthetic) textile mills, leaving them wheezing for the rest of their lives. We have known about the origins of this disease since the beginning of the industrial revolution, but OSHA had not done anything about it until recently.

In addition, administrative agencies answerable to the president (including both EPA and OSHA) have been required since 1976 to prepare and consider in their decisions "Inflation Impact Statements" (under Ford) or "Economic Impact Statements" (under Carter) that estimated costs and benefits of particular orders. At this writing, Congress is considering new legislation that would require such statements from the independent agencies that report to Congress (such as the ICC and the FCC). Many of these statements have been perfunctory, but OSHA took them quite seriously. For instance, OSHA's proposed cotton/dust standard was estimated to cost about $200,000 per case of byssinosis avoided. You can judge for yourself whether preventing something like asthma (but seldom early death) for about a quarter of the cotton textile workers is worth that much. Properly done, these studies would require the regulatory agencies to evaluate their standards in terms of costs and benefits.

Other sorts of safety and health regulation that will not be covered in this book deserve some comment. The National Highway Traffic Safety Administration's early rules apparently did reduce auto deaths significantly, assuming that the lower death rates on later-model cars are ascribable to safety devices. The Consumer Product Safety Commission claims responsibility for a greatly reduced rate of child overdoses on drugs owing to those infernal new drug bottle tops. The Food and Drug Administration has certainly saved lives and prevented tragic personal disabilities at least by keeping thalidomide off the American market. On the other hand, its requirement since 1962 that new drugs be effective as well as safe has been accompanied by a sharp drop in the number of "new chemical entities" (wholly new drugs) introduced each year. To some extent the decline may simply mean that many of the new drugs introduced earlier were ineffective, but it is probably also partially due to the greater risk and delay in introducing new drugs under the new rules.

Finally, in the late 1970s another sort of regulatory reform was under way in the field of utility rates. Although there was virtually no chance that deregulation was in the offing, by 1980 eight states, with a third of the nation's population, were basing rates explicitly on estimates of marginal costs. It seems likely that these estimates often missed the mark, but several improvements in ratemaking did result. First, marginal costs were generally based on current rather than past costs, so consumers got more accurate signals about what costs their consumption imposed on society today. Second, practically all the new rates were higher at peak periods than at off-peak periods, which meant that, because of the resulting slower growth in peak-period demand, the utilities had to build fewer plants. Finally, some states eliminated or greatly reduced the declining block rates that existed down to the mid-1970s. All three changes probably led consumers to make more economic decisions about their consumption of electricity.

THE REST OF THIS BOOK

Altogether, the late 1970s were an important time for the field of regulation. This book will report on nine cases of regulatory reform that took place during this period. These cases do not by any means exhaust the subject, but they are among the most important. Although many of the results of these reforms will not be seen until the 1980s, a few payoffs are visible already, especially in the cases of competitive brokerage rates and unregulated airlines. It should be interesting to follow performance in the 1980s, when many of the regulatory reforms will be in place.

The rest of this book will be devoted to economists' comments on regulation in nine sectors and to what actually happened. In Case 1 Hans Stoll explores the effects of competitive brokerage rates ordered by the SEC. In Case 2 Theodore Keeler tells the remarkable story of airline deregulation. In Case 3 Bruce Owen discusses what economists said about FCC regulation of cable TV and what the FCC did about it. In Case 4 Ann Friedlaender summarizes what we know about freight regulation and what has been done about it so far. Case 5 contains Ronald Braeutigam's analysis of public policy toward natural gas and the probable effects of the new legislation in that field. In Case 6 David Montgomery discusses these same problems as they apply to oil regulation. Cases 7 and 8 are devoted to two of the most important agencies involved in the "new regulation." In Case 7 Albert Nichols and Richard Zeckhauser discuss OSHA, and in Case 8 Larry Ruff analyzes the EPA. Finally, in Case 9 Leonard Weiss explores marginal-cost pricing for utilities at the state level.

CASE 1

Revolution in the Regulation of Securities Markets: An Examination of the Effects of Increased Competition

Hans R. Stoll
Vanderbilt University

INTRODUCTION

Since passage of the Securities Act of 1933, regulation of securities markets has been concerned primarily with providing for full disclosure and eliminating fraud and manipulation in order that securities prices resulting from the free interplay of market forces may as nearly as possible reflect fundamental values. The primary means employed to assure this objective have been the new-issue prospectus and continuing reporting requirements of corporations and direct regulation against fraud and manipulation.

For many years, under the principle of self-regulation, relatively less attention was paid to the internal workings of stock exchanges and the efficiency with which brokers and dealers provided transactions ser-

Copyright © 1981 by Hans R. Stoll. This paper is based on a study prepared for the United States Senate Committee on Governmental Affairs as part of its study of federal regulation. An updated version of that study appears in monograph 1979-2 of NYU's *Monograph Series in Finance and Economics*. The helpful comments of Donald Farrar and Leonard Weiss at various stages of the study are greatly appreciated.

vices. The public pays for transactions services in two ways. First, the broker, who acts as an agent, is compensated by a commission for the services of communicating with other traders and executing, clearing, and recording the transaction. Second, when another investor cannot be found for the other side of a transaction, a dealer is compensated by the bid-ask spread for the service of acting as a principal. This study is concerned with the brokerage function.

Under long-standing New York Stock Exchange practice, unchanged by federal regulation until May 1, 1975, commissions for brokerage services were fixed above the competitive level, and membership on the Exchange was limited to a fixed number of "seats." Fixed commission rates were justified by market-failure arguments and arguments based on equity considerations. Without fixed commission rates, it was alleged, continuing economies of scale and a fixed-to-variable-cost ratio conducive to "destructive competition" would lead to monopolization of the industry or its domination by a few large brokerage firms. Small and regional firms, not necessarily the least efficient, would fail, and the industry's capital and therefore its capacity to serve the public would be impaired. Markets would also fail because all costs and benefits could not be internalized. NYSE members, unwilling to bear the costs of running the exchange without receiving high fixed commissions, would leave the Exchange; this would fragment markets and reduce liquidity. Research would decline because the cost of producing it would not be recaptured under competitive rates; the first recipient could resell the research at less than costs of production. Competitive rates were said to be undesirable on equity grounds because they would lead to discrimination against the small investor, who would not have the bargaining power of institutional investors.

The arguments against fixed commission rates are the arguments against cartel pricing of any service: competition would lead to lower prices and a higher level of output. Competitive rates would eliminate roundabout and costly procedures for rebating commissions and would reduce the production of unrelated services that not all investors desire. Potential conflicts of interest that arise in the provision of some services to institutional investors would be lessened. Market fragmentation would not result; instead, investors would have a greater incentive under lower competitive rates to channel transactions to the NYSE. Finally, competition would eliminate inefficiency and lead to greater innovation in the provision of brokerage services.

On the basis of extensive hearings and studies conducted between 1968 and 1975, the Securities and Exchange Commission and committees of the House and Senate reached the conclusion that the evidence did not support the argument for fixed commission rates. On May 1, 1975, fixed rates of commission were abolished.

Empirical investigations of the arguments for and against competitive rates and the experience since the introduction of competitive rates indicate, almost without exception, that competitive rates have been beneficial to consumers · without resulting in the harmful and disruptive effects anticipated by the opponents of competitive rates.

According to the Securities and Exchange Commission, commission rates have declined an average of about 15 percent under competition, which is equivalent to an annual saving for consumers of about $400 million. Commissions have declined much more on transactions of institutional investors and hardly at all on transactions of individuals. However, both institutions and individuals have the opportunity to pay commissions lower than the average when fewer services are required, an opportunity not available under fixed rates. There is no evidence that discrimination against small investors has occurred.

Reduced commissions have been made possible in part through the elimination of brokerage firm monopoly profits (a fact reflected in much lower NYSE seat prices); in part through the elimination of unnecessary services, particularly to institutional investors; and in part through the expanded volume of trading that has somewhat offset the reduced revenue per transaction. Brokerage firms specializing in institutional customers were hardest hit, suffering revenue declines of over 30 percent, but even these firms have been able to adjust quickly by finding new customers and new lines of business, by reducing costs, or by merging with other firms.

The fear that one firm would dominate the industry and that, in particular, small and regional firms would be driven out of business as a result of competitive rates has not been realized. Although there has been an increase in the share of commission revenue going to the very largest firms, this is a longer-term trend not affected by the introduction of competitive rates. In fact the trend has been less pronounced since the introduction of competitive rates. The trend appears to reflect some economies for national full-line brokerage firms and the use of mergers to bail out failing firms. The evidence on the firms leaving the NYSE in 1975 through 1977 indicates that both large and small firms failed; the growth in market share of the very largest cannot be said to be at the expense of the smallest firms. Furthermore, the cost structure of the industry does not exhibit the high level of fixed costs usually associated with destructive competition that might lead to domination by one firm. Except for occupancy and equipment costs, brokerage costs are quite variable, and this fact has helped the industry to adapt so well to competitive rates. There is also no indication that large firms cut commission rates more than small firms in an attempt to drive small firms out of business. In fact, it appears that the innovators in discount commissions for individual investors have been small brokerage firms.

Markets have not become fragmented as a result of competitive rates. The trend is to more rather than less trading on the NYSE. Use of commission dollars to buy research has apparently declined, although one cannot say that the amount of research produced has declined. It does seem clear that fixed commissions are not necessary for effective compensation of those who produce research. Finally, measures of the liquidity afforded large-block transactions and more general measures of market quality do not indicate any deterioration since the introduction of competitive rates.

While the issue of competitive brokerage commissions has been satisfactorily resolved, a key remaining issue for the securities markets is the structure of the computerized national market system and the ease of access to it. Currently, access to trading on the floor of the NYSE is limited to members. This benefits floor members such as specialists (dealers) because they have privileged access to the flow of orders. Whether the SEC will promote a system that permits effective competition from dealers outside the NYSE has yet to be determined.

The successful introduction of competitive pricing of brokerage services has been accomplished without the "destructive competition" and other harmful effects predicted by the brokerage industry. In view of the fact that similar harmful effects are predicted in other industries where competitive pricing is proposed, the successful transition to competition in the brokerage industry serves as a useful example and guidepost.

BACKGROUND

Functions of Securities Markets and Criteria of Efficiency

The function of securities markets is to allocate new funds to those industries and firms that can most effectively use them and to provide liquidity to investors who wish to make portfolio adjustments. The market is said to be allocationally efficient and fair if information available to investors is as correct and complete as it can be and if prices of securities quickly and accurately reflect that information.[1] In an allocationally efficient market, investors are assured of achieving liquidity at prices that reflect underlying values, and corporations who most need funds have the best chance of getting additional funds.*

---

* The price of its stock will affect the ease with which the corporation can sell a new issue, but it will also affect less direct sources of financing, such as the ability to get a bank loan or the decision to retain earnings.

Public policy ought, therefore, to be concerned with assuring that information is complete, accurate, and timely and that there is an absence of manipulation or fraud that might distort prices. One important aspect of SEC regulation of securities markets has been to require corporate disclosure through the new-issue prospectus and periodic reports, and to forbid activities that are fraudulent or would cause prices to be manipulated. Whether these regulatory requirements produce an allocationally more efficient market than would exist otherwise has only recently come under scrutiny, and the verdict is not unanimous.[2]

However, issues of allocational efficiency are not the main purpose of this study, and the reader is referred to the cited works. The main concerns here have to do with operational or transactions efficiency of the securities markets.

Operational efficiency is concerned with the prices of the services of the securities industry brokers and dealers who facilitate trading and not with the underlying prices of the securities that are being traded. Since the net price of a security to the buyer or seller depends on commissions and other charges he must pay, operational efficiency, of course, also affects allocational efficiency. In other words, information may be complete, accurate, and timely, yet investors can achieve liquidity only at unfair prices because commission costs are too high; or corporations may choose not to seek additional funds because underwriting spreads are too high.

Three services of the securities industry may be distinguished: (1) communication and execution, (2) clearing and record keeping, and (3) market making. There must be a mechanism by which investors who desire to trade find each other and establish mutually satisfactory prices. This is accomplished through the services of a broker, who is an agent, and by the use of various communications devices ranging from face-to-face communication on the floor of an exchange, to telephones, to sophisticated computer communications systems. After a transaction has been agreed upon, title and money must change hands and various records of the transaction must be established. This service is performed (generally by the broker) with varying degrees of sophistication ranging from physical transfer of certificates of ownership to transfer via book entries in a computer. Since investors are not always able (through brokers) to find other investors with whom to trade, the services of a market maker or dealer, who stands ready to buy or sell for his own account as a principal, may be required. The dealer must be compensated for his costs, which include the risk associated with keeping inventories of securities.

The broker is compensated by a commission. The market is operationally efficient if that commission corresponds to the least-cost basis for providing the services. The principal concern of this study is to assess the arguments for and against the desirability of fixing these commission charges and to examine the effects of their competitive determination. The dealer is compensated by buying at the bid price and selling at the ask price.

Markets Today

An exchange market is a physical location where trading takes place. The principal exchanges in the United States are the New York Stock Exchange (NYSE), the American Stock Exchange (AMSE), and the regional stock exchanges (PBW, Midwest, Pacific, Boston, Cincinnati). The NYSE accounts for the large bulk of trading in common stocks. Before the summer of 1976 the NYSE and AMSE listed different securities and agreed not to compete. The regionals are small and account for about 10 percent of trading in listed stocks. Because the NYSE has dominated the industry, the emphasis of this paper is on the role of this exchange.

The beginnings of the NYSE can be traced to the much-quoted Buttonwood Tree Agreement signed on May 17, 1792, by 24 brokers:

> We the undersigned, brokers for the purchase and sale of public stocks, do hereby promise and pledge ourselves to each other that we will not buy or sell from this date for any person whatever, any kind of public stocks at a less rate than one quarter of one percent commission on the specie value, and that we will give preference to each other in our negotiations.

Although this was an informal agreement, its key ingredient — to charge fixed commissions and to give preference to signatories over nonsignatories — are central features of any cartel whose purpose is to fix a monopoly price and to enforce that price by controlling its members and preventing the entry of outside competitors who wish to share in the monopoly profits. The modern New York Stock Exchange (NYSE) was founded in 1869 as the result of a merger with a successful competitor. It had 1,060 "seats," and for the first time these seats were salable. One potential rival to the NYSE — the curbstone crowd — was diffused rather than merged or eliminated. By renouncing trading on NYSE listed issues, the curbstone crowd received the support of the Exchange. In 1910 the curbstone crowd formally organized as the New York Curb Market Association, which eventually became the American Stock Exchange (ASE). Until 1976 the rules of the new exchange prohibited trading in NYSE issues. Competition between the exchanges has not increased greatly since then, in part because most members of the ASE are also members of the NYSE.

An alternative type of market is an over-the-counter (OTC) market. The OTC market in stocks is not a physical location; rather, it is a communication network using computers and the telephone. It is a dealer market. Over-the-counter trading in common stocks is limited primarily to the smaller, less actively traded companies except for those listed companies that are also traded OTC. The OTC market in stocks also traded on exchanges is called the third market. Today trading in about 2,600 OTC stocks is facilitated by the use of an automated quotation system called NASDAQ, which has the capability of simultaneously displaying the bid-ask quotations of the dealers in a stock.

Regulation

Federal regulation of the securities markets rose out of the stock market crash of 1929 and the reports on pools and other manipulative devices made by the Senate Committee on Banking and Currency, whose investigation was spearheaded by Ferdinand Pecora. Not surprisingly the Securities Act of 1933 and Securities Exchange Act of 1934 were concerned primarily with attempting to assure that prices of securities did not reflect misinformation, fraud, or manipulation; that is, the major concern was with allocative efficiency. There was less concern with the questions of operational efficiency — the efficiency with which brokers and dealers provided their services and the charge for these services. To the extent that business conduct of brokers and dealers was regulated, the emphasis was in preventing manipulative or fraudulent activities. Thus, relatively little attention was paid to anticompetitive behavior of the exchanges, such as fixed commissions, which had existed for many years. The principle of self-regulation established by the 1934 Act as administered by the SEC largely left matters of internal conduct to the exchanges themselves with only general oversight by the SEC.

Under the 1934 Act the exchanges retained disciplinary power over their members. Direct rule-making authority was given to the SEC only in certain limited cases — by the antimanipulative section 10 and by section 14, which gave the Commission authority to make rules with respect to off-floor trading by members and the operations of specialists and odd-lot dealers. Indirect rule-making authority — the power to require the exchanges to adopt rules (after hearings) — was given by section 19 with respect to thirteen areas that included commission rates and other charges, financial responsibility of members, reporting of transactions, and "similar matters." The power to request changes in commission rates was not used until 1968, when SEC pressures forced the NYSE to adopt a volume discount (before a formal ruling became necessary). Until that time commission rate increases were accepted by the SEC without comment. Finally in 1975 the SEC did use its rule-making power to abolish fixed commission rates. Rule 19b-3 became effective May 1, 1975, and it is the principal purpose of this paper to assess the effects of that rule.

Also in May 1975 Congress passed the Securities Acts Amendments of 1975.[3] The amendments mandate a national market system for securities in which competitive forces will play a much larger role. They oblige the SEC to abrogate rules of exchanges that are anticompetitive and are not necessary for a legitimate regulatory objective [sections 6(b), 19(b), and 19(c)]. Section 23(a) prohibits promulgation of rules by the SEC that impose a burden on competition not necessary to achieve the purposes of the Exchange Act. The amendments explicitly mandate in section 6(e)(1) that "no national securities exchange may impose any schedule or fix rates of commissions, allowances, discounts or other fees to be charged by its members" except that floor brokerage fees are exempt until May 1, 1976. The SEC is given "failsafe" authority to reimpose fixed commissions if it finds it necessary. An important provision is section 28(e), which explicitly permits "paying up" for research. This section permits brokers to charge commission fees above those of other brokers in cases where research services are performed. "Brokerage and research services" are defined, and the section implies that the services must be provided by the member firm receiving the commissions; that is, the give-up* is not permitted.

CARTEL PRICING OF
BROKERAGE SERVICES
BEFORE MAY 1, 1975

Before May 1, 1975, the rules and regulations under which member firms of the NYSE operated to provide brokerage services to the public satisfied the classic definition of a cartel: (1) prices of brokerage services were fixed, (2) entry into the business was limited by the number of seats available, which prevented new entrants from capturing the monopoly profits earned by members of the NYSE, (3) a panoply of rules and regulations prohibited price cutting and rebates by members

---

* The give-up would allow the firm receiving commissions to compensate another firm for providing nonbrokerage services by "giving up" to it part of the commission.

and limited the output of brokerage services per seat so that monopoly profits would not be competed away by member firms.

Fixed Commissions

Before December 5, 1968, commissions per share or as a percent of value depended only on the price of the stock and were independent of the number of shares traded. For example, commissions on 10,000 shares of a $40 stock were $3,900, which is 100 times the commission on 100 shares. Costs were not 100 times as great. Table 1 reports estimates of profits on transactions of various sizes on a $40 stock. Cost estimates are based on a survey of firms for 1969. For the purposes of this discussion, concern is less with the absolute level of costs (which appears to be too high in view of the fact that firms were accepting small orders) and more with the relationship among costs of orders of different sizes. Clearly, large orders were extremely profitable relative to small orders.

In the 1960s and 1970s, with the growth of trading by investment companies, bank trust departments and other institutions, large orders became ever more frequent, and the institutional side of the business became extremely profitable. A volume discount instituted on December 5, 1968, reduced these profits, but not substantially. Further reductions were accomplished by the SEC-mandated requirement that

Table 1. Profits on a $40 Stock by Size of Order

Share per Order	Commissions[a]	Costs[b]	Profits
100	39.00	54.62	− 15.62
200	78.00	90.26	− 12.26
300	117.00	123.21	− 6.21
400	156.00	154.21	1.79
500	195.00	183.65	11.35
1,000	390.00	315.73	74.27
5,000	1,950.00	1,191.14	758.86
10,000	3,900.00	2,283.54	1,616.46
100,000	39,000.00	20,580.51	18,419.49

[a] Commissions based on pre–12/5/68 schedule.

[b] Cost estimates as calculated by National Economic Research Associates. *Stock Brokerage Commission: The Development and Application of Standards of Reasonableness for Public Rates* (July 1970), Vol. II, Table XI-2. Costs based on survey for 1969.

commissions be negotiated on that portion of the order over $500,000 (as of April 5, 1971) and later (April 24, 1972) on that portion of the order over $300,000. NYSE surveys indicated that commissions on the negotiated portion of the order were reduced by 30 percent relative to the fixed commission. What is surprising is that further reductions in commissions on large orders proved possible with the introduction of fully competitive commission rates in May 1975.

Limited Membership

Membership in the NYSE is limited to 1,366 individuals, each of whom owns a "seat." Membership entitles one to do business on the floor of the NYSE, to pay a share of the costs of running the exchange, and to own a pro rata share of the assets of the exchange — primarily the real estate and building. As of 1978 the 1,366 members were grouped into about 500 firms, of which about 365 did business with the public. In 1978 most members (741) were affiliated with a member firm and did not derive their primary source of income from activity on the floor of the NYSE. The remaining members were primarily floor members — floor brokers, registered traders, and specialists. The specialist provides the dealer function on the NYSE. As of 1978 there were 395 individual specialists grouped into 63 specialist units.

An important characteristic of NYSE membership is its salability. This permits more efficient firms to expand by buying seats from less efficient ones and tends to ensure that the level of services rendered is rendered efficiently (even though prices may be too high and the level too low). The market price of a seat depends on the monopoly profits (over and above all costs and a normal profit) that a potential buyer could earn. Annual profits are

$$(P - C)V$$

where

P = commission in cents per share
C = average cost of supplying brokerage services in cents per share; includes a normal profit
V = number of shares traded by seat holder.

The price of a seat is the discounted value of expected profits (plus the value of NYSE property). End-of-month seat prices reached a high point of $500,000 in 1929,* fell to a low of $18,000 in 1942, reached an

---

* Adjusted for a seat dividend of one-third of a seat per member.

all-time high of $515,000 in 1968 and 1969, fell to $45,000 in December 1977, and had recovered to $210,000 by August 1979.

Since profits are related to the volume of trading and commission rates, seat prices have tended to be related to volume of trading and commission rates, because individuals base their expectations of the future on current events. Only the recent advent of competitive commission rates has broken this association. Figure 1 plots a simple form of this relationship — namely, seat prices and contemporaneous dollar volume of trading. Each variable is an annual average of monthly values. The association over time is quite close until 1970, when seat prices and volume diverge. At that time there was good reason to expect the introduction of negotiated rates and a more competitive national market system, which would tend to eliminate monopoly profits and therefore reduce the value of seats.[4] The recovery in seat prices in 1979 reflects the fact that NYSE membership was still valuable in giving brokers access to the order flow and that a national market system in which non-NYSE members would have equal access had not yet been successfully established.

Since new members must pay to join the cartel an amount equal to the capitalized value of expected monopoly profits, the only clear beneficiaries of a cartel are the original founders. New members benefit if they are more efficient than those selling a seat, or if actual profits exceed those expected. The resistance to competitive rates is easily understood when one recognizes that many members bought seats at price ranges as high as $515,000. Elimination of fixed commissions imposes a windfall capital loss. (A large portion of that loss is realized when the intention to have competition is announced.)

Rules and Regulations

A cartel is an agreement among many firms to raise prices and limit output. Since a monopoly profit is earned on each transaction, each member of the cartel has an incentive to expand output in order to increase his level of monopoly profits. Rules prohibiting price cutting and limiting output are therefore generally found in cartels. On the NYSE, rebating any part of the commission to a nonmember was prohibited. Rule 394 prohibited members from trading away from the NYSE and therefore made impossible price cutting off the exchange.[5] Limits on output are set by the rule that allows only members to trade on the floor. This effectively limits output per seat to the physical capacity of that individual to carry out transactions. If a member were able to hire other individuals to act for him on the floor, no limit on the output per seat would exist, and the value of a seat could be com-

Figure 1. New York Stock Exchange Volume of Trading and Seat Prices

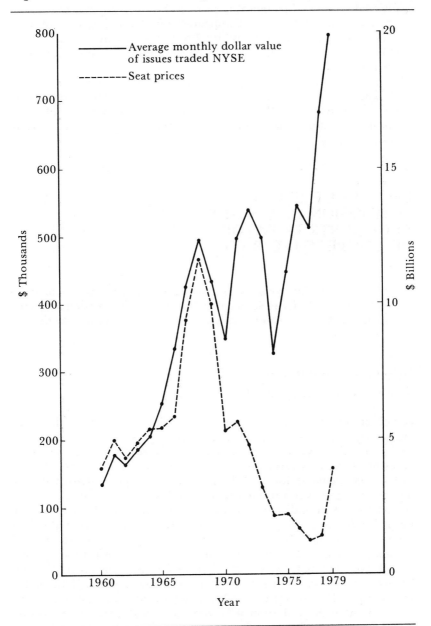

peted away. Under current rules a firm doing more business must buy additional seats. Technological improvements, such as wire connections to the floor, also require NYSE approval. The limited number of seats, the limit on output per seat, and the limit on nonmember access to the NYSE order flow explain why seats have value even with competitive commissions.

NYSE rules were reasonably effective because of explicit or implicit SEC sanction. Nevertheless, rules did not exist for all contingencies, and members of the NYSE cartel found means, albeit very complicated, to cut prices and increase output in an attempt to capture a larger share of the monopoly profits.

EFFECTS OF FIXED COMMISSION RATES AND ARGUMENTS IN FAVOR OF COMPETITIVE RATES

On May 1, 1975, Congress and the SEC eliminated a key element of the cartel — the ability to set fixed commissions. This section states the arguments in favor of competitive commissions and examines the evidence since 1975.

Effects of Cartel Pricing on Trading Costs and Trading

Cartel pricing introduces an operational inefficiency into the stock market by imposing higher trading costs than would otherwise exist. As a result the investing public finds it more costly to make portfolio adjustments and to carry out savings or dissavings decisions. To the extent that demand for brokerage services has price sensitivity, the higher price causes less trading than would otherwise exist.

The evidence indicates that competition brought about a substantial reduction in trading costs after May 1, 1975. However, reductions were not uniform. They varied according to transaction size, level of services desired, and whether the investor was an institution or individual. An SEC monthly survey of 70 brokerage firms accounting for 55 percent of total securities commission income shows that, in the period April 1975 to December 1978, commissions as a percent of the value of the order fell from 0.84 percent to 0.43 percent for institutional investors and from 1.73 percent to 1.48 percent for individual investors.[6] Brokers are able to achieve substantial economies in handling large orders or a steady flow of small orders. Since institutions are able to place such orders (and often make specific arrangements with particular brokers to systematize trading), their commissions have fallen by nearly 50 percent of the fixed commissions. Commissions on large orders of individuals have also fallen substantially. However, most individual orders are small, and on orders of less than 200 shares commissions have in fact risen slightly since 1975 (by 5.4 percent).

Hidden in the average trend is the fact that, under competition, commission rates vary across brokers according to the services offered. Those individuals willing to accept a lower level of service have the opportunity to achieve substantial reductions in commissions on small orders by using a "discount broker." Such a choice was not generally available under fixed commissions.

Nonprice Competition among NYSE Members under Fixed Rates

When price competition is stifled, nonprice competition takes place in an attempt by each firm to capture a larger share of the market. In principle, such competition can raise costs of each firm by enough to eliminate monopoly profits. The high prices of seats during much of the fixed-commission era suggest that nonprice competition was not complete. The reason was that limitations on nonprice competition under NYSE rules would not allow clearly unrelated services to be rendered and imposed other restrictions.*

Nonprice competition induced by fixed commissions is undesirable because it is inefficient, it is discriminatory, and it creates conflict-of-interest situations. It is inefficient because firms produce nonbrokerage services simply to attract commission business, not because they are best qualified to produce the service. It is discriminatory because all investors pay the minimum commission, even though some cannot use the nonbrokerage services offered in return. It leads to conflicts of interest because investment managers, rather than the owners of the assets being managed, may benefit from nonbrokerage services rendered in return for commissions.

Institutional investors, the source of the majority of commission dollars, particularly in the lucrative large transactions sizes, were the recipients of the highest level of services. The major institutional money managers are the bank trust departments and the investment

---

* For example, Rule 436 prohibits interest on customer credit balances "created for the purpose of receiving interest thereon."

advisory complexes that manage mutual funds. Of lessor importance are the insurance companies and self-administered foundations, endowments, and employee benefit plans. The NYSE Public Transaction Study of 1974 reports that 44.60 percent of the share volume of trading on the NYSE originates from institutions and intermediaries.*

The variety of ancillary services rendered in return for commission dollars is limited only by one's imagination and NYSE rules. The principal forms of services were research, sale of mutual funds, and maintenance of idle demand deposits. In return for commission business, brokers offered research that ranged from general analyses of the economy to specific studies of industries and companies. Indeed, certain brokerage firms became specialized research "boutiques." Since 1975 there has been some unbundling, so that order execution and research are priced separately. The sharp reduction in institutional commission rates reflects this unbundling. Many institutional investors, however, still "pay up" in their commission for research as explicitly permitted in Section 28(e) of the Securities Acts Amendments of 1975. Brokerage firms in the past also offered to recommend to customers a particular mutual fund rather than some other fund in return for the commission business generated by the investment advisor in managing the fund. This procedure, in effect, charges existing shareholders of a fund (who pay the brokerage) for increasing the fund's size — a practice that is not in their interest.† The practice has recently been banned. Finally, the principal item that brokers could offer banks in return for commission business was the deposit of idle demand deposit balances by the broker at the bank. The Institutional Investor Study (IIS) documents the association between broker deposits at banks and commissions from banks.[7] Since commissions are generated by trust department accounts, while idle bank deposits benefit the commercial side of the bank, there is an obvious conflict of interest here. In principle, the conflict could be overcome by reducing the management fee on the trust accounts by the amount of the benefit to the bank of the idle deposits. In practice, this was difficult to do or to enforce. Instead, the use of idle deposits declined as a result of publicity and legal challenges, and a "wall" has been established between commercial and trust activities of banks.[8] With competitive commissions, bank trust departments have been quite active in negotiating lower commissions rather than seeking services from brokers.

---

* Of the remainder 31.1 percent came from public individuals and 24.3 percent from NYSE members.

† It should be noted that brokers also received a sales "load" when selling shares of a mutual fund. Recently no-load funds, which are not sold through broker-dealers, have grown in importance.

Because brokers differ in the skill with which they can provide ancillary services, it is often desirable to buy ancillary services from another broker than the one executing the transaction. During the fixed-commission era, rather byzantine and costly procedures arose to channel excess commission dollars from the executing broker to the one providing ancillary services. The simplest of these was the give-up. Although NYSE rules prohibited rebates to nonmembers, a member was permitted to give up part of the commission he received to another member who rendered services to the customer. The magnitude of the give-up on institutional-size orders reached 60 percent, and this indicates the extent to which commissions exceeded the costs of execution as well as the existence and the viability of competition as to price long before negotiated rates were instituted. The complicated procedure necessary to channel these commissions to brokers rendering services indicates the inefficiency of this procedure necessary under fixed rates.

Competitive commissions have simplified interbroker competition. Competition is with respect to price where previously it was with respect to the amount to be given up to another broker or the level of ancillary services to be rendered. Record keeping necessary to channel give-ups has been eliminated.

Institutional Membership

Fixed commissions encouraged institutions not interested in ancillary services of brokers to join exchanges by forming brokerage subsidiaries to recapture for themselves the excess commissions being paid. While the NYSE responded by making institutional membership almost impossible, certain other exchanges (such as the PBW) admitted institutional members to build up and maintain trading volume. Although an institution might recapture excess commissions, there was no guarantee that commission savings would be passed on to customers rather than be retained by the institution. Indeed, there was the danger that institutions might "churn" accounts to make profits for their brokerage subsidiary.

Competitive commissions greatly reduced the pressures for institutional membership because reduced commissions could be negotiated directly. They therefore also reduced the conflict of interest inherent when investment and brokerage activities are combined. However, Congress also prohibited brokers from carrying out transactions for affiliated institutions or for accounts over which the broker had investment discretion in Section 11(a) of the Securities Acts Amendments of 1975. This provision has caused considerable difficulty and has been interpreted to mean that the affiliated broker can handle all upstairs and back-office aspects of transactions but cannot carry out the actual transactions on the exchange floor.

Market Fragmentation

An important effect of fixed cartel prices is the encouragement of competition from nonmembers of the cartel who provide the same services as the cartel at lower cost. The outside competition to the NYSE has been the third market, an over-the-counter market in listed stocks made by dealers who are not members of the NYSE. The potentially harmful effect of such a competitor is the diversion of volume that may impair liquidity — that is, reduce the speed or raise the cost at which a transaction can be carried out on the exchange. Such diversion is actually difficult to achieve, since the likelihood of a fair and speedy transaction increases with the number of transactions carried out in a market. Thus, in the absence of a communications mechanism that permits orders at different physical locations to be exposed to each other, there is a natural tendency for orders to go to that physical location to which most investors send their orders. Despite this natural tendency, and because of the incentive to avoid paying high commissions, the third market increased its market share from 2.9 percent of NYSE volume in the first quarter of 1966 to a peak 9.3 percent in the fourth quarter of 1971.

The institutional users of the third market were able to avoid any reduction in the depth and liquidity of the market because they maintained instantaneous communications with both the exchange floor and third-market brokers. In the proposed national market system, reconciliation of the liquidity objective and the objective of competition among rival physical locations is to be achieved by a communications system that allows orders in all physical markets to be exposed to orders on the other side in all physical markets, thereby converting them into a single market.

Competitive commissions have eliminated the principal economic rationale for the third market. Contrary to arguments of the NYSE that competitive commissions would increase market fragmentation, the market share of the third market has dwindled to about 2 or 3 percent since the introduction of competitive rates.

Inefficiency

It is argued that fixed commissions protected inefficient firms and restrained innovation and change. There are two possible sources of inefficiency: (1) the inefficiency of the NYSE and the rules and procedures by which trading is conducted, and (2) the inefficiency of individual firms that operate on the exchange.

It seems clear that the NYSE rules and regulations that promoted a mechanism of trading based on face-to-face communication on the floor of the exchange restrained the development of more efficient trading techniques. Thus the NYSE, attuned to handling small order flows of individuals, was not in a position effectively to bring large buyers and sellers together on the floor, and this business was moved to "upstairs" market makers. Major innovations in automating trading, such as the Autex, Instinet, and NASDAQ systems, were developed outside the NYSE. The NYSE has reacted to and accepted some of these innovations but has rarely initiated them.

While NYSE rules induced certain inefficient behavior by all member firms, competition among firms in the cartel tended to eliminate firm-specific inefficiencies. That is, within the constraints of NYSE rules, the normal incentives existed for member firms to be as efficient as possible, since efficiency would lead to higher profits. Furthermore, the salability of NYSE seats provided a mechanism by which efficient firms were able to buy up seats of inefficient firms. The efficient firm could pay an amount in excess of the present value of profits expected by the inefficient firm. Thus, while the NYSE cartel did foster generally inefficient procedures for trading as a result of limits on price competition, it did not protect the individually inefficient firm.

ARGUMENTS AGAINST COMPETITIVE COMMISSION RATES

The position against competitive commission rates was put forward primarily in reports by the NYSE (1968, 1973) and in NYSE testimony at the SEC Commission Rate Hearings. The key element in the argument was that competitive rates would lead to "destructive" competition for a variety of reasons — natural monopoly of the individual brokerage firms, predatory price cutting, and the existence of high fixed costs and fluctuating demand. At a minimum broker revenues and profits would be adversely affected. All of this was undesirable because firms would lose capital and fail to provide the necessary excess capacity to meet surges in demand. Destructive competition might go so far as to endanger the solvency of brokerage firms and threaten the stability of the American financial system. Furthermore, small and

regional brokerage firms would be the first to be hurt, and this was undesirable because these firms had the most to do with raising new
funds for new small companies.

In this section these arguments are analyzed in light of the events
since 1975. It is a fair generalization that very few, if any, of the harmful and disruptive effects predicted by the opponents of competitive
rates have in fact materialized.

Structure of the Securities Industry and Destructive Competition

Natural Monopoly of the Brokerage Firm. A natural monopoly exists
if marginal cost of producing another unit of output is below average
cost at every output level. This means that the average-cost curve decreases as output increases. Since, under competition, firms price at
marginal cost and since this is below average cost, firms would suffer
losses and eventually go out of business until one firm dominated the
industry. The NYSE (1968) argued that the average-cost curve for the
brokerage firm (not the brokerage industry as a whole) did fall, and
therefore that competitive commission rates would lead to the failure
of many firms, particularly small and regional firms. It is not clear, of
course, why that is an undesirable result: in a natural monopoly the
least-cost output level is achieved by a single firm. It may be desirable
to regulate that firm by setting maximum prices (not minimum prices),
but it is certainly not desirable to encourage production by many firms,
each operating at too small a scale.

In the discussion of the existence of economies of scale, substantial
computer time and statistical expertise were applied in attempting to
determine the shape of the cost function of NYSE brokerage firms. The
NYSE argued that economies of scale existed primarily on the basis of
a regression equation relating total expenses per firm and number of
transactions per firm using data for 369 firms in 1966.[9] Others provided
contradictory results. For example, Mann, using the same data, argued
that the NYSE data suffered from heteroskedasticity and that correction
for this resulted in diseconomies of scale.[10] The results are clearly quite
ambiguous, and to the extent that economies of scale did exist they
would be very small beyond output of 300,000 transactions.* In another
study using data for 1968 and 1970, Friend and Blume (1972) also
achieve inconclusive results in direct tests of their cost function.

What one can expect from such statistical analyses of cost functions

---

* The NYSE equation implies that a doubling of output to 600,000 transactions
reduces costs by about 5 percent.

is highly questionable. First, there are problems with the data: Do the accounting data accurately reflect economic concepts of costs and revenues? Are fixed costs allocated properly? How does one account for the fact that firms are not homogeneous in all respects except size, and that different firms have different product mixes and therefore different cost functions? Does a variable such as the number of transactions properly reflect all influences on the cost of executing such transactions?

Second, there is no clear rationale why the introduction of competitive rates should affect the structure of the industry. If indeed there are economies of scale, the industry need not wait for the introduction of competitive rates to become more concentrated. The salability of memberships allows one firm to buy out other firms and expand output. That is, to the extent that economies of scale exist (as maintained by the NYSE), an incentive exists, under fixed as well as competitive rates, for lower-cost firms to buy seats of higher-cost firms. If those economies exist over the entire range of industry output, one firm would eventually dominate the industry as readily under fixed commissions as under competitive commissions.

Finally, it is difficult to conclude from cross-section studies carried out for one year whether the long-run equilibrium cost curve has been estimated. Given the adjustments possible through the sale of membership, it is difficult to believe that over 500 firms could exist in the presence of an opportunity to achieve a natural monopoly. The estimated downward-sloping cost function may reflect certain temporarily high-cost firms in transition toward an optimal output or, in the case of some firms, the presence of specialized (but limited) factors that are related to output. In neither case is there a natural monopoly.

An alternative approach to estimating optimum firm output and the optimum number of firms in an industry is the survivorship approach. This technique attempts to determine whether there is a tendency for an industry to become more concentrated over time. If such a tendency exists in the long term, it suggests that the optimum scale of operations is increasing. Our concern is whether the introduction of competitive commissions has caused or accelerated a trend toward greater concentration.

Table 2 contains data on the proportions of securities commission income (SCI) earned by the largest four, eight, etc. firms. The annual data for 1965–1970 are from Friend and Blume (1972) and are based on consolidated income and expenses of NYSE firms carrying public customer accounts. The data for 1972–1977 are based on unconsolidated revenues and expenses of members doing a public business. The more recent figures are based on the new NYSE Joint Regulatory Report for all NYSE firms doing public business. Since the number of firms doing a public business exceeds the number carrying public accounts, the

Table 2. Measures of Concentration of Securities Commission
Income (SCI)

	Percent of SCI Accounted for by the Following Numbers of Firms						Total SCI (Millions)	Total No. of Firms
NYSE I & E [a]	*1*	*8*	*14*	*20*	*26*	*32*		
1965	11	29	39	47	52	56	1,413.2	374
1966	11	29	39	47	51	55	1,766.1	371
1967	10	28	38	45	50	55	2,519.6	374
1968	8	24	34	41	47	52	3,245.4	386
1969	8	24	34	41	47	52	2,563.0	379
1970	9	27	37	44	51	56	2,079.0	331
1971 NA								
NYSE JRR [b]	*4*	*8*	*14*	*20*	*26*	*32*		
1972	18.1	26.4	35.3	42.5	47.9	52.5	3,223.7	498
1973	19.1	27.6	37.0	46.7	52.8	57.6	2,659.6	467
1974	21.1	31.3	40.9	48.7	54.6	59.0	2,271.2	430
1975	23.8	34.8	44.9	52.9	59.0	63.3	2,924.5	411
1972								
Q1	18.6	27.3	36.1	43.0	48.6	53.4	949.6	500
Q2	18.3	26.7	35.4	42.5	47.8	52.3	836.7	500
Q3	17.6	25.8	34.8	42.1	47.7	52.3	669.3	497
Q4	17.8	25.7	34.8	42.2	47.6	52.0	768.1	494
1973								
Q1	18.3	26.5	35.9	43.7	49.5	54.1	703.2	481
Q2	18.6	27.1	36.3	51.6	57.7	62.3	562.5	474
Q3	19.3	28.0	37.4	45.2	51.6	56.5	547.8	463
Q4	20.0	28.9	38.3	46.2	52.5	57.3	846.1	449
1974								
Q1	20.0	29.8	38.7	46.4	52.7	57.2	651.3	438
Q2	20.4	30.3	39.7	47.4	53.5	58.2	520.8	432
Q3	21.5	32.1	41.9	49.7	55.1	59.5	508.5	428
Q4	22.3	33.0	43.2	51.1	56.9	61.2	590.6	421

	Percent of SCI Accounted for by the Following Numbers of Firms						Total SCI (Millions)	Total No. of Firms
NYSE JRR [b]	4	8	14	20	26	32		
1975								
Q1	22.9	34.2	44.9	53.0	59.0	63.6	791.5	405
Q2	24.2	34.9	45.0	53.0	59.1	63.5	880.5	414
Q3	24.1	35.4	44.9	53.0	59.0	63.2	641.4	412
Q4	24.3	35.0	44.8	52.8	58.7	62.9	611.1	414
1976								
Q1	26.4	38.7	48.8	56.9	62.1	66.8	1,041.9	398
Q2	23.9	35.1	45.8	54.0	59.3	63.2	707.7	395
Q3	24.0	35.6	46.3	54.6	60.1	64.0	678.5	387
Q4	23.7	35.2	46.0	54.6	60.1	64.2	735.4	384
1977								
Q1	23.0	33.8	44.4	52.4	57.8	62.0	759.9	375
Q2	22.9	34.2	46.0	54.8	60.9	65.2	692.9	371
Q3	24.0	35.4	46.8	55.9	61.8	66.0	684.1	371

[a] From Friend and Blume (1972), p. 37. Based on NYSE Income and Expense Reports which are *consolidated* revenues and expenses of NYSE members *carrying* public customer accounts.

[b] Based on NYSE Joint Regulatory Report, which reports *unconsolidated* quarterly revenue and expenses of NYSE members *doing* a public business. Number of firms differs between JRR and I & E primarily because of firms that do a public business but do not carry public accounts. Tabulations were provided by the SEC.

two sets of figures are not directly comparable. Two trends are evident in the table. First, concentration of SCI has increased. In the first quarter of 1972 the top four NYSE firms accounted for 18.6 percent of SCI. This figure increased to 24.2 percent by the second quarter of 1975 and has stabilized since then with the exception of the upward "blip" in the first quarter of 1976 (due to high trading volume). A similar pattern is evident for the top eight firms. Second, at the same time, the number of firms declined from 498 to 371. At issue is whether these trends are due to the introduction of competitive rates or to other factors.

The decline in the number of firms does not appear to be affected by the introduction of competitive commission rates. Rather it appears to represent a trend due to other factors with some sensitivity to lagged net income of NYSE member firms.[11] Indeed, the annual rate of decline in the number of firms was greater before competitive rates (1972 quarter 1 to 1975 quarter 1: −7.8 percent) than after competitive rates (1975 quarter 1 to 1977 quarter 3: −3.7 percent). Similarly, the trend in concentration of SCI does not appear to be affected by the introduction of competitive rates, except perhaps for the top four firms. That concentration ratio increased from 22.9 percent to 24.2 percent between the first and second quarters of 1975 — a fairly sharp change, exceeded only once in the first quarter of 1976. However, there may be factors specific to those four firms that could equally well explain the change.* It can readily be determined from Table 2 that the annual increase in concentration is substantially greater before competitive rates than afterward, a relationship that holds for all groups of firms in the table. For example, between the first quarter of 1972 and 1975 the top eight firms increased their market share at an annual rate of 8.4 percent, whereas between the first quarter of 1975 and the third quarter of 1977 the annual rate of increase was only 1.4 percent.

The long-term trend in concentration itself is difficult to explain. Part is due to the simple fact that as some firms leave the industry other firms increase their revenues. If the output of departing firms were shared proportionally by the remaining firms, all firms would increase market share in proportion to their prior share. However, the percentage increase in market share is greater for the large firms than the small.† This trend may reflect a permanent increase in the optimum size of some brokerage firms due to recent technological changes involving the computer and the movement toward a national market system. Since national full-line firms are the largest firms, the economies seem to be specific to these firms. A second explanation for the increased market share of the largest firms is that it is a transitory phenomenon reflecting the merger of certain financially troubled firms. Such mergers have usually involved the largest brokerage firms.

Finally, it should be noted that with 360 brokerage firms on the NYSE and over 2,000 nonmember firms, the securities industry is not concentrated by usual standards. The establishment of new brokerage firms, such as the discount brokerage houses, testifies to the ease of entry and the viability of firms of all sizes.[12]

Predatory Price Cutting. An element in the destructive-competition argument is that firms with large resources could afford to cut prices

* For example, DuPont Glore Forgan Inc. was liquidated and absorbed by other firms in this period.

† It should be noted that the category of top eight firms involved twelve different firms over time. That is, four new firms entered that group at various points in time. Firms that left returned three times, twice because of mergers that increased their size.

to drive smaller firms out of the securities business. These initial losses would be made up by raising prices once control of the industry was achieved. Critical to this argument is the ability to raise prices once competitors have been driven out. This depends on collusion by the remaining firms and limitations on reentry of other firms. Neither condition is readily satisfied in the securities business, except when imposed artificially by regulation or self-regulation, as by a stock exchange.

The empirical evidence also does not support the argument that competitive commissions would bring about predatory price cutting by large firms. Comparisons among firms of commissions charged for April 1975 (before competitive rates) and December 1975 (after competitive rates) showed that size of the firm as measured by gross revenue had no significant effect on commissions of that firm either before or after negotiated rates. The results of cross-section regressions of commissions (cents per share or percent) against transaction characteristics (shares per order and price per share) and firm size (measured by gross revenue) are in Table 3. They show that commissions of large firms are no lower than commissions of other firms for transactions of the same characteristics. Shares per order and price per share consistently have a significant negative effect on percentage commission rates, but firm size is never statistically significant. Not included in the regressions are the new discount brokers. These are small, not large, firms.

High Fixed Costs, Fluctuating Demand. The third element in the NYSE destructive-competition argument is that brokerage firm costs are structured in such a way as to lead to large price fluctuations in response to demand fluctuations. Brokerage firms are characterized by high fixed costs relative to variable costs. As a result, in a period of slack demand for brokerage services, prices would be cut to marginal cost. Since marginal cost of another transaction is less than total average cost when fixed costs are large, "losses" would ensue; that is, there are periods in which fixed costs would not be covered.

Questions of fact and questions of logic arise in this argument. The question of fact is whether fixed costs are indeed a large fraction of total costs and whether there are not many industries operating under competition for which fixed costs are substantially higher. The NYSE argued that 44 percent of expenses were fixed in 1966 and included in that amount clerical and administrative salaries, communication costs, occupancy and equipment costs, and other expenses including promotion, licenses, dues, and assessment (NYSE, 1968, pp. 64, 65). Friend and Blume (1972) find that all categories of expenses except occupancy and equipment costs fall in response to declines in revenues. They conclude that only these are fixed, and these expenses accounted for only

Table 3. Cross-section Regressions of Commission Rates Against Transaction Characteristics and Firm Size (Coefficients, t Values in Parentheses)

	Dependent Variable	Independent Variables				r^2	Obs.
		Shares per Order, s/n	Price per Share, V/s	Gross Revenue, R	Constant		
INSTITUTIONAL CUSTOMERS							
April 1975	% Commission, C/V	−0.008945 (7.286)	−0.01647 (8.152)	−0.01523 (−1.111)	1.583 (24.21)	0.72	65
December 1975	% Commission, C/V	−0.01339 (6.512)	−0.01892 (4.992)	−0.009797 (.528)	1.451 (12.50)	0.56	65
April 1975	Commission per share, C/s	−0.2645 (7.275)	+0.2411 (4.030)	−0.3481 (.857)	24.80 (12.81)	0.50	65
December 1975	Commission per share, C/s	−0.4060 (7.159)	+0.2055 (1.966)	−0.1568 (.306)	19.70 (6.153)	0.45	65

INDIVIDUAL CUSTOMERS

April 1975	% Commission, C/V	−0.06044 (6.469)	−0.04544 (9.677)	+0.01340 (.597)	2.707 (30.41)	0.74	62
December 1975	% Commission, C/V	−0.08065 (6.179)	−0.04368 (8.861)	+0.04577 (1.453)	2.607 (27.95)	0.71	62
April 1975	Commission per share, C/s	−1.234 (7.437)	+0.6369 (7.637)	+0.4108 (1.031)	21.82 (13.80)	0.59	62
December 1975	Commission per share, C/s	−1.535 (6.005)	+0.3939 (4.079)	+0.6964 (1.128)	23.61 (12.92)	0.40	62

Source: SEC Survey of Commission Charges on Brokerage Transactions. Regressions performed by the SEC Office of Economic Policy and Research.

Variables: C = dollar commissions received by firm; V = dollar value of securities traded in hundreds; n = number of orders processed; t = number of transactions; s = number of shares traded in hundreds; R = 1975 gross revenue of firm in millions of dollars.

Data: All data are monthly — April 1975 or December 1975. Except for R all variables have different values according to customer category — institutional or individual. There are about 65 firms in the sample.

9.1 percent of all expenses in 1970. Since office space and computers can be rented out, even those costs could easily be considered at least partially variable. In an update of the Friend and Blume study through 1976, Stoll (1979) also concludes that less than 10 percent of expenses are fixed even in the short run. Compared to other industries, this is not a large percentage.

Questions of logic arise in that the presence of high fixed costs has never been accepted as an argument for fixing prices so long as sufficient firms exist to ensure competition. (The existence of sufficient firms depends on economies of scale, an argument considered earlier.) Fixed costs are a large fraction in capital-intensive manufacturing industries. Yet one does not argue that prices should be fixed there. Firms enter such an industry because the losses during periods of slack demand are made up by profits in periods of high demand.

Broker Revenues and Profits

While the argument that competitive commissions would entail "destructive" competition has not proved convincing, the reduction in commission rates that has occurred has had some effect on securities industry revenues and profits. What has been that effect and how have the industry as a whole and the various types of brokerage firms responded?

In the Aggregate. The SEC calculated the effect on broker profits of commission rate reductions under the assumption that the level of trading would have been the same at higher fixed rates as it was with negotiated rates. Figures on all NYSE firms are in Table 4. They show, for example, that in the first quarter of 1976, NYSE firms collected $139 million less in revenues (12.3 percent) than they would have under the fixed rates at the level of trading existing in the first quarter of 1976. Since security commission income constitutes about 50 percent of total revenue of NYSE firms, the percentage effect on total revenues is about half that shown by the percent decline in commission revenue in Table 4 or of the order of 6 to 7 percent.

To the extent that there is any elasticity in the demand for brokerage services, the revenue loss estimated by the SEC is overstated. Since the demand for a product usually rises when its price falls, one would expect some increase in revenues due to increased trading, and this could offset the loss in revenues estimated by the SEC due to the decline in commission rates. Estimates of the elasticity of demand are difficult because many variables affect the volume of trading. Based on the work of Epps (1976, p. 192), an elasticity of -0.25 is reasonable.

Table 4. Estimated Revenue Foregone due to Competitive Commission Rates for All NYSE Firms, All Markets

Period	% Decline Commission Rates	Commission Revenue ($ million)	Est. Rev. Foregone ($ million)
May-June 1975	7.0	556	42.0
Q3 1975	10.0	611	67.5
Q4 1975	13.0	582	87.2
Q1 1976	12.3	989	139.0
Q2 1976	13.8	672	107.2
Q3 1976	14.5	644	109.1
Q4 1976	15.7	700	130.0

Source: SEC, "The Effect of the Absence of Fixed Rates of Commissions," Fifth Report to Congress, May 26, 1977. All data are based on SEC survey of 70 brokerage firms accounting for about 55 percent of all security commission revenue. Figures in table are projected NYSE totals based on this sample.

This would imply that a commission rate reduction of 12 percent would increase trading by about 3 percent. This in turn implies that a revenue reduction of 12 percent estimated by the SEC ought to be 9 percent because it is offset by a 3 percent increase in volume. It is important to recognize that increased volume on the NYSE can, in large part, come from a decline in volume on other exchanges and the third market and does not depend on increased trading activity by all investors. Furthermore, the elasticity and volume would tend to increase over time as investors have the opportunity to adjust trading patterns to take advantage of the lower NYSE commissions. Thus, later revenue reductions shown in Table 4 tend to be more overstated than earlier ones.

To the extent that expenses are the same as they would be in the absence of competitive rates, revenue losses are fully and directly reflected as reductions in broker profits. Using as a basis the historical relation between total expenses and security commission income, it does not appear that expenses were reduced in response to the estimated revenue reduction when firms are viewed in the aggregate.[13] This implies that the revenue reduction did have an effect on profits. Since expenses are largely variable and could have been reduced, this evidence implies that the pressure of competition maintained the level of services in the face of reduced revenue.

A second source of evidence that profits have been affected by competitive rates is the behavior of seat prices. As was seen in Figure 1, the historical relation between seat prices and dollar trading volume appears to have been broken in 1970, a point in time when negotiated rates were first perceived as a distinct possibility. Of course, a number of other adverse factors affected the industry at that time. However, even though volume recovered and the general health of the industry improved, seat prices did not recover until 1979, and then not nearly to the extent that volume recovered. The drop in seat prices represents in large part the present value of cartel profits lost due to negotiated rates.*

The net implication of these findings is that the reduction in commissions produced a loss in revenue, although not as great as implied by the SEC estimates. Costs in the aggregate did not fall, and therefore the revenue loss resulted in lower profits, which are also reflected in lower seat prices. From our earlier discussion, costs could have been adjusted downward. Since they were not, the continued incurrence of costs appears to be a voluntary one. This implies that brokers are continuing to earn at least a normal return and that the profit loss has come out of monopoly profits, the loss of which is reflected in the lower seat price. SEC figures on profitability suggest that this may indeed have been the case. Profit margins in 1975 were 13.7 percent for the industry as a whole. Return on equity was 31.6 percent. Both figures were higher than for any year since 1971.[14] Profit margin and return on equity rose slightly in 1976 (to 14.2 percent and 32.9 percent, respectively). In 1977 margins declined to 6.2 percent. Such fluctuations can be expected and are no more severe than experienced before the introduction of competitive commission rates.

By Type of Firm. Revenue losses differed substantially among firms as a result of substantial differences in the impact of commission rate cuts.[15] Since the largest commission rate reductions took place in institutional orders, brokerage firms depending primarily on institutions suffered the greatest revenue losses according to SEC estimates. By the first quarter of 1976, the SEC estimates that commissions of institutional firms were 31.6 percent below what they would have been under fixed commissions (again assuming that commission rate reductions do not increase trading volume). On the other hand, national full-line firms that have a greater proportion of individual customers suffered a discount of only 6.3 percent. However, institutional firms reacted with speed to the reduction in revenues. Some firms merged, but many stayed in the institutional business and were able to cut costs and

---

* A drop from a level of $450,000 in 1968 to $80,000 in 1976 implies a capital loss for all 1,366 members of $505.4 million. At a 10 percent rate of interest, this corresponds to an annual profit loss of $50.5 million for the industry.

diversify their product line. As a result, in the four quarters immediately after introduction of competitive rates, institutional firms had a profit margin of 12.9 percent as compared with a profit margin of 14.2 percent for national full-line firms. These figures attest to the flexibility of costs in this industry and the responsiveness to changing demand conditions.

Other Consequences Related to Destructive Competition

Small and Regional Firms. The NYSE argued that competitive commissions and the resulting destructive competition would have a particularly adverse effect on small and regional firms. This prediction has not proved correct because firms of all sizes have failed. Although direct evidence on failures is not available, evidence on 72 NYSE firms discontinuing membership between January 1975 and December 1977 is presented in Table 5. In this period large firms did not discontinue membership unless they failed or were pushed into a merger because of imminent failure. Small firms discontinued membership for the additional reason of retirement of the owner of the firm. The table shows that while 10 percent of all NYSE firms had security commission income (SCI) above $10,802,000, 14 percent [(3 + 7)/72] of the firms discontinuing membership were of this size. In view of the small sample size, the fact that SCI will be lower for firms about to fail, and the fact that small firms are more likely to discontinue membership for reasons other than failure, the table does not suggest that the size distribution of failing firms is different from that of surviving firms.

The profitability and viability of regional firms also does not appear to have been impaired. According to SEC surveys, regional firms that are members of the NYSE have retained their market share of SCI. In addition, share volume of regional exchanges as a percentage of share volume in all markets has not declined since 1975.

Capital and Capacity. The NYSE argued that destructive competition would lead to a loss of capital and failure of firms, which in turn would reduce the ability of the industry to provide excess capacity to meet surges in demand for brokerage services. The validity of this position is not clear. First, under competitive rates, firms will still compete in the provision of services, and well-managed firms will seek to capture market share by being prepared and able to handle surges in demand. Second, under competitive rates, price changes can help to mitigate strains on capacity. If price is allowed to ration demand, there is less likelihood of queuing, and capacity is more likely to be at the socially

Table 5. Size Distribution of Firms Discontinuing NYSE Membership, by Security Commission Income, January 1, 1975 to June 30, 1976, and July 1, 1976 to December 31, 1977

1974[a] Security Commission Income (thousands)	Percent of NYSE firms with equal or greater security commission income in 1974	Number of firms in security commission income class discontinuing membership[b]	
		1/1/75 6/30/76	7/1/76 to 12/31/77
$10,802	10	3	7
4,754	20	2	3
2,820	30	5	3
1,804	40	8	3
1,247	50	1	4
827	60	1	3
516	70	8	4
258	80	8	0
89	90	3	4
0	100	1	1

Source: SEC.

[a] Decile values on annual security commission income are sum of quarterly decile values for NYSE firms doing a public business. Summing quarterly decile values to get annual decile values exaggerates the dispersion of decile values over what it would be if deciles were calculated directly on annual security commission income of firms. This in turn biases downward the number of firms in the extreme deciles. Only firms with positive security commission income were classified. The number of such firms by quarter was: Q1, 437; Q2, 431; Q3, 424; and Q4, 420. Total security commission income of firms doing a public business was: Q1, $651,300,000; Q2, $520,800,000; Q3, $508,500,000; and Q4, 590,600,000.

[b] Firms were classified by the latest SCI figure available for each firm. Since most firms discontinued membership under some form of distress, SCI tended to be below normal. This bias is offset by the fact that decile values in column one are based on 1974 SCI, which was lower than in subsequent years.

optimal level. Under fixed rates more capacity may be provided, but all investors, including those who would be willing to postpone trading, pay for it. Under competitive rates, capacity is less, and only investors who need it pay for it.

There is no evidence that capital has been eroded since 1975. Indeed, equity capital of NYSE firms, including the value of seats, increased from $2,736 million in the second quarter of 1975 to $3,427 million in the fourth quarter of 1978. One should not expect a great effect. There may, in theory, be a reduction in capital that reflects the decline in seat values due to the elimination of monopoly profits. However, this windfall loss would not discourage firms from staying in business to seek a normal profit that is as good as or better than other alternatives open to the firm.

Stability of the Financial System. Brokerage firms are like financial intermediaries such as commercial banks in that they hold customer funds. It was argued that one goal of United States economic policy was to minimize the risk of failure of financial institutions and that the minimum commissions applied to NYSE transactions were essential to the effective implementation of this policy.

First, it is not at all clear that commercial banks and other financial intermediaries should be protected against failure, since such protection has the undesirable side effects of inefficiency and misallocation of resources. Second, it is not clear that brokers are related in the same way as banks to the stability and integrity of the nation's payment system, since they are not involved in the creation of the nation's money supply. Third, it is not clear that minimum commissions create a "profit cushion" and protect against failure. Since the profits generated by high commissions are capitalized in the price of the seat and since purchasers of the seat view the cost of the seat as a cost of doing business, new entrants earn a normal return and do not have a profit cushion, and old firms bear opportunity costs of holding onto the seat and have no reason to treat the return to it as a "cushion." Fourth, to the extent that the argument is valid, a more effective method has been found to protect the integrity and stability of the financial system — namely, the insurance of customer accounts by the Securities Investor Protection Corporation established in 1970. Like the insurance of bank deposits, insurance of customer funds at brokers protects against runs on brokerage firms that might cause cumulative failures of firms. Finally, there is no evidence that in the period since 1975 competitive commission rates have in any way adversely affected the stability and integrity of the United States financial system.

Market Fragmentation

A second major element in the NYSE argument against competitive rates was that competition would cause brokers to leave the NYSE and take their orders elsewhere, thereby fragmenting markets and reducing liquidity. The first firms to leave would be those that do no floor execution and clearing and are members mainly to avoid paying the nonmember commission rate. Others would leave to avoid regulation by the NYSE and to avoid the costs of running the exchange. This argument has little validity. With competitive rates, investors have less incentive to trade away from the NYSE to save commissions. If their customers wish to trade on the NYSE — the most liquid market in the absence of efficient intermarket communications — brokers will remain members of the NYSE. Since 1975 trading in NYSE stocks in the OTC market has indeed declined substantially, and the major third-market traders have gone out of business or substantially curtailed their trading in NYSE stocks.

Discrimination Against Small Investors

Another argument against competitive rates was that trading costs for small investors would rise because under fixed rates small investors had been subsidized by institutional commissions and because the weak bargaining power of small investors would make it difficult to negotiate favorable rates at the advent of competitive commissions.

There is no economic rationale in this case for subsidizing one class of customer by charging higher fees to another class, particularly in view of the fact that the individuals investing through institutions are likely to be "smaller" than those individuals that trade for their own account. Thus, if a subsidy existed, competitive rates would have the beneficial effect of removing it. Under competition, prices tend to reflect costs, and so long as that is the case, discrimination in an economically meaningful sense cannot be said to exist. The large drop in institutional commissions since 1975 as compared with individual commissions shows that individuals investing through institutions were discriminated against under fixed rates as compared with individuals investing directly.

Research

Another argument in favor of fixed minimum commissions was that, without minimum commission rates, information, research, and advisory activities on the part of brokerage firms would be sharply curtailed; the discount-house concept, which ignores service, would probably become dominant in the securities business. This argument is based on the position that one cannot charge separately for research: it would be difficult to recapture the costs of producing research, since those who did not incur the costs of production could resell the information at a lower price than the producer.

The opposing argument is that research can be unbundled from execution and charged for separately. Indeed, many research organizations and firms do just that. Furthermore, research supplied in return for commission dollars can as readily be resold as research supplied in return for hard dollars. Finally, it should be noted that it is theoretically possible for research to increase under separate pricing. If the market is given a choice as to the proportions of execution and research that can be purchased, more of both can be bought.

Experience since 1975 indicates that the production and delivery of research has changed somewhat. Institutions and individuals capable of doing their own research now do so and pay lower commissions. However, many investors still choose to "pay up" for research in their commissions. For a product as intangible as research it is difficult to judge whether the aggregate level of research has declined. Under fixed commissions much research was in fact difficult to distinguish from advertising, and it appears there has been a salutary reduction in such "research."

REVOLUTION IN SECURITIES MARKETS REGULATION: FUTURE PROBLEMS AND PROSPECTS

The revolution in securities markets regulation has stemmed from a change in philosophy on the part of the SEC and the Congress toward relying more heavily on competition than on direct government regulation or self-regulation by exchanges. The greater reliance on competition has resulted in part from the difficulties experienced by the SEC in regulating detailed aspects of the securities markets and from the undesirable forms that competition took under fixed exchange rates. In part it has resulted from underlying economic forces — institutionalization of the stock market and the third market — that were undermining fixed rates anyway. And in part it has resulted from direct legal challenges of the fixed-commission system by individual citizens and the Justice Department.

The implication of this change in philosophy, however, goes beyond the legislation of competitive commissions. A key aspect of the Securities Acts Amendments of 1975 calls for a national market system (NMS) characterized by the absence of unnecessary regulatory restrictions, fair competition among brokers, dealers, and markets, the availability to all of information on transactions prices and dealer price quotations, the linking of markets, and the ability to execute orders in the best market. In other words, Congress and the SEC have recognized that technological advances permit the establishment of a single national market that is not restricted to a specific physical location and in which communication and trading through a computer replace face-to-face communication and trading on an exchange floor. Any qualified broker or dealer could join such a system by buying or renting the necessary computer terminals.

There are three key elements of an NMS:[16] (1) a computerized national transaction reporting system that records and reports all transactions (price and quantity) wherever they take place; (2) a computerized national central limit order file (CLOF) that lists limit order prices and quantities of investors as well as bids and offers of dealers (an investor leaves a limit order when he wishes to trade at a price better than the prices currently available from other investors or market makers); (3) a mechanism to "lock in" a transaction on the computer when an acceptable price is observed in CLOF.

While some of the elements, such as the national transactions reporting system, are in place and while there are no technological obstacles to any remaining elements of the system, it is not expected that the ideal system will soon be in operation. The costs of implementing such a system and, more important, the vested interests benefiting from current trading procedures hinder the speedy establishment of NMS and the greater access and competition that NMS would imply. The SEC has tended to let NMS "evolve" for fear of imposing a system that is not necessarily the most efficient. But control of such an evolutionary process is likely to be in the hands of vested interests that benefit most from the old ways of routing orders.

With the demise of fixed commissions, brokerage firms doing a public business now need no longer see their fortunes tied to those of the NYSE, which in the past enforced high commissions. Indeed these firms are more properly viewed as intermediaries between the public and the various processes for executing transactions. They seek the most efficient method of trading. If the evolving national market system (NMS) provides a lower-cost method for completing transactions, brokerage firms will use it. If not, they will continue to channel transactions to the floor of the NYSE as they have in the past. Support for the existing methods of trading comes from the floor community of the NYSE that benefits most from the order flow that is channeled there. The battle over Rule 390, which restricts off-floor dealer trading, and other regulatory policy is a battle for the order flow. It is in the interests of the specialists and other members of the floor to retain the order flow, even if other methods of trading would be more efficient. Thus the major regulatory issue before us now is the appropriate market structure for the provision of competitive dealer services as called for in the Securities Acts Amendments of 1975. Whether the SEC will in fact promote a system that facilitates competition among dealers or whether specialists will continue to have a privileged access to the order flow is yet to be determined.

The ideal national market system is like a national highway system on which anyone willing to pay the cost of the vehicle may drive. In the NMS the danger is that some of the drivers may also own the road. Government policy must balance the desirable objective of letting private initiative and ingenuity determine the most efficient market structure against the need to intervene to prevent particular interests from controlling access to the market and restricting the degree of competition.

NOTES

[1] See I. Friend (May 1972).

[2] See papers by Benston (1973, 1975), Friend and Westerfield (1975), Stigler (1964), and Friend and Herman (1964).

[3] The issues leading up to the Amendments are effectively presented in U.S. House, Subcommittee on Commerce and Finance of the Committee on Interstate and Foreign Commerce, *Securities Industry Study* (August 1972); and U.S. Senate, Subcommittee on Securities of the Committee on Banking, Housing and Urban Affairs, *Securities Industry Study* (February 1973).

[4] More elaborate models of the determinants of seat prices are in Doede (1967) and Schwert (1975).

[5] As of March 31, 1976, Rule 394 was replaced by Rule 390 pursuant to SEC Rule 19C-1, which requires that exchange members, when acting as agents, be permitted to execute transactions on other exchanges or the OTC market, provided only that they may be required to satisfy limit orders left with the specialist.

[6] For more detailed information see Stoll (1979); U.S. SEC, "The Effect of the Absence of Fixed Rates of Commission" (December 1, 1975; March 29, 1976; August 10, 1976; May 26, 1977); and U.S. SEC, "Staff Report on the Securities Industry in 1978" (July 26, 1979).

[7] IIS, Vol. 4, p. 2281; Vol. 2, pp. 469–471 and Table V-25.

[8] See Farrar (1974) and Herman (1975), Chap. IV. An important signal of possible legal action was the speech by Donald I. Baker, Antitrust Division, U.S. Department of Justice, "Banking and Bigness: and the Search for a Better Tomorrow" (Federal Bar Association Convention, Washington, D.C., September 17, 1970), cited in Farrar (1974).

[9] The result (NYSE, 1968, p. 61) is:

$$X_1 = 476.393 + 31.34X_2 - 0.000001082X_2^2; \qquad r^2 = 0.934$$

$$\quad (2.79) \qquad (40.39) \qquad \quad (-6.54)$$

where X_1 = total expenses per firm in 1966
$\quad X_2$ = number of transactions per firm in 1966.

Dividing through by X_2 yields average cost, which will be declining as a function of X_2.

[10] As reported in West and Tinic (1971) and Mann (1975).

[11] Analysis of quarterly data from the first quarter of 1972 to the third quarter of 1977 shows that changes in the number of firms were not significantly related to the introduction of competitive rates. There was a significant positive association with lagged income. The regression results follow:

$$\Delta N = -6.09 - 11.91D_1 + 3.77D_2 + 0.0188Y_{t-1}$$

$$(-3.93) \quad (-4.51) \qquad (1.11) \qquad (2.29)$$

$$\text{adj. } r^2 = 0.538, \qquad DW = 3.01, \qquad \text{obs.} = 22$$

where ΔN = change in number of firms
$\quad D_1$ = dummy variable taking the value 1 in quarter 1 because significant changes in number of firms took place between fourth and first quarters; 0 otherwise
$\quad D_2$ = dummy variable taking the value 1 in each of the first three quarters of 1975 to reflect introduction of competitive rates; 0 otherwise
$\quad Y_{t-1}$ = prior quarter's aggregate net income.

The regression shows that the quarterly time trend was a decline of 6.09 firms per quarter except for the first quarter of each year, when the drop, on average, was 18.0 firms. The response to lagged income, Y_{t-1}, is statistically significant. The dummy variable reflecting the introduction of competitive rates is insignificant.

An alternative regression in which D_2 is set equal to 1 from the second quarter 1975 onward yields the same conclusion:

$$\Delta N = -6.125 - 11.69D_1 + 0.679D_2 + 0.020Y_{t-1}$$

$$(-3.55) \quad (-4.24) \qquad (0.25) \qquad (2.24)$$

$$\text{adj. } r^2 = 0.507, \qquad DW = 2.72, \qquad \text{obs.} = 22$$

[12] For a recent debate on the causes and seriousness of concentration in the brokerage industry, see the papers by Schaefer and Warner (1977) and West and Tinic (1978).

[13] The relation between quarterly changes in total expenses and quarterly changes in security commission income (SCI) for the period first quarter 1972 to first quarter 1975 is as follows:

$$\Delta y = 0.3583 + 0.5705 \ \Delta X$$
$$\quad\quad (0.03) \quad (8.157)$$

$$r^2 = 0.8133, \quad \text{obs.} = 12$$
$$DW = 2.116, \quad \sigma \text{ of residuals} = 41.9$$

where y = total expenses
X = security commission income.

Then $y = 830.69 + 0.5705X$, where the constant is given by $\bar{y} - 0.5705\bar{X}$. Predicted expenses for the quarters after introduction of competitive rates are then as follows, using the "levels" equation:

Quarter	Actual SCI + Revenue Loss	Predicted Expense $(\hat{y})$	Actual Expense (y)	Actual − Predicted
2/75	880.5 + 42.0	1,356.98	1,343.7	−13.28
3/75	641.4 + 67.5	1,235.12	1,213.6	−21.52
4/75	611.1 + 87.2	1,229.07	1,273.4	44.33
1/76	1,041.9 + 139.0	1,504.39	1,505.7	1.31

Actual expenses appear to be about the same as would have been predicted under continuation of fixed rates.

[14] SEC profit-margin figures (in "The Effect of the Absence of Fixed Rates of Commissions," Reports to Congress) cited in the text are income after partners' compensation but before taxes divided by gross income.

[15] The SEC publications cited above give statistics for seven different types of brokerage firms.

[16] For a more extensive discussion of the national market system see Peake (1978), Mendelson and Peake (1979), and SEC Release No. 34-15671, "Development of a National Market System" (March 22, 1979).

BIBLIOGRAPHY

Baxter, W. F., "NYSE Fixed Commission Rates: A Private Cartel Goes Public," *Stanford Law Review*, 22 (April 1970), 675–712.

Benston, G. J., "Required Disclosure and the Stock Market: An Evaluation of the Securities Exchange Act of 1934," *American Economic Review*, 63 (March 1973).

———, "Required Disclosure and the Stock Market, Rejoinder," *American Economic Review*, 65 (June 1975).

Benston, G. J., and Hagerman, R., "Determinants of Bid-Asked Spreads in the Over-the-Counter Market," *Journal of Financial Economics*, 1 (March 1974).

Doede, Robert W., "The Monopoly Power of the New York Stock Exchange," unpublished Ph.D. dissertation, Department of Economics, University of Chicago, 1967.

Epps, T. W., "The Demand for Broker's Services: The Relation Between Security Trading Volume and Transaction Cost," *Bell Journal of Economics*, 7 (Spring 1976), 163–194.

Farrar, D. E., "The Coming Reform on Wall Street," *Harvard Business Review*, 50 (September–October 1972).

———, "The Martin Report: Wall Street's Proposed 'Great Leap Backward,' " *Financial Analysts Journal* (September–October 1971).

———, "Toward a Central Market System: Wall Street's Slow Retreat into the Future," *Journal of Financial and Quantitative Analysis*, 9 (November 1974).

Friedman, M., "Comment," in Stigler (ed.), *Business Concentration and Price Policy*. Princeton: Princeton University Press, 1955, pp. 230–238.

Friend, Irwin, "The Economic Consequences of the Stock Market," *American Economic Review*, 52 (May 1972), 212–219.

——— and Blume, M., "The Consequences of Competitive Commissions on the New York Stock Exchange," Rodney White Center for Financial Research, the Wharton School, University of Pennsylvania, Philadelphia, April 1972.

——— and ———, "Competitive Commissions on the New York Stock Exchange," *Journal of Finance*, 28 (September 1973).

Friend, Irwin, and Herman, E., "The SEC Through a Glass Darkly," *Journal of Business*, 37 (October 1964).

Friend, Irwin, and Westerfield, R., "Required Disclosure and the Stock Market, Comment," *American Economic Review*, 65 (June 1975).

Greenwich Research Associates, *Annual Report on Institutional Brokerage Services*, Greenwich, Conn., 1976.

Herman, Edward S., *Conflicts of Interest: Commercial Bank Trust Departments*. New York: Twentieth Century Fund, 1975.

Institutional Investor Study Report of the Securities and Exchange Commission (IIS), 92d Congress, 1st Session, House Document No. 92–64, 7 vols., March 10, 1971.

Kraus, A., and Stoll, H., "Price Impacts of Block Trading on the New York Stock Exchange," *Journal of Finance*, 27 (June 1972).

Mann, H. Michael, "The New York Stock Exchange: A Cartel at the End of Its Reign," in Phillips, A. (ed.), *Promoting Competition in Regulated Markets*. Washington, D.C.: Brookings Institution, 1975, pp. 301–327.

Mayer, Martin, *Conflicts of Interest: Broker-Dealer Firms*. New York: Twentieth Century Fund, 1975.

Melnik, A., and Ofer, A., "Price Deregulation in the Brokerage Industry: An Empirical Analysis," *Bell Journal of Economics*, 9 (Autumn 1978).

Mendelson, Morris, "From Automated Quotes to Automated Trading: Restructuring the Stock Market in the U.S.," *The Bulletin*, NYU Graduate School of Business Administration, March 1972.

———, and Peake, Junius, "The ABC's of Trading on a National Market System," *Financial Analysts Journal*, September–October 1979.

National Economic Research Associates, Inc., *Stock Brokerage Commissions: The Development and Application of Standards of Reasonableness for Public Rates*, A Report to the Cost and Revenue Committee of the New York Stock Exchange, July 1970, 2 vols.

New York Stock Exchange, *Economic Effects of Negotiated Commission Rates on the Brokerage Industry, the Market for Corporate Securities, and the Investing Public*, A Report submitted to the SEC, August 1968.

———, A Staff Analysis of Issues Affecting the Structure of a Central Exchange Market for Listed Securities, July 1973.

———, *Fact Book*, annual.

———, "Public Transaction Study," 1969, 1974.

———, "Research Report on: Impact of Competitive Rates: A Monitoring Program Report," December 9, 1975.

Peake, Junius W., "The National Market System," *Financial Analysts Journal*, July–August, 1978.

Robbins, Sidney, *The Securities Markets*. New York: Free Press, 1966.

Schaefer, Jeffrey, and Warner, Adolph, "Concentration Trends and Competition in the Securities Industry," *Financial Analysts Journal*, November–December 1977.

———, "Rejoinder," *Financial Analysts Journal*, May–June 1978.

Schwert, G. W., "Public Regulation of National Securities Exchanges: A Test of the Capture Hypothesis," unpublished Ph.D. dissertation, Graduate School of Business, University of Chicago, 1975.

Smidt, Seymour, "Which Road to an Efficient Stock Market?" *Financial Analysts Journal*, September–October 1971.

Smith, Caleb, "Survey of Empirical Evidence on Economies of Scale," in Stigler (ed.), *Business Concentration and Price Policy*. Princeton: Princeton University Press, 1955, pp. 213–230.

Stigler, G. J., "Public Regulation of the Securities Markets," *Journal of Business*, 37 (October 1964).

Stoll, H. R., "Dealer Inventory Behavior: An Empirical Investigation of NASDAQ Stocks," *Journal of Financial and Quantitative Analysis*, September 1976.

———, "The Supply of Dealer Services in Securities Markets," *Journal of Finance*, September 1978.

———, "The Pricing of Security Dealer Services: An Empirical Study of NASDAQ Stocks," *Journal of Finance*, September 1978.

———, "Regulation of Securities Markets: An Examination of the Effects of Increased Competition," *The Monograph Series in Finance and Economics* 1979-2 (December 1979), NYU Graduate School of Business Administration.

Tinic, Seha, "The Economics of Liquidity Services," *Quarterly Journal of Economics*, 86 (February 1972).

——— and West, R., "Competition and the Pricing of Dealer Services in the Over-the-Counter Market," *Journal of Financial and Quantitative Analysis*, 7 (June 1972).

U.S. Department of Justice, "Memorandum of the U.S. Dept. of Justice on the Fixed Minimum Commission Rate Structure," brief submitted to the SEC in January 1969, File No. 4–144.

———, "Proposal to Adopt Securities Exchange Act Rules 19b–3 and 10b–22, SEC File No. 4–176, Comments of the U.S. Dept. of Justice," December 10, 1974.

U.S. Securities and Exchange Commission, "Statement of the Securities and Exchange Commission on the Future Structure of the Securities Markets," mimeo, February 2, 1972.

———, "Policy Statement of the Securities and Exchange Commission on the Structure of a Central Market System," printed in *Securities Regulation and Law Report*, No. 196 (April 4, 1973).

———, "The Effect of the Absence of Fixed Rates of Commission," Reports to Congress December 1, 1975; March 29, 1976; August 10, 1976; May 26, 1977.

———, Staff Report on the Securities Industry in 1978, July 26, 1979.

———, Release No. 34-15671, "Development of a National Market System," March 22, 1979.

———, Statistical Data:
1. Statistical Bulletin.
2. Statistical Reference Tables.

U.S. House, Subcommittee on Commerce and Finance of the Committee on Interstate and Foreign Commerce, *Securities Industry Study*, 92d Congress, 2d Session, August 1972.

U.S. Senate, Subcommittee on Securities of Committee on Banking, Housing and Urban Affairs, *Securities Industry Study*, 93d Congress, 1st Session, February 1973.

Warren, James T., Jr., "An Empirical Examination of the Transition Period in Brokerage Commissions from Fixed to Negotiated," unpublished paper, Computer Directors Advisors, Inc., Md., and University of Maryland, June 14, 1976.

West, R., and Tinic, S., "Minimum Commission Rates on New York Stock Exchange Transactions," *Bell Journal of Economics and Management Science*, 2 (Autumn 1971), 577–605.

——— and ———, *The Economics of the Stock Market.* New York: Praeger, 1971.

——— and ———, "Concentration Trends and Competition in the Securities Industry, An Alternative Viewpoint," *Financial Analysts Journal*, May–June 1978.

CASE 2

The Revolution in Airline Regulation

Theodore E. Keeler
University of California, Berkeley

INTRODUCTION

Since its birth fifty years ago the airline industry has experienced rapid growth and dramatic technological change. Yet for most of that period public regulatory policies toward the industry — a set of tight controls on fares and firm entry devised during the Great Depression — remained largely unchanged. In the late 1970s, however, after a long buildup of studies and proposals advocating modernization, public policy toward the industry changed drastically, and the market was suddenly given free play. The hope was that the forces of the marketplace, rather than the controls of regulation, could best satisfy the needs of the traveling and shipping public.

This paper will follow and analyze these changes in regulatory policy. What were they, and are they for the better in economic terms? They are so recent that their full impact has not yet been determined. Markets have not had a chance to respond fully to the dramatic changes recently instituted in Washington. But enough has happened to make an analysis of the changes worthwhile.

Copyright © 1981 by Theodore E. Keeler. The author is Associate Professor of Economics at the University of California, Berkeley, and Senior Fellow at the Brookings Institution. He acknowledges the assistance of Richard Rocke and the support of the Transportation Policy Research Center and the Alfred P. Sloan Foundation through grant 78-4-1 to the Department of Economics, University of California, Berkeley. Any opinions, findings, conclusions, or recommendations expressed in this paper are those of the author and do not necessarily reflect the views of the Alfred P. Sloan Foundation or the sponsors of the Transportation Policy Research Center.

We need first to know something about the industry and about the development of regulatory policies that preceded the revolution in the late 1970s. We shall begin with a brief description of the industry as it now stands: who carries whom and what between what places.

THE AIRLINE INDUSTRY
IN A TIME OF TRANSITION

In trying to classify airline firms in these times of change, one is reminded of Voltaire's quip about the latter-day Holy Roman Empire: "It is neither holy, nor Roman, nor an Empire." [1] Similarly, the functional characterizations of different types of airlines in the old regime apply at best loosely now. A set of classifications will be offered here nevertheless as a useful framework, with some indication of where a caveat in the manner of Voltaire is appropriate.[2]

Based on traditional classifications, domestic United States airline service is provided by several different types of carriers, each with a different function. The major carrier types and the traffic they account for are summarized in Table 1.

As Table 1 reveals, the domestic trunk carriers account for the overwhelming majority of passenger-miles. They are the larger airlines, serving high-density, nonsubsidized routes, primarily in domestic service. The CAB traditionally regulated these carriers domestically, and what few foreign routes they possessed were controlled by the CAB, the International Air Transport Association, the Office of the President, and the relevant agencies of the foreign countries involved.

The CAB also controlled the local service carriers, nine airlines whose original aim was to serve smaller cities and towns across the

Table 1. Air Carrier Types and Traffic in the United States, 1978

Airline Type	Revenue Passenger-Miles (billions)	Percent of Total
Domestic trunk airlines	217.5	89.0
Local service carriers	17.6	7.2
Regional and feeder airlines	4.9	2.0
Intrastate carriers	4.5	1.8
Total	244.5	100.0

Source: Air Transport World, March 1979, pp. 14, 98–99.

country and to serve as feeders to the trunk system. The local service carriers have the right to federal subsidies, allocated and distributed by the CAB. Very similar in function are the Alaskan and Hawaiian carriers, who also receive federal subsidies for serving the two noncontiguous states.

Finally, the CAB has also regulated the cargo and supplemental (charter) carriers, but neither of these types has traditionally been allowed to provide scheduled passenger service.

In the traditional scheme of things, there are two other types of carriers, neither of which has been controlled by the CAB. The commuter carriers provide low-density, short-haul service (both scheduled and taxi) with small aircraft (capacity under 60 passengers and 25 tons gross takeoff weight). Even when the CAB had the full power to regulate these carriers, it gave them an exemption from regulation. With deregulation, they are receiving subsidies and supplanting the traditional role of the local service carriers. The other carriers not previously controlled by the CAB are the intrastate carriers, which developed within the states of California, Texas, and Florida, and which for many years in the former regime provided short-haul, high-density service at fares well below CAB levels.

Having summarized the various carrier types and the traffic they carry, we can paraphrase Voltaire: the domestic trunks are not domestic; the local service carriers do not provide local service; the supplemental carriers are no longer supplemental; and the intrastate carriers are not intrastate. In other words, almost all the domestic trunks now have extensive international route structures, in addition to their domestic networks. The local service carriers have concentrated more and more on high-density routes, leaving the local service traffic increasingly to the commuters (thus, one local, Allegheny, abandoned practically all its local routes to commuters, went off subsidy, and to eliminate its regional image changed its name to US AIR). The supplementals are now being granted scheduled routes. And the intrastate carriers have now all been awarded interstate routes, expanding the same types of low fares and no-frills service to what were trunk routes. The changes we now observe are probably only the forerunners of more to come.

AIRLINE REGULATION: A BRIEF HISTORICAL SKETCH [3]

In their earliest days in the late 1920s and early 1930s the scheduled airlines operated primarily to haul mail, and they were paid for that purpose by the Post Office. As planes got larger and at least somewhat more reliable, in the early 1930s they began taking on passengers, although relative to the train and private auto their share of the market remained negligible. The Postmaster General of the time was very much an aviation enthusiast, and in giving out postal subsidies he showed a clear interest as well for promoting the carriage of passengers by air. Rather than awarding airmail contracts on the basis of lowest bids, however, he sat down with groups of airline executives and parceled out routes without bids, on the basis of a desire to develop route systems for each airline. This might conceivably have been in the interests of passengers, in the sense that the right route system could entail more convenient travel for most passengers. But it was outside the spirit and the letter of the law as it related to airmail carriage, and it caused a scandal.

The outcome of this procedure was the Airmail Act of 1934, which assured competitive, sealed bids for airmail contracts on a given route. A year after an airline had initiated service on a route, it was in a position to win changes in rates (supposedly based on changes in costs) from the Interstate Commerce Commission, without the need for a second-round bidding process. This combination of incentives, along with the carriers' desire to preserve their original route structures, produced an unfortunate result: each airline made an extremely low bid (as low as 0.1 cent per aircraft-mile) to maintain its existing routes, with the hope that the ICC would allow it to raise rates later.

There were two basic outcomes to this bidding process: first, each airline kept the route structure previously negotiated with the Postmaster General. Second, nearly every airline went to the brink of bankruptcy, given that rates were so far below costs. The ICC, sensing it was neither legal nor fair to allow rate increases immediately after the bidding process, and not being in the habit of acting quickly anyway, failed to grant rate increases soon enough to prevent financial disaster for some carriers.

In the years since this unfortunate competitive bidding process occurred, the outcome has been cited as clear evidence that the airline industry cannot function without government regulation — that destructive competition would occur without continuation of the government controls that were afterward imposed. The current viability of the airline industry without government regulation of fares and of firm entry is a topic we shall discuss later in detail. For now, two things are worth noting: first, the airline industry has changed considerably since the 1930s. Most notably, in the 1930s the industry was not economically viable without government subsidies, whereas now, on the high- and medium-density routes, many carriers survive quite comfortably without subsidies.[4] Second, as pointed out by Caves, even with government subsidies the bidding process devised in the Airmail Act of 1934 was ambiguous: it set up incentives to make low bids, with the hope of getting subsidy increases later, but it was ambiguous as to whether those subsidies were forthcoming. Taking these two things into account, there is good reason to doubt that the failure of the bidding process in the 1930s has any bearing on the viability of competition in the airline industry in the 1970s and 1980s.

Whatever its current relevance, this bidding experience made it clear in the 1930s that the Air Mail Act of 1934 was not adequate or appropriate for those times. Legislation was drafted that placed the industry under the control of a totally new and largely independent agency, charged with controlling the airline industry not simply for the purposes of the Post Office but for all the potential uses that commercial aviation might have to society. This legislation, the Civil Aeronautics Act of 1938, provided the basic principles behind federal control of commercial aviation for the next four decades.

More specifically, the 1938 Act set up the Civil Aeronautics Authority (changed in 1940 to the Civil Aeronautics Board), which had broad powers over the airlines. It was given complete control over entry of new firms, maximum and minimum rates (for passengers, air mail, and freight), subsidy allocations, route structures of existing firms, and aviation safety. (Safety regulation was transferred in 1958 to the Federal Aviation Agency; its name was changed in 1966 to the Federal Aviation Administration.)

What was the CAB to do with these powers? Title I of the Act states:

In the exercise and performance of its powers and duties under this Act, the Board shall consider the following, among other things, as being in the public interest, and in accordance with the public convenience and necessity:

(a) The encouragement and development of an air transportation system properly adapted to the present and future needs of the foreign and domestic commerce of the United States, of the Postal Service, and the national defense;

(b) The regulation of air transportation in such a manner as to recognize and preserve the inherent advantages of, assure the highest degree of safety in, and foster sound economic conditions in such transportation, and to improve the relations between, and coordinate transportation by, air carriers;

(c) The promotion of adequate, economical, and efficient service by air carriers at reasonable charges, without unjust discriminations, undue preferences, or unfair or destructive competitive practices;

(d) Competition to the extent necessary to assure the sound development of an air-transportation system properly adapted to the needs of the foreign and domestic commerce of the United States, of the Postal Service, and of the national defense;

(e) The promotion of safety in air commerce; and,

(f) The promotion, encouragement, and development of Civil Aeronautics.[5]

Not only are these provisions somewhat vague, but they have the potential for contradiction. There may, for example, be a contradiction between "economical, efficient service by air carriers at reasonable charges" and "sound economic conditions" in the air transportation industry. Nor is it clear that the needs of the postal service are totally in line with, say, the needs of the national defense.

Overall, then, there was considerable need for interpretation of this law. Rather than going into all possible interpretations here, we shall concern ourselves with the broadest and most economically relevant interpretation that the CAB itself applied.

From this law the CAB took as perhaps its major goal the development of a nationwide airline system, serving practically all communities of significant size, at a minimum cost in government subsidies (there is, as we shall see, subsequent evidence that this is what Congress wanted).

How was the CAB to meet this goal? Consider first the question of fares. For many years rail was the airlines' dominant competition (at least into the early postwar years), so that airline fares were largely determined by first class rail fares.[6] Unlike rail costs, however, airline costs per seat- or plane-mile decline considerably with length of haul. As a result, long-haul traffic was considerably more profitable (or, at the very beginning, incurred less of a loss) than short-haul traffic. Similarly, because high-density routes generally operated with more seats full than low-density routes, they tended to be more profitable than low-density routes.

Under these circumstances, the CAB found it increasingly attractive during the 1930s, 1940s, and early 1950s to use profits from high-density and long-haul routes to cross-subsidize losses from low-density and short-haul routes. This approach was attractive politically because it enabled the airlines to provide service over an extensive route structure with relatively little direct subsidy.[7]

Several market forces, however, if allowed to take their course, will make this politically attractive policy of cross-subsidization fail.

First, a profit-maximizing airline would much rather keep the profits from its more lucrative routes than give them away to operate unprofitable routes. Second, there will be incentives for new firms (or airlines not currently serving a given route) to enter the route, reduce fares, and thereby eliminate the profits needed to cross-subsidize. Third, an airline entering a route need not even reduce fares to drive away profits on that route; it can compete in various service dimensions as well. In fact, all these forces came into play over the years, especially after 1950, and they tended to subvert the achievement of the CAB's goals of cross-subsidization.

During World War II and thereafter, the longer-haul and higher-density routes were consistently profitable. The trunk carriers thus had an incentive to withdraw from unprofitable routes and keep the profits from their remaining routes rather than giving them away. As a result, by 1952 all the trunks except Northeast went off subsidy (though, as Caves argues, the industry likely benefited from indirect subsidies, through airports and airways, for many years thereafter, and probably still does).[8] To replace the trunks a new class of carrier, the local service carriers, came into existence in the late 1940s and early 1950s. These received subsidies of the same sort the trunks had received earlier. But once the local service carriers were on subsidy they faced pressure from Congress, and from the Eisenhower and Kennedy administrations, to reduce the need for direct subsidies.[9] Thus, the CAB began awarding high-density routes to the local service carriers, in hopes that they would be able to use them to cross-subsidize low-density routes. Predictably, the local service airlines have in recent years been abandoning low-density routes to the commuter carriers, and at least one local service carrier has gone off direct subsidy. The point is that the carriers have little if any incentive to cross-subsidize: they are better off keeping the money as profit. But that is only the first reason why policies of cross-subsidy did not work.

Second, there is an incentive for carriers to enter high-density routes and make profits by reducing fares. With two exceptions, the CAB was able to prevent this from happening. First, in the late 1940s, a group of small carriers entered various markets, using war-surplus aircraft and war-trained pilots. Because the CAB prevented them from providing scheduled service, they operated on irregular schedules — hence the term applied to them: "nonskeds." By use of higher seating density than the trunks, these carriers had distinctly lower costs. For several years the CAB resisted the trunks' pleas to provide similar service with similar seating densities. In 1949, however, it allowed the trunks to match the densities of the nonskeds and to nearly match their fares on some routes. The result was the first coach or economy service, which in turn drove the nonskeds out of all but charter operations (they subsequently became known as supplementals). Although coach service made fares lower than the theretofore-available first class, they were in the end at least as profitable; the higher densities reduced costs. So this lowering of fares did not harm airline profitability on high-density routes.

Much more damaging to airline profits on high-density routes was service-quality competition; the CAB controlled fares, but it placed no controls on capacity or service competition. And, as long as a route was generating excess profits, there were incentives to add capacity; extra frequencies generated extra business in the same way a price cut generates extra business for a newly entered firm.

There is some evidence that this frequency and capacity competition, possibly along with lesser competition in service dimensions such as meals, had the same effect on aggregate airline profits as price competition in other industries: it drove them down to a normal level — a level similar to that which the corporate sector as a whole earns — even though in the early 1950s trunk carriers largely abandoned money-losing routes for which cross-subsidies would be necessary.[10]

In short, it can be argued that CAB policies failed at their main objective of supporting a larger airline system than the market would support without using government revenues to cover the full cost of doing so. At the same time, the relatively high fares charged on long-haul and high-density routes were not being used to cross-subsidize low-density routes; they were instead dissipated in service-quality competition. This would give us reason to suspect that passengers, especially on long-haul and high-density routes, were paying more than they would have to pay in the free market, though they may have been getting better service as a result. On the basis of evidence presented so far, however, this is just conjecture. More detailed evidence on airline fares and service qualities under regulation is presented in the next section. This evidence should also indicate the benefits that deregulation promised, which can in turn be compared with the benefits that have materialized.

BEFORE THE CHANGE: THE EFFECTS OF AIRLINE REGULATION BY THE MID-1970s

The effects of airline regulation on the structure and conduct of the industry in the 1970s have already been discussed; no totally new firms were allowed into interstate markets from 1938 to 1978, except local service carriers. Fares, by and large, were set based on CAB formulas, and while certain types of discount fares were allowed from time to time, the CAB had allowed little by way of unrestricted discount fares since the introduction of coach service. Thus, competition occurred in the dimension of service quality. On many routes the CAB did authorize entry by existing firms from time to time, but that resulted simply in enhanced service competition in the routes involved.[11]

The most critical question relating to CAB regulatory policy by the mid-1970s related to its effects on fares. Fortunately, the development of intrastate carriers in California, Texas, and Florida suggested what would happen with deregulation in interstate routes. The relevant state regulatory authorities took a more permissive attitude toward fare reductions and entry of new firms than did the CAB, and so the intrastate markets offered a laboratory in which the likely effects of deregulation on a nationwide basis might be predicted. We shall focus on the intrastate markets of California and Texas, which by 1974–1975, were better developed than those of Florida.

In California, both fares and firm entry were almost totally unregulated until 1965, except that a new firm had to meet safety standards set by the Federal Aviation Administration, and the California Public Utilities Commission (PUC) could set maximum rates, but not minimum ones. In 1965 the PUC was given the right to control both fares and entry of firms, with the aim of achieving an "orderly, efficient, economical, and healthy intrastate air network" along with stability, low fares, and frequent service.[12]

The Texas Aeronautics Commission (TAC) had complete control over entry of firms, as did the California PUC, but very limited control over fares. Technically, it had control over an intrastate carrier's fares, but it claimed no control over the fares of intrastate operations of interstate carriers, so it effectively allowed pricing freedom for both carrier types.[13] The law required the TAC to "further the public interest and aeronautical progress by providing for the protection, promotion, and development of aeronautics." [14]

In both states the relevant regulatory agencies were considerably more liberal than the CAB in allowing new firms to enter and in allowing downward price competition. Thus, before 1965, sixteen new carriers entered the California market, and after 1965 two more. Of these eighteen carriers, however, only two important ones, Pacific Southwest Airlines (PSA) and Air California, survived.[15] In Texas one carrier, Southwest Airlines, entered the market, and then only after lengthy court litigations, for although the Texas Aeronautics Commission favored its entry from the beginning, Texas law allowed court appeal of TAC decisions by interested parties, including carriers already serving the routes proposed for service by Southwest.[16]

The numbers of intrastate carriers succeeding in each market (one in Texas and two in California) may seem small. But even these small numbers would seem to be enough to instigate vigorous price competition. They cut fares sharply and forced the CAB-regulated carriers to match the cuts for intrastate traffic.[17] As a result, fares on every intrastate route were significantly below fares on CAB routes of equivalent length and traffic density.

Fare Differences

Table 2 presents some 1975 California and Texas intrastate fares (and yields per mile) alongside equivalent figures for routes of similar length on CAB-regulated interstate routes. The results indicate that fares on interstate routes were consistently greater than fares on equivalent California routes by 70 to 120 percent. Thus, the (trunk) fare for the Chicago-Minneapolis route (339 miles) was $38.89, or over 100 percent greater than the (intrastate) Los Angeles-San Francisco fare of $18.75 (for a trip of 338 miles). Similarly, the (trunk) fare from Detroit to Philadelphia, a distance of 454 miles, was $45.37, or 73 percent greater than the (intrastate) San Francisco-San Diego fare of $26.21 (for a trip of 456 miles). As the reader can verify, the results are more or less the same for comparisons of any of the other comparable city-pairs.

Similar fare savings were available in Texas. Between Dallas and Houston, a distance of 239 miles, the 1975 fare was $23.15 on weekdays before 7 P.M., and $13.89 for evenings and weekends.[18] This compares with a fare of $28.70 for the Las Vegas-Los Angeles route, a distance of 236 miles (Table 2).

The low fares provided by the intrastate carriers in California and Texas were not achieved at the cost of aircraft safety or modernity. The intrastate carriers use aircraft identical to those of interstate carriers on equivalent routes, and their safety records were and are excellent in comparison with CAB-certificated carriers.[19] Furthermore, it is not clear that the service quality provided by the intrastate carriers was overall inferior to that provided in coach service on equivalent routes by interstate carriers. Both carriers generally used coach seats 18 inches wide pitched 34 inches apart. Although the intrastate carriers do not serve meals, the trunk carriers do not generally serve meals or free snacks on the hops of 65 to 350 miles served by the intrastate carriers. With regard to flight frequency, the evidence from intrastate routes would suggest that the low fares charged by intrastate carriers had induced sufficient new demand to support more flights than the higher fares previously charged by CAB-certificated carriers. Finally, the intrastate carriers have made considerable use of "satellite" airports, providing service to and from more points in a metropolitan area than generally occurs on interstate routes and making for a higher level of

Table 2. Comparison Between Interstate and Intrastate Fares, 1975

City Pair	Fare[a]	Miles
Los Angeles-San Francisco[b]	$18.75	338
Chicago-Minneapolis	38.89	339
New York-Pittsburgh	37.96	335
Los Angeles-San Diego[b]	10.10	109
San Francisco-Sacramento[b]	9.73	86
Portland-Seattle	22.22	129
Los Angeles-Sacramento[b]	20.47	373
Boston-Washington	41.67	399
San Francisco-San Diego[b]	26.21	456
Detroit-Philadelphia	45.37	454
Dallas-Ft. Worth-New Orleans	44.44	442
Dallas-Ft. Worth-Houston[b]	23.15/13.89[c]	239
Dallas-Ft. Worth-San Antonio[b]	23.15/13.89[c]	248
Las Vegas-Los Angeles	28.70	236
Chicago-St. Louis	29.63	258

Sources: Kennedy Committee Report (1975, p. 41); Official Airline Guide, February 1, 1975.
[a] Interstate markets: coach fare. Intrastate markets: economy fare.
[b] Intrastate route.
[c] Night and weekend fare.

passenger convenience. It thus does not appear that intrastate passengers have inferior service compared to interstate coach passengers.

How have the intrastate carriers achieved these lower fares? Certainly not by accepting lower profits than the CAB-certificated carriers. Once start-up costs were covered, intrastate carriers have consistently enjoyed profits as great as or greater than those of CAB-certificated carriers. Thus, in the years 1972 through 1974, Air California earned a return of over 24 percent after taxes on its equity investment.[20] Over the same period PSA earned 4 to 6 percent after taxes, which, although it may seem low, is not out of line with earnings of CAB-certificated carriers in the same years.[21] And Southwest Airlines, once heavy start-up costs were covered, also became profitable, earning a return on investment of 12.6 percent in 1974.[22]

How, then, did the intrastate carriers achieve profits in combination with fares substantially lower than those charged by the CAB-certificated carriers? The answer lies in a number of considerations, but most importantly in two: the seating capacity of the aircraft, and the load factor. Thus, in the case of the Boeing 727-200 (one of the most widely used aircraft ever built), PSA puts 158 seats in each aircraft, compared with 120 to 133 seats in trunk aircraft.[23] Does this mean that the passenger enjoys less space on intrastate aircraft? In the case of coach passengers, any space improvements provided by interstate carriers on short-haul routes are minimal, for the six-abreast seating with 34-inch pitch* used by PSA is common among the trunk and local-service carriers on short hauls. The difference in seating capacity would seem to be accounted for by two things: first class service on trunk carriers (but not PSA), and galley space (but, as we have already noted, meal service to coach passengers on trunk routes is rather rare for the short hauls of relevance here). Air California and Southwest Airlines (in Texas) get similarly larger numbers of seats into their Boeing 737s.[24]

As regards load factors, all three intrastate carriers have consistently achieved higher load factors than have the interstate carriers. Over the early 1970s Air California achieved an average load factor of 70 percent; PSA achieved a load factor of 60 percent or more on all its high-density routes, which in turn accounted for over two-thirds of its traffic. After its start-up period Southwest Airlines achieved a load factor of 58 percent in 1974 and 62 percent in the first three quarters of 1975. The trunk carriers, on the other hand, consistently achieved lower load factors: 52.1 percent in 1972, 51.9 percent in 1973, 55.7 percent in 1974, and 54.8 percent in 1975.[25]

It might be argued here that the lower load factor provided by CAB-regulated carriers did produce a superior service quality by making it easier to get a reservation at the preferred time.† If such benefits occurred, however, they accrued exclusively to the privileged 10 percent of interstate passengers who flew first class. In 1974 and 1975 alike, the *coach* load factor was nearly 59 percent, roughly the same as that achieved by PSA and Southwest.[26]

Evidence from the intrastate markets, then, strongly supports the contention that interstate trunk fares were being set "artificially" high by the Civil Aeronautics Board, and that the potential excess profits from these high fares were being competed away through service-quality and flight-frequency competition.

It might be argued that special operating or other considerations enabled the intrastate carriers to achieve these low fares. Yet the interstate carriers generally matched the intrastates when the latter reduced

---

* Pitch is the distance from a given spot on one seat to the same spot on the seat in front of it or behind it.

† This matter is discussed in more detail later in this paper.

fares. Furthermore, research by the present author in the early and mid-1970s indicates that the interstate carriers could have achieved coach fares similar to those of the interstates on a wide variety of trunk routes, based on interstate operating costs.[27]

This result was based on a cost model estimated on data for the trunk carriers, but adjusting load factors and seating configurations to those achieved on intrastate routes. One test of the accuracy of the results of this procedure was its ability to predict California Intrastate Fares, even though it was based on trunk costs. In fact it came quite close to predicting California fares. For the Los Angeles-San Francisco route it estimated a fare of $13.87, compared with an actual 1968 fare of $13.50. For the Los Angeles-San Diego route it predicted a fare of $6.50, compared with an actual fare of $6.35. In each case the model came within 3 percent of predicting actual fares. Although there were no long-haul intrastate routes with which to compare the model's results, it is worth noting that it came within a similar percentage of predicting World Airways' first proposed unrestricted transcontinental fares as of 1967. Thus, for three perhaps special cases, the model did a reasonably good job of predicting what unregulated, unrestricted fares would have been on interstate routes as of the late 1960s.

On the regulated routes, fares exceeded predicted unregulated ones by margins ranging from 20 percent on the shortest hauls, such as New York-Boston, to over 90 percent in other cases, such as New York-Miami. Thus, CAB-regulated trunk fares exceeded estimates of feasible unregulated fares by 20 to 90 percent.

Updated to autumn of 1974 this model indicated that fares on the same CAB routes were anywhere from 30 to 56 percent higher than potential unregulated fares would be.[28] In other words, the spread of "markups" had narrowed by the mid-1970s, and specifically the correlation between markup and length of haul had diminished considerably. Nevertheless, it would appear overall that CAB regulation, as of 1974–1975, continued to extract a toll in higher coach air fares than would have existed in its absence.

Arguably, however, CAB regulation produced not only higher coach fares but also the benefits of service-quality competition: more frequency, easier obtaining of reservations during crowded periods, less crowding, and more amenities. Considerable research has been done in this area, most especially by Douglas and Miller.[29] Surprisingly, the provision of these benefits to air travelers, especially in coach, is not so evident as one might expect.

First, consider flight frequencies. It is true that the high CAB fares did induce lower load factors and hence higher frequencies than would otherwise prevail *for the number of passengers traveling at CAB fares*. But it is also true, as previously indicated, that a reduction in the fare level to intrastate levels should induce extra demand. Offhand, it is not clear which effect should dominate.

Second, consider the matter of crowding and the ease of getting reservations during peak periods. It is true that CAB regulation resulted in lower load factors than would otherwise prevail. But these lower load factors existed almost exclusively in the first class compartments of aircraft. In the coach section, load factors were roughly the same in intrastate and trunk interstate markets from the late 1960s to the mid-1970s: around or just below 60 percent. On the other hand, first class load factors were consistently under 40 percent on interstate routes. The present author has previously presented evidence indicating that, unlike coach, first class fares were not fully compensatory relative to the long-run cost of providing the space.[30] Thus, CAB regulation did result in less crowding, more space, and greater ease of getting reservations during peak times. But it can be argued that these benefits accrued almost exclusively to the 10 percent of all passengers who traveled in the first class compartments of trunk aircraft.

It could be argued, then, that CAB regulation caused not inefficiency, but rather redistribution of income from coach to first class passengers. Such an argument, however, assumes that first class passengers would be willing to pay for the benefits of riding in spacious compartments with only 35 percent of the seats full, on average, and that the high coach or economy fares had no impact of discouraging demand in those lower classes. Neither assumption is plausible.

By the mid-1970s numerous economic studies indicated that less reliance on the CAB and more reliance on the marketplace in air transportation would produce substantial benefits for the traveling public. It remained for this evidence to be translated into policy. The next section tells how that happened.

REGULATORY REFORM AND THE STEPS LEADING TO IT

That unregulated air service could produce dramatically lower fares was not lost on academics; Caves (1962) and, even more forcefully, Levine (1965) reviewed the situation, especially in California, and put forth the case. Further studies by Purvis (1969), Jordan (1970), Keeler (1971, 1972), Douglas and Miller (1974), and others all confirmed the desirability of airline deregulation.[31]

Academic studies gave way by the mid-1970s to policy studies.

Senator Kennedy in 1974 mounted a detailed study of the potential airline deregulation, in 1975 produced a strong report in its favor, and shortly thereafter produced a Senate bill aimed at achieving deregulation.[32] In 1975 the CAB, which in the past had been outright hostile to deregulation, produced a staff report favoring it.[33] At roughly the same time the Department of Transportation in the Ford administration proceeded to study the same topic and to issue similar, detailed reports favoring deregulation. The CAB Chairman at the time, John Robson, unlike his predecessor Stuart Tipton, favored looser regulation, but he felt that a legislative mandate was needed to change the policies of the CAB on a large scale.

In 1977 President Carter appointed to the CAB two economists, Alfred E. Kahn (Chairman) and Elizabeth Bailey. After these appointments (and those of various proderegulation economists to various CAB staff positions) the Board proceeded to allow the airlines many fare reductions that previous Boards had blocked. Most of these reductions were restricted, with advance-purchase and minimum-stay requirements (i.e., Super Saver), but some were unrestricted, such as Western's heavy cuts in fares between Miami and Los Angeles (on which route Western was a new entrant) and Continental's "Chicken-feed Fares." [34]

However, it was still felt that a legislative mandate (i.e., a regulatory reform bill) would be desirable, first because the CAB feared that otherwise its policies would not stand up in the courts, and second because it felt that the 1938 law itself did not grant it enough leeway when it came to allowing new firms to enter routes. Furthermore, it was not clear that all subsequent Boards would be as procompetitive as the current one. Without further legislation, subsequent Boards could go back to the old policies of high fares and restricted competition.

The loosening of the CAB's policies in 1977 helped to bring on subsequent legislative reform. It became increasingly clear that deregulation could indeed induce lower fares, while at the same time opponents of deregulation were beginning to believe that competition was workable. Some airlines, such as United, that had originally opposed deregulation came to favor it. Some legislators, such as Senator Cannon (especially powerful in this context, because he was Chairman of the Senate Committee on Commerce), whose initial support of deregulation was at best lukewarm, came to support it. Senators Kennedy and Cannon sponsored a joint bill for deregulation that had the support of consumer groups, the Administration, and some (but not all) airlines. As a result, the Senate passed the Cannon-Kennedy Bill on April 19, 1978; the House passed a slightly amended version on September 21 of the same year. A conference synthesis of the original and amended bills was passed by both houses by October 15 and signed by the President October 24.[35]

Thus, airline deregulation had become a national policy: what had been regarded by many only a few years back as politically infeasible had in fact occurred. We shall look now at some specific legislative changes involved, and in the next section we shall consider how they have been implemented so far by the CAB.

The Statement of Purpose in the 1978 Act emphasizes the goal of safety in air transport, and the development of a system suited to the needs of commerce, the Postal Service, and the National Defense. Furthermore, it specifically mentions the need to provide service to small, isolated communities, with federal support, if necessary. It differs strikingly from its predecessor 40 years earlier, however, in that it explicitly recognizes the desirability of low fares and the usefulness of the market mechanism in achieving them. Thus, the goals include "the availability of a variety of adequate, economic, efficient, and low-priced services by air carriers, . . . the placement of maximum reliance on market forces and on actual and potential competition, . . . the encouragement, development, and maintenance of an air transportation system relying on actual and potential competition to provide efficiency, innovation, and low prices, and to determine the variety, quality, and price of air transportation services."

Furthermore, the 1978 Act gives as a goal "the encouragement of entry into air transportation markets by new air carriers, the encouragement of entry into additional air transportation markets by existing air carriers, and the continued strengthening of small carriers so as to assure a more effective, competitive industry."

The CAB thus received the legislative mandate that it was seeking to permit lower fares and the entry of new firms. Furthermore, in order to assure the benefits of deregulation, the Act also allowed for automatic entry of existing carriers (including intrastate carriers) onto interstate routes on a limited basis during 1979–1983. More specifically, each firm was free to enter automatically one new route in 1979 and another in 1980, with two additional routes per year in 1981 and 1982. (Each carrier, however, was free to block automatic entry on one route apiece in each of these years; this was added as a safeguard to help make the effects gradual.)

But there was another way, more potent in the short term, in which this legislation allowed entry of certificated carriers onto new routes. There were many routes on which various airlines were certificated to fly but did not in fact fly on a regular basis. If existing airlines did not start service on these routes within six months of passage of the Act, other airlines were allowed to get their certificates on a first-come-first-served basis. Effectively, this opened up a vast number of new routes to existing firms, as will be discussed in more detail below.

In a similar way, the Act specifies in detail a fare policy that does not rely solely on the Statement of Purpose to achieve liberalization of fares. More specifically, it directs the Board to find a "standard industry fare level," based on 1977 fares and adjusted at least twice a year for cost changes. It also states that the CAB must not find unreasonable a fare no more than 5 percent above or 50 percent below the "standard industry fare." The Act does not block moves outside this zone, but simply requires that moves within it be allowed. This gives airlines great latitude for fare reductions of the order of magnitude that could be expected as a result of deregulation; it also allows more flexibility for upward fare revision in a time of rapidly rising costs.

Although they are perhaps not so important economically, a number of other provisions in this revised Act differ sharply from those of the earlier one. For example, the Act sets a six-month limit on CAB regulatory proceedings for entry; it provides a detailed procedure to assure that small communities receive "essential" service; as a "plum" to the airlines it provides for government-guaranteed loans to assist in fitting aircraft with noise and pollution controls; and it has elaborate provisions for the protection of employees who might be harmed by deregulation. Finally, and strikingly, it contains a "sunset provision," requiring that by 1985 the CAB provide a detailed study of its success or failure under regulatory reform, with recommendations either justifying its existence, recommending abandonment of the agency itself, or proposing specific reforms so as to better meet the legislative goals in the Statement of Purpose. This provision was included to prevent the continuation of outmoded policies, which many felt occurred under the 1938 Act, or the long-term deterioration of the industry due to deregulation policies that for some reason did not work as they were expected.

This, in brief, is the legislation. What have been its effects? How have the industry and the traveler fared under these new policies? To those questions we now turn.

THE EFFECTS OF DEREGULATION ON AIRLINE MARKETS AND FARES

In response to the Deregulation Act the CAB has indeed permitted entry of new firms into many markets — on so grand a scale that the expansion is difficult to summarize. In case after case it has opened up routes to all carriers who were "fit, willing, and able" to provide service on those routes. Systematic evidence of this entry is provided below. The CAB has also allowed considerable fare flexibility, both upward and downward. Thus, while keeping the 50 percent zone of downward flexibility, the CAB in May of 1980 allowed carriers to raise fares to as much as 130 percent of the standard industry fare level on hauls of 400 miles or more, 150 percent on hauls of 200–400 miles, and with no regulatory ceiling on hauls under 200 miles. Movement outside these bounds is permitted only with prior CAB approval.[36] The CAB expected that the forces of competition would keep fares well below these ceilings.

Given the large number of routes involved and the fact that changes are still occurring in the industry, it is impossible to present definitive evidence on the overall effects of deregulation. For this reason we shall concentrate on a sample of the 90 highest-density interstate trunk routes (actually, the sample is based on the top 100, but of those, ten were intrastate, and hence unlikely to be affected by deregulation). We shall provide evidence on fares and entry of firms on these routes as of August 1980, as shown in Table 3. Entry of firms and reduction of fares occurred on many other routes (we shall discuss some here). But this table at least provides statistical evidence on some routes — perhaps the routes on which entry of new firms is easiest, given their size.

In its fourth column, Table 3 lists the routes that have had entry of firms since 1975 and the firms that have entered. It is worth noting that over half these routes have had newly entrant firms during this period and that a number of other routes are soon to be entered by new firms as well. In a number of cases more than one firm has entered a market.

Table 3 also offers evidence on plane fares. Before considering this, we should note that between 1975 and 1980 air transportation costs rose sharply, owing to general inflation and, more especially, to a dramatic increase in fuel prices. As a result, it is inappropriate, therefore, to compare direct fare levels over this period; rather, fares should be compared with some reference point, some cost index for air transportation. The difficulty, of course, is that one cannot be sure which changes in costs are due to factor price changes and which are due to deregulation. Aid in resolving the difficulty is provided by the "CAB standard fare level." The CAB standard fare between two points is determined now, as it was in 1975, by airline costs, holding load factor constant at 55 percent, with a trunk airline seating configuration more or less as it existed in 1975.[37] As a result, this CAB fare level provides a useful reference point. As we shall see, most fares in 1975 were set at or near this level, and, to the extent that they stay at this level currently, that is a sign that they are not dropping in response to deregulation.

To analyze the effects of deregulation on the fare level in the 90 top interstate markets then, Table 3 shows the ratio of the lowest unrestricted daytime airfare in each market to the standard formula CAB

Table 3. Fares and Firm Entry on High-density Routes

City Pair	R75 [a]	R80 [a]	Firms Entering since 1975
New York-Boston	80.6	52.6	Braniff
Chicago-New York	101.4	66.9	
New York-Washington	78.8	95.1	
New York-Miami	98.9	57.2	TWA, Air Florida
New York-Los Angeles	100.6	29.9	Continental, World, Capitol, Eastern
New York-Ft. Lauderdale	100.0	52.6	Air Florida, TWA
New York-San Francisco	96.8	37.6	Continental, World, Eastern
Chicago-Los Angeles	90.5	39.8	
New York-Detroit	100.0	99.0	TWA, Pan American
Los Angeles-Las Vegas	94.3	71.8	Air California, PSA
New York-Pittsburgh	100.0	50.6	Northwest
Boston-Washington	100.0	59.3	Braniff, Northwest, World
New York-Atlanta	100.0	105.1	
Chicago-Minneapolis	100.0	55.7	American
Chicago-Detroit	97.1	59.3	Midway
New York-Cleveland	100.0	111.8	
New York-Buffalo	100.0	105.4	
Los Angeles-Honolulu	70.4	42.1	Braniff, World
Chicago-Washington	100.0	63.5	Piedmont, Midway
New York-Tampa	98.9	72.6	TWA
Chicago-St. Louis	100.0	52.9	Midway
Chicago-San Francisco	86.7	41.9	Continental
Chicago-Miami	100.0	65.6	United
New York-Dallas	100.9	105.0	
Los Angeles-Seattle	89.5	57.0	Northwest
Boston-Philadelphia	102.6	103.3	
Los Angeles-Denver	87.5	73.1	Hughes Airwest
New York-Orlando	103.5	105.7	TWA
New York-Rochester	102.8	101.4	
San Francisco-Seattle	89.7	75.2	Alaska, Northwest, Hughes Airwest
Los Angeles-Washington	101.2	48.6	Continental, World
New York-Houston	99.1	64.2	Continental, Pan American
Chicago-Philadelphia	100.0	108.0	
Chicago-Cleveland	100.0	56.0	Midway, Braniff
Chicago-Denver	90.4	78.8	
New York-West Palm Beach	100.0	54.2	Air Florida, TWA
Los Angeles-Phoenix	87.2	71.8	Braniff, PSA
New York-St. Louis	100.0	112.7	Ozark

[a] Ratio of lowest unrestricted daytime airfare in each market to the standard formula CAB fare in September 1975 (R75) and August 1980 (R80).

Table 3. Fares and Firm Entry on High-density Routes (*cont.*)

City Pair	R75 [a]	R80 [a]	Firms Entering since 1975
Chicago-Dallas	100.0	74.8	
San Francisco-Honolulu	74.4	43.3	World
New York-Denver	100.0	60.8	Continental
Philadelphia-Pittsburgh	100.0	111.5	
Chicago-Kansas City	89.8	57.8	Midway
Los Angeles-Boston	100.0	40.5	World
New York-Syracuse	100.0	106.6	
Chicago-Pittsburgh	100.0	107.7	
Houston-New Orleans	90.2	49.3	Southwest
Chicago-Tampa	98.9	74.4	United
Chicago-Ft. Lauderdale	101.0	103.2	United
New York-Minneapolis	100.0	101.8	American, TWA
San Francisco-Washington	96.6	43.1	Continental, World
Chicago-Las Vegas	100.0	101.8	American, Continental
Atlanta-Chicago	100.0	102.6	
New York-New Orleans	100.0	77.7	Texas International
Boston-Chicago	100.0	103.4	
Los Angeles-Dallas	99.0	52.1	Braniff, Texas International
Atlanta-Washington	100.0	52.3	
Atlanta-Miami	100.0	101.7	Northwest
Los Angeles-Houston	88.6	56.5	Hughes Airwest, Texas International
Chicago-Phoenix	99.2	78.7	
Los Angeles-Detroit	100.6	60.4	
Miami-Philadelphia	100.0	105.5	TWA
New York-Cincinnati	100.0	105.0	
Los Angeles-Minneapolis	100.0	82.7	
Portland-Seattle	88.5	70.8	Alaska, Braniff
Boston-Miami	99.1	66.8	TWA, Braniff
Miami-Washington	100.0	55.6	Air Florida, TWA
Chicago-Houston	98.8	74.7	
Columbus-New York	100.0	104.9	
Los Angeles-Philadelphia	100.6	73.0	
Los Angeles-Miami	89.6	77.7	Western
Detroit-Washington	100.0	103.4	
San Francisco-Denver	89.5	50.3	Continental
Seattle-Spokane	88.2	72.6	
San Francisco-Boston	97.4	39.3	World
Los Angeles-Portland	89.7	93.1	
Chicago-Cincinnati	102.8	105.8	
San Francisco-Portland	90.0	95.5	

[a] Ratio of lowest unrestricted daytime airfare in each market to the standard formula CAB fare in September 1975 (R75) and August 1980 (R80).

City Pair	R75 [a]	R80 [a]	Firms Entering since 1975
New York-Charlotte	100.0	100.9	
Detroit-Tampa	98.9	90.7	
New York-Norfolk	100.0	102.8	
New York-Indianapolis	100.0	100.0	
Los Angeles-St. Louis	99.2	58.6	Texas International
Chicago-Orlando	97.8	107.3	
Boston-Ft. Lauderdale	101.0	106.8	
New York-Las Vegas	100.0	100.0	Continental
Los Angeles-Salt Lake City	98.4	42.6	PSA
Atlanta-Tampa	98.0	64.4	
New York-Raleigh-Durham	100.0	101.0	
Ft. Lauderdale-Philadelphia	101.1	73.5	TWA

[a] Ratio of lowest unrestricted daytime airfare in each market to the standard formula CAB fare in September 1975 (R75) and August 1980 (R80).

fare in that market for September 1975 and August 1980. Before we consider these fares in more detail, we should examine the criteria used to select fares. First, it was necessary that the fares be unrestricted in the sense that they contain no round-trip or length-of-stay requirements. Arguably, providing a round trip with a minimum one-week stay and a requirement for advance purchase is not cheaper than providing two one-way trips.* Much more likely, such restrictions represent an attempt at price discrimination, not generally characteristic of competitive markets: travelers willing to make plans in advance and stay at least a week are likely to be vacation travelers with high demand elasticities, whereas those requiring flexibility and shorter lengths of stay are likely to be business people with low demand elasticities. It is understandable that firms with market power should want to discriminate between the two markets, and it is arguable, as well, that all consumers are better off if airlines are allowed to offer these discount fares relative to a single fare level based on the high, CAB-formula fare.[38] However, this sort of discrimination is neither characteristic of competitive markets nor observed in intrastate markets where the forces of competition have been allowed fairly free play for some time. Therefore, as a gauge of how competitive markets have become as a result of deregulation, we have considered unrestricted fares only. To qualify, all fares

* These are the restrictions of excursion and super saver fares now in effect. Since most travel is not migration, most people will at some point return, eliminating the need for a round-trip requirement to fill the planes.

had to be available on an unrestricted daytime basis, with either a non-stop flight or a one-stop flight with either single-plane service or a single on-line transfer. Thus, while the fares shown here are not necessarily available on every flight on any route, they should nevertheless be easily accessible to all those who shop for them.

As is evident from Table 3, on many routes the lowest available fares fell sharply relative to the standard CAB level from 1975 to 1980. In 1975 the average route had a fare of 96.8 percent of the normal CAB level. In 1980, on the other hand, the average route had a minimum unrestricted fare of only 76.6 percent of the CAB level. This difference is not only readily observable, but it is also statistically significant.[39] Similarly, in 1975 only four of the ninety unrestricted routes had discount fares of 15 percent or more, whereas in 1980 fifty-six, or over 60 percent of the routes, had them, and there is every reason to believe that they will become even more widely available in the future. Based on this relatively small sample, then, there is plenty of evidence that deregulation is conducive to lower, unrestricted fares. But the evidence presented here suggests a further important question. Why is it that some routes have had sharp fare reductions and others have not? What are the implications of these results regarding the prospects for further fare reductions in the future?

A glance at Table 3 suggests that the entry of new firms is closely connected with the reduction of unrestricted fares. Unlike an existing firm, a new entrant has an incentive to reduce fares to all passengers, for it has very little to lose from the cut. An existing firm, however, has plenty to lose; it would prefer to cut fares only for that extra business it can win by doing so. More detailed and sophisticated statistical analysis suggests that the entry of new firms is indeed strongly and significantly related to the propensity of fares to fall in a given market.[40] Furthermore, entry of new firms has a separate effect, also tending to reduce fares, but different from the one mentioned above: as more firms share a market, they find it more difficult to coordinate prices at levels higher than the free market would permit. Thus, independent of entry, markets with many firms are more likely to have fares below the CAB level than markets with few firms (this result has also been shown to be statistically significant in an earlier study).

Overall, then, it would appear that the CAB's policy of allowing new and existing firms to enter new markets had been achieving the very results it was intended to achieve.

Nevertheless, it would appear that not all newly entrant firms behave the same when it comes to fare reductions. Some have reduced fares little if at all in new markets, whereas others have sharply reduced fares in practically every market they have entered.

Large, well-developed trunk carriers, such as United, American,

Delta, and Eastern, have been quite uninclined to reduce fares on their new routes (which in any event are relatively few). These carriers may fear they have the most to lose if the rate level falls significantly.

At the opposite extreme are the totally new firms, such as World and Midway, and the intrastate carriers newly expanding to interstate markets, such as PSA, Air California, Southwest, and Air Florida. These carriers have consistently reduced fares sharply for all seats they sell in all the markets they enter. Apparently these firms feel they have the most to gain by sharply reducing fares.

Almost as aggressive in reducing fares as the new firms and intrastates have been local service carriers expanding onto new, high-density routes. The most aggressive have been Texas International and Frontier. These two carriers have recently initiated substantial fare cuts, not only on the routes shown in Table 3 but also on a large number of other routes radiating out of the hub cities of Denver, Dallas, and Houston.[41] Some, such as Dallas-Los Angeles and Denver-Salt Lake City, are relatively high-density; others, such as Oklahoma City-Denver, Tulsa-Dallas, Tucson-Denver, Las Vegas-Denver, and Las Vegas-Dallas, are not by any calculation among the highest-density trunk routes. In any event, the majority of these routes are of lower density than those shown in Table 3.

Some trunk carriers also have been quite aggressive in reducing fares. Thus, as Continental has expanded its route system from Denver to various cities on the East Coast, it has initiated fairly sharp fare reductions both between Denver and the cities involved and for one-stop and connecting trips between East and West Coast cities through the Denver hub. And Continental has been even more aggressive in reducing fares internationally in the South Pacific, a market it has entered recently.[42]

The remaining carriers, basically small and medium-sized trunks, plus a number of local service carriers, have been aggressive in reducing fares in some markets, but not in others. Braniff, for example, has reduced fares sharply on the Atlantic and Pacific routes it has recently entered, while showing little tendency to reduce fares domestically even on its vast number of newly acquired routes. Western and Northwest have reduced fares dramatically on some new routes, while keeping fares up at the CAB level on most routes.

If there is a single group of routes not enjoying the benefits of deregulation so far, it is that group of trunk routes serving exclusively the Northeast and Midwest; connecting Boston, New York, and Washington with relatively nearby cities in the East, Midwest, and South. (A look at Table 3 supports this observation.) There are a number of possible explanations. First, these markets are not growing the way many markets in the South and West are (and it is worth noting that fares are going down between cities in the Northeast and more distant ones in the South and West). Second, it is quite possible that most patrons of these routes value service quality more than low fares, as indicated by the popularity of Eastern's Air Shuttle. Third, and closely connected, much of the high-priced service of concern here uses close-in airports (most specifically La Guardia and National) that are saturated to capacity, both in the number of flights using them and in the terminal space used. It is difficult to say for sure, but the relatively high fares in and out of these airports may represent scarcity rents on the value of the close-in service provided. If this is true, we should expect to see lower fare service develop from less-crowded airports such as Newark and Baltimore. Indeed, as this work went to press, a new airline, People Express, had proposed to enter many of these northeastern routes from Newark airport, at sharply reduced fares.[43]

Regarding the northeastern routes, it is also worth noting that only on a few of these routes (and some connecting the Northeast and the South) have airlines taken advantage of their newly granted authority to raise fares above the standard industry fare level. That would make these routes likely targets for entry by price-cutting firms. The fact that fares went up on so few routes and down on so many seems to vindicate the CAB's belief that market forces make regulatory fare ceilings unnecessary.

Overall, then, the evidence from high-density routes supports the claims of those who favored deregulation; it indicates that fares have fallen substantially on many routes relative to earlier CAB levels (adjusted for cost changes); and it gives good reason to believe that these fare reductions will spread onto more routes in the future.

What of the potential disadvantages of deregulation? To what extent have they been a problem? To those matters we now turn.

POTENTIAL PROBLEMS WITH DEREGULATION: THE EVIDENCE SO FAR

Opponents of deregulation warned of several problems that could occur[44] — most importantly, (1) a loss of service on lower-density routes and, more generally, to smaller communities; (2) a need (in the opinion of some) to dramatically "restructure" the industry (through mergers) to a form "better suited" to the environment of deregulation; and (3) a reduction in safety. We have not had deregulation long enough to be able to judge whether these problems have arisen. However, it is still worth summarizing the evidence so far.

Consider first the matter of loss of service to smaller communities. It is not clear a priori why deregulation should have this result: in very few circumstances was a carrier required to serve a route against its will, and to the extent that some routes were profitable and others were not, it is difficult to see why profit-maximizing airlines would give away stockholders' money to operate unprofitable routes. Furthermore, given service-quality competition, it is not clear how much excess profit was available from high-density routes to pay for low-density ones. So it is not clear how much service loss for small communities should be expected as a result of deregulation.

Systematic evidence regarding service to small communities since deregulation would be highly desirable, but as yet none is available. Certainly, many smaller cities around the United States have enjoyed considerable improvement in service since deregulation. These include such places as Toledo, Ohio; Redding, California; Santa Ana, California; and Reno, Nevada. On the other hand, some cities, such as Providence, Rhode Island, have lost some service. Those in the industry who have looked at the matter have been unable to determine whether, on balance, smaller cities have gained or lost.[45] For the sake of argument, let us look closely at what many regard as the "worst-case" outcome among smaller cities: Bakersfield, California.

The problem with Bakersfield occurred basically because the trunk airline serving the community, United, abandoned service there shortly after deregulation. Although it is not clear that the move is due to deregulation (higher fuel costs are likely to make short-haul flights less economic because takeoffs and landings are more fuel intensive), deregulation is widely seen as the culprit here. Whatever may be the causes of these service changes, the situation in Bakersfield has not deteriorated nearly so much as many would claim. More specifically, though United and Hughes Airwest have discontinued service to Bakersfield, they have been replaced by other carriers specializing in low-density service. And these carriers are now providing Bakersfield with service more frequent than United and Hughes Airwest did. More specifically, as of July 1975 Bakersfield had a total of six flights daily each way to Los Angeles (four daily on weekends) and four daily each way to San Francisco.[46] As of March 1980 Bakersfield had twelve daily flights each way to Los Angeles and three to San Francisco. It is true that the aircraft used in 1980 were smaller than those used in 1975, but a large portion of them were turboprops of the same size used by local service airlines all around the country, seating 40 to 50 passengers per plane.[47] Given the much greater frequencies which Bakersfield now enjoys, it is not clear why residents should consider themselves worse off as a result of deregulation. If Bakersfield represents the "worst case" of what could happen to smaller cities with airline deregulation, then deregulation has not done badly on this count.

In any event, it is worth noting that if a community loses service after implementation of the Deregulation Act of 1978, there are provisions to subsidize the service directly up to an "adequate" level, now determined by the Board to be two flights daily each way in and out of the community.* While some communities may not feel that this fairly represents "adequate" service, such a debate should be made directly in the political arena. The matter here is whether federal and state taxpayers are ready to directly subsidize service to smaller communities to a higher degree. As previously stated, it is difficult to make a moral or ethical argument that travelers on high-density routes should be making under-the-table payments to support a higher level of service to small communities, and it is on this implicit argument that support for regulation as a method of enhancing low-density service is usually based.

A second problem warned of for the airline industry under deregulation stems from a possible need to restructure it in order to adapt to the changed market environment. This claim has been made with regard to the recent merger movement in the industry, a movement that the CAB has sanctioned in some cases and disapproved of in others.

There are a number of potential arguments in favor of airline mergers of the sort sought in 1978 and 1979, but the following line of reasoning is arguably the most important.[48]

First, from the viewpoint of traveler satisfaction, an airline that integrates a number of connecting routes has an advantage over a set of airlines over which interline connections must be made to complete the same trip. Thus, if a traveler between, say, Salt Lake City and Memphis had a choice of a through plane stopping in Denver, and a change of planes in Denver for the same trip, he would probably choose the through plane, all other things equal; changing planes has a certain cost in inconvenience, time, and risk of missing connections that travelers would prefer to avoid if necessary. Similarly, if a traveler must change planes on such a route, he is likely to prefer an online (same airline) connection to an interline one; the walk between flights is likely to be shorter, the probability that the baggage will make it with the passenger is higher, and the chances of making the connection are often considerably better. If this is the case, it becomes clear that airlines with large, integrated route systems are likely to have a service advantage over smaller airlines with only regional or corridor route systems.

Under deregulation, we should therefore expect a number of car-

---

* The Deregulation Act of 1978, discussed on pages 67–69, gives the CAB the right to determine an appropriate level of service. As of this writing, the CAB's proposals were tentative and subject to debate.

riers to expand onto new routes in an attempt to build an integrated route system. There is considerable evidence that a number of airlines have attempted to do so, including Braniff, Continental, Delta, Eastern, Frontier, Texas International, and TWA to name a few.

If airlines can create integrated, nationwide route systems through internal expansion, why should they want to merge? There are at least two reasons. First, merging allows quick achievement of the full benefits of an integrated route structure, whereas internal expansion can take longer. Second, there may not be enough "room" on major routes for every airline in the country (for there to be such room, major routes would have to accommodate over a dozen carriers apiece). If that is the case, in order to avoid the losses connected with overentry, it has been argued that mergers are likely to be necessary. Proponents of mergers argue further that entry of new firms into the airline industry is relatively easy, so that if mergers increase market power of existing firms to any significant degree, new firms will enter and lower fares.

Opponents of airline mergers counter these arguments on several grounds. First, they note that in many markets there is room for specialized regional or corridor carriers that do not have integrated, nationwide route structures and that, by and large, do not go after connecting traffic. These include such profitable carriers as Pacific Southwest, Southwest, and Air California. So it is by no means clear that every airline in the country must have an integrated, nationwide route structure.

Second, opponents of mergers note that entry of new firms into a market is one of the most powerful forces in achieving lower fares. If firms want integrated route structures but cannot achieve them through mergers, internal expansion is the only path available, and the resultant entry of new firms is likely to result in lower fares. It is true that entry of totally new firms into the industry is another method of achieving the same benefits, and while entry into the industry indeed does seem easy relative to, say, entry into steel or automobiles, nevertheless, evidence so far indicates that it is by no means a trivial problem in the short run. Since deregulation, three airlines have entered into scheduled operations on a major trunk level for the first time; so far, none has had an easy time of it, and in each case the entry has taken a period of years to work out (including assembling the work force, acquiring the capital, purchasing aircraft, solving labor disputes, and so on), and the success of each venture is at this time unclear.*

Finally, opponents of mergers note that we currently do not know just how many firms will "fit" into a given market. Would it not be

* The three major airlines entering into scheduled domestic service are Midway, Capital, and World.

better to allow the marketplace to determine that, rather than to pre-judge it by allowing the mergers?

It is thus possible to make strong arguments both for and against airline mergers of the sorts applied for over 1978 and 1979. Currently, there is not enough evidence to determine who is right.

But it is possible to make a few suggestive judgments based on the evidence so far. First, if a persuasive argument could be made that the relevant airlines could not achieve the desired integration through internal expansion, and if the merger were not anticompetitive in that it created monopolies in any important markets, the merger should probably be approved. On the other hand, if there is some reason to believe that the relevant airlines could, for the time being, achieve their route integration through internal expansion, there is strong reason to believe that the merger should at least be delayed. If the threat of bankruptcy loomed for a carrier, merger would remain a potential avenue in the future.

In fact, the CAB has decided merger cases in a way consistent with this reasoning: it allowed mergers of North Central and Southern, two very small local service carriers, which showed little evidence of ability to expand internally on the scale that the merger would achieve. And the shares held by each firm in the relevant markets were so small as to make the anticompetitive effects of the merger negligible.[49] The Board judged similarly in the case of the merger between Pan American and National; internal expansion was simply not judged to be a feasible alternative for either carrier. In the two cases of Western-Continental and Eastern-National, on the other hand, the Board decided the firms could expand internally, and that in the latter case the merger would have been anticompetitive.

On a closely related topic, it is worth asking whether the airline industry, in its first year of deregulation, has earned "adequate" profits. Some in the airline industry feared that deregulation would induce a "ruinous" competition, making it impossible for many airlines to raise capital. On the face of things, one might be tempted to believe that deregulation has not had a salutary effect on airline earnings: trunk airline profits fell from $642 million in 1978 to $282 million in 1979.[50] However, it would be a serious mistake to attribute this sharp decline in profits to deregulation. As most Americans know, fuel prices rose sharply in 1979 (they doubled for trunk airlines), and given that airlines make intensive use of fuel, the sharp rise in costs made some short-run decline in profits inevitable.[51]

In fact, if anything, deregulation enabled the airlines to mitigate the effects of fuel cost increases through rapid fare increases more readily than they could have done under the old regulatory regime. The best evidence for this comes from the President of TWA, C. E.

Meyer.[52] Before passage of the 1978 Act, he had been one of the most ardent opponents of deregulation. But in February 1980 Meyer said he wished deregulation would move even faster, allowing the airlines to cope even better with the changing situation; and he observed that in international markets his company had fared worse in the face of fuel cost increases than in the deregulated domestic market. These views, coming from an airline executive initially opposed to deregulation, give strong evidence that at least so far, low airline profits cannot be attributed to deregulation, and that deregulation has been, if anything, beneficial from the viewpoint of airlines.

Another potential problem seen by some in airline deregulation was that of reduced safety. It was argued that with price competition, fares would be driven down in markets to the point that airlines would be tempted or perhaps even forced to cut corners on aircraft maintenance and perhaps staff training. On the basis of a superficial glance at evidence so far, one might be tempted to claim some truth to this. The most striking case in point would be the crash of an American Airlines DC-10 in Chicago in May 1979, wherein faulty (and cost-cutting) maintenance procedures on the part of American were cited by the Federal Aviation Administration as directly connected with the accident. The difficulty with this argument is that the maintenance procedures connected with the accident were used for years before the accident occurred, and it was indeed only for that reason that the equipment was faulty. Thus, the maintenance procedures responsible for the accident occurred as much under the regime of CAB regulation as under the subsequent regime of deregulation.

A more accurate and systematic indicator of the degree of safety of the industry is that of passenger deaths per 100 million passenger-miles per year. There is a consistent record of these statistics for commercial aviation in the United States over a long period, and the measure thus provides a good benchmark. Table 4 provides a comparison of deaths per passenger-mile over the past decade in the industry.

As Table 4 indicates, although seven of the previous ten years did indeed have lower fatality rates than 1979, three did not: 1974, 1971, and 1973. Furthermore, 1969 and 1972 had fatality rates very little below those of 1979. Thus, despite the tragic air accidents that occurred in 1979, the fatality rate for air transportation in that year was well within the range found during the previous decade of relatively regulated transportation. Furthermore, it is worth noting that many of the effects of deregulation began for practical purposes in 1978, and that year experienced the second-lowest fatality rate during the eleven-year period. Overall, then, it would be difficult to argue that deregulation is responsible for a decrease in air-travel safety.

Table 4. Airline Passenger Fatality Rates, 1969–1979

Year	Passenger Deaths per 100 Million Passenger-Miles
1969	0.100
1970	0.001
1971	0.119
1972	0.100
1973	0.115
1974	0.197
1975	0.065
1976	0.019
1977	0.031
1978	0.005
1979	0.115

Source: U.S. National Transportation Safety Board, reprinted in *Aviation Daily,* 247 (February 22, 1980), p. 292.

CONCLUDING COMMENTS

So far, airline deregulation is doing by and large what it was intended to do: it is encouraging entry of firms into new markets, along with price competition, which in turn is reducing fares on a very large number of routes significantly below what they would otherwise be. This has been accomplished so far without what was thought to be a major drawback of deregulation: a marked deterioration of service on low-density routes. Furthermore, evidence so far indicates that air-passenger safety has remained well within the range travelers enjoyed during the previous decade of regulation. And while 1979 was not the most profitable of years for the airlines, airline executives themselves claim that their profit situation would be worse under the old regime of regulation.

Despite this rather sunny picture, it is important for producers and consumers of airline service not to expect too much of deregulation: high fuel costs have cut into the industry's profits, and in 1980 recession threatened to cut into them further. If, indeed, times do worsen for the airline industry, it will be important for producers to remember that deregulation does not per se guarantee high profits, and that coping with such difficult times would also be difficult under a regime of regulation. Similarly, it is important that consumers keep in mind that despite the sharp escalation in airline fares due to the run-up in fuel costs, fares are, in a real sense, falling in a large number of markets.

In short, airline deregulation as the 1980s began faced a severe test, imposed on it by fuel cost increases and the business cycle. Those who believed in its long-term benefits could only hope that it would pass that test.

NOTES

1 *Essay sur les Moeurs,* 1756.

2 More detailed (but already somewhat outdated) descriptions of the industry can be found in Theodore E. Keeler, "Domestic Trunk Airline Regulation: An Economic Evaluation," in U.S. Senate, Committee on Governmental Affairs, *Study of Federal Regulation,* Vol. VII, *Case Studies,* pp. 73–160. See also Douglas and Miller, *Economic Regulation of Domestic Air Transport* (Washington, D.C.: The Brookings Institution, 1974), pp. 187–205.

3 For a more detailed discussion of these issues, see Richard Caves, *Air Transport and Its Regulators* (Cambridge, Mass.: Harvard University Press, 1962), Chap. 6, and Michael E. Levine, "Regulating Airmail Transportation," *Journal of Law and Economics,* 18 (October 1975), 317–359. See also Keeler, *op. cit.,* pp. 80–87, and Douglas and Miller, pp. 187–192.

4 With the exception of Northeast, which had some local service routes, the trunk carriers went off subsidies in 1952. However, as Caves has shown, indirect subsidies through underpriced airport and airways facilities persisted long after that. See *Air Transport and Its Regulators,* pp. 411–418.

5 Stat. 102, 72, Stat 140, USCA 1303.

6 Caves, *op. cit.,* p. 357.

7 A more detailed documentation of policies of cross-subsidization on the part of the CAB may be found in Keeler, pp. 90–93, and Caves, pp. 402–411.

8 Cf. note 4 above.

9 Caves, pp. 224–229, and George Eads, *The Local Service Airline Experiment* (Washington, D.C.: The Brookings Institution, 1971), p, 107.

10 For returns up to 1962 see Caves, p. 392. For returns past that time see Theodore E. Keeler, *Resource Allocation in Intercity Passenger Transportation,* Ph.D. Dissertation, Massachusetts Institute of Technology, 1971, pp. 20–22, and for an up-to-date, state-of-the-art study, see B. Starr McMullen, "Profits and the Cost of Capital to the United States Trunk Airline Industry," Ph.D. Thesis and Working Paper SL-7205, University of California, Berkeley, June 1979.

11 Statistical evidence that this is so is provided in George Eads, "Competition in the Domestic Trunk Airline Industry: Too Much or Too Little?" in A. Phillips (ed.), *Promoting Competition in Regulated Markets* (Washington, D.C.: The Brookings Institution, 1975), pp. 13–54.

[12] Simat, Helliesen, and Eichner, *An Analysis of the Intrastate Air Carrier Regulatory Forum*, submitted to U.S. Department of Transportation, Washington, January 1976, Vol. I, p. 11.

[13] Testimony of Charles A. Murphy, Executive Director, Texas Aeronautics Commission, before U.S. Senate, Committee on the Judiciary, Subcommittee on Administrative Practices and Procedures, February 14, 1975, 94th Congress, First Session, Vol. II (Washington, D.C.: U.S. Government Printing Office, 1975), p. 528.

[14] Simat, Helliesen, and Eichner, Vol. I, p. 11.

[15] It is worth noting, however, that the carriers that went out of business in California tended to be very small and short-lived (under a year, usually). Thus, this experience does not indicate that a well-established carrier would be likely to go out of business with deregulation. See William Jordan, *Airline Regulation in America* (Baltimore: Johns Hopkins University Press, 1970), pp. 14–33.

[16] Simat, Helliesen, and Eichner, Vol. I, pp. 17–18.

[17] A full discussion of this pricing behavior may be found in Jordan, Chap. 5, for California, and in Simat, Helliesen, and Eichner, Vol. II, Chaps. 2 and 3, for California and Texas, respectively.

[18] From the *Official Airline Guide*, February 1, 1975.

[19] Testimony of J. Barnum, *Hearings on Oversight of Civil Aeronautics Board Practices and Procedures*, Vol. I, p. 10.

[20] William T. Coleman, *Statement to the Aviation Subcommittee on Commerce Regarding the Aviation Act of 1975* (Washington, D.C.: U.S. Government Printing Office, 1976), p. 75.

[21] *Ibid.*, p. 75.

[22] Simat, Helliesen, and Eichner, Vol. I, p. 8.

[23] *Ibid.*, Vol. II, p. IV-4.

[24] Air California puts 115 seats into a 737-200, and Southwest puts 110 into the same aircraft (Hearings of Subcommittee on Administrative Practices and Procedures, Vol. I, p. 450, and Vol. II, p. 1243). On the other hand, United and Western's 737's seat only 95. See Simat, Helliesen, and Eichner, p. II-75.

[25] Intrastate load factors come from Simat et al., Vol. I, pp. 4, 8. Interstate load factors come from U.S. Civil Aeronautics Board, *Air Carrier Operating Statistics*, December 1973 and December 1975.

[26] See U.S. Civil Aeronautics Board, *Air Carrier Operating Statistics*, December 1975, for interstate load factors; PSA and Southwest load factors are mentioned above. A full discussion of the impact of CAB regulation on coach service quality will be presented below.

[27] See T. Keeler, "Airline Regulation and Market Performance," *The Bell Journal of Economics*, Autumn 1972, pp. 399–424.

[28] T. Keeler, prepared statement, Hearings, U.S. Senate Subcommittee on Administrative Practices and Procedures, Vol. II, pp. 1302–1305.

[29] *Economic Regulation of Domestic Air Transport*, Chaps. 4–6.

[30] "Domestic Trunk Airline Regulation: An Economic Evaluation," pp. 159–160.

[31] All these studies have been previously cited, save for M. E. Levine, "Is Regulation Necessary: California Air Transportation and National Regulatory

Policy," *Yale Law Journal*, 75 (July 1965), 1416–1447; and Michael Pustay, *The Effects of Regulation on Resource Allocation in the Domestic Trunk Airline Industry*, Ph.D. Dissertation, Yale University, 1973.

[32] U.S. Senate, Committee on the Judiciary, Subcommittee on Administrative Practices and Procedures, *Civil Aeronautics Board Practices and Procedures* (Washington, D.C.: U.S. Government Printing Office, 1975).

[33] R. Pulsifer, L. Keys, P. Eldridge, J. McMahon, and W. L. Demory, Regulatory Reform: Report of the CAB Special Staff (Washington, U.S. CAB, 1975).

[34] "Cutting Confusion in Air Fares," *Business Week* (April 24, 1978), p. 64.

[35] Public Law 95-504, 92 Stat. 1705.

[36] James Ott, "Fare Flexibility Expanded by Board," *Aviation Week* (May 19, 1980), pp. 26–27.

[37] Keeler, "Domestic Trunk Airline Regulation: An Economic Evaluation," p. 94.

[38] This point is made by Robert H. Frank in a memo to the Board dated January 4, 1980.

[39] A comparison of the two means generated a difference significant at the 1 percent level.

[40] See Theodore E. Keeler and Michael Abrahams, "Market Structure, Pricing, and Service Quality in the Airline Industry under Deregulation," Working Paper SL-7902, University of California, Berkeley, November 1979, pp. 18–26.

[41] See the *Official Airline Guide*, March 1, 1980.

[42] Fares and services on international routes are available from the Official Airline Guide, International Edition.

[43] "A New Line Flies Against the Odds," *Business Week* (August 18, 1980), pp. 27–28.

[44] Some of these matters are discussed in Keeler, "Domestic Trunk Airline Regulation: an Economic Evaluation," pp. 129–135. Others are discussed in Keeler and Abrahams, pp. 1–18.

[45] In February 1980 *Aviation Week* held a conference on the effects of deregulation after one year. This was the conclusion regarding service to small communities by its editors. See *Aviation Week*, February 18, 1980, p. 28.

[46] *Official Airline Guide*, July 1, 1975, and March 1, 1980.

[47] This includes, for example, the Convair 500.

[48] See Keeler and Abrahams, pp. 1–18.

[49] D. W. Carlton, W. M. Landes, and R. A. Posner, "Public Policy toward Airline Mergers: A Case Study," 1979, unpublished.

[50] *Aviation Week*, February 18, 1980, p. 31.

[51] Michael Feazel, "Fuel Pivotal in Trunks' Earnings Slump," *Aviation Week*, February 18, 1980, pp. 31–32.

[52] *Aviation Week*, February 18, 1980, p. 29.

CASE 3

The Rise and Fall of Cable Television Regulation

Bruce M. Owen

Duke University and
United States Department of Justice

INTRODUCTION

Since 1955 the number of cable television subscribers has grown at an average rate greater than 20 percent per year. In 1980 one out of five households subscribed to cable service. The explosive growth of cable in the 1960s and 1970s led to a major confrontation among several industries, refereed by the Federal Communications Commission. The rise and fall of cable television regulation over this period is a story rooted in economic conflict between cable television operators, TV stations and networks, and Hollywood program producers. The broadcast industry and its allies saw cable as a destructive force that threatened to diminish their profits and the public interest in "free" over-the-air broadcasting. Cable television companies and most outside observers saw cable as an opportunity to achieve a vast increase in consumer service, freedom of viewer choice, and economic competition in broadcasting.

Television is the major entertainment industry in America. The A. C. Nielsen Company estimates that the average American family watches more than six hours of television per day. More than 98 percent of all households in the United States have at least one TV set. Billions of dollars are spent yearly on TV advertising and TV program production. Viewers would be willing to pay billions more in order to retain even the present level of programming.

Copyright © 1981 by Bruce M. Owen. The author is Director of Economics, Antitrust Division, United States Department of Justice, on leave from Duke University. The views expressed here are those of the author and should not be taken as representing the position of the Department of Justice.

Cable television, despite its rapid growth, is still comparatively small. There are about 15 million cable subscribers, and the industry has revenues of about $2 billion per year.

Figure 1 shows the physical design of a cable system. The typical system has twelve channels, devoted mainly to rebroadcasting local TV signals in order to improve the quality of reception. Some systems carry a local origination channel, mostly programmed with time and weather forecasts. Most systems also carry, to the extent permitted by FCC rules, TV signals from distant cities that cannot be received by rooftop antennas in the area. These signals are "imported" by microwave relay or by communication satellites. A growing number carry one or more special channels with new movies, for which a separate charge is made.

Figure 1. Physical Design of a Cable System

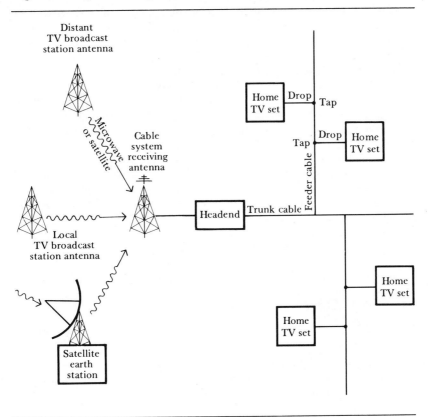

These are "pay-TV" channels, whose operation was closely regulated by the FCC until 1977. About 15 percent of all cable subscribers subscribe to such a pay-TV service. A few entrepreneurs are providing other innovative program services. For example, C-SPAN, Inc., provides live satellite feeds of sessions of the House of Representatives and other public affairs events to hundreds of cable systems. The largest cable system in the country is in San Diego, with about 100,000 subscribers. The top 50 cable companies (multiple-system operators) serve more than 70 percent of all cable subscribers. The largest such company is TelePrompter Corporation, with more than one million subscribers.

Cable systems tend to have the characteristics of natural monopolies in their local areas. Costs decline as the number of subscribers within a given area increases. The higher the ratio of subscribers to homes "passed" by the cable, the lower the cost per subscriber. This does not preclude the existence of two or more cable systems in a city, provided that they serve different areas. The financial viability of a cable system depends on population density, income levels, quality of over-the-air reception, number of over-the-air signals, and so on, all of which may vary considerably within a television market. Hence, cable may be viable in some parts of a market and not in other parts.

The TV rating services list over 200 TV "markets" in the United States, defined roughly by the coverage areas of TV stations assigned to a city or adjacent cities. Most TV revenues and profits go to VHF network affiliates in the top 100 markets. This is not surprising, given the distribution of population: one-third of all TV households are in the top ten markets, 68 percent in the top 50, and 87 percent in the top 100. TV stations are in the business of selling audiences to advertisers. The larger the audience, the more advertisers are willing to pay. Therefore TV revenues are greater in larger cities than in smaller ones. Of course, there are important differences within TV "markets," some of which are quite varied internally, so that the quantity and quality of TV service and the extent of economic demand for cable is not a constant within markets.

HISTORY OF CABLE REGULATION

The historical development of federal regulation of cable television can only be understood in the broader context of radio and television regulation. In 1927 Congress nationalized the radio spectrum and in

1934 granted regulatory authority over wire and radio communications to the Federal Communications Commission. As demand for television programs grew after the war, the FCC was faced with the problem of allocating spectrum to this new service.

At first the commission seriously underestimated demand for television channels and allocated only eleven VHF channels to the new service. Moreover, it continued its policy of "localism" in allocating these channels, attempting to maximize the number of localities served by a station rather than the number of signals available to the population. Assigning a frequency to a city meant that that frequency could not be assigned to nearby cities without causing interference. This created an excess demand for licenses, which began to change hands at prices far in excess of the value of tangible property involved. Competition was restricted and local licensees were granted monopoly power over advertising prices.

The undersupply of spectrum to television service had a number of effects, aside from the production of excess profits for VHF licensees. First, the market responded with supplementary technologies: boosters, satellite stations, translators, and cable television systems — all means of improving reception in rural areas. Second, the FCC responded by allocating a relatively large number of new channels to television service. Unfortunately, these channels were allocated in the UHF band, where stations were at a technical disadvantage vis-à-vis VHF stations. Not only did most sets manufactured in the fifties and early sixties lack UHF tuners, but UHF signals do not travel as far or as clearly as equally powerful VHF signals. This "UHF handicap" has persisted despite the FCC's efforts to eliminate it. (The efforts included a requirement that all TV sets have UHF tuners, and later, that they have "click-stop" tuning dials.) It is generally agreed that the FCC made a serious error in its UHF decisions; if the Commission had shifted all TV broadcasting to the UHF band, or if it had not mixed UHF and VHF stations in the same markets, the resulting abundance of channels might have reduced the need for cable television. This would have eliminated the handicap that UHF stations have in competing with VHFs. However, by the late 1950s, when the implications of the FCC's error became apparent, the VHF broadcasters were politically too powerful to dislodge. An effort to "deintermix" the VHF and UHF stations was abandoned.

The net result of these events was that TV viewers in most cities were limited to three or four viewable channels and that VHF TV broadcasters were practically guaranteed substantial excess profits by the lack of competition.

The supplementary technologies that grew up in the fifties were designed to bring TV signals to rural fringe areas where the primary signals were weak or plagued with interference. Boosters, satellites,* and translators receive these weak signals and rebroadcast them with greater power. Cable telvision systems do the same but use wires rather than rebroadcasting the signals. Cable television systems are much more expensive than satellite antennas and translators for small numbers of channels, but they have two overwhelming advantages: (1) because they use wire, cable companies can at relatively little expense charge consumers for the service they provide by excluding those who don't pay, and (2) because of the technical characteristics of coaxial cable, they can carry a relatively large number of channels. Cable systems typically have twelve channels, many more than the number of over-the-air stations available to most viewers. There is no technical limit to the number of cable channels; some systems are being built with twenty or more channels.

The selling point of cable systems during the fifties was simply the provision of clear signals; this service was uncontroversial and even was welcomed by broadcasters, because it increased their audiences. In 1959 the FCC refused to accept regulatory jurisdiction over cable, asserting that it was neither a broadcast facility nor a wire common carrier.

Between 1959 and 1966 the situation changed radically. Cable operators discovered that they could increase the demand for their service by "importing" distant TV signals using microwave relay systems. Subscribers were willing to pay to receive these additional nonlocal signals, and there was plenty of capacity on the coaxial cable. Distant-signal importation aroused the ire of broadcasters, because by increasing the choices available, it "fragmented" their audiences. This reduced local advertising revenues. The new audiences gained by the distant station were of little value to the imported station's own local advertising clients. Local advertising accounts for a third of the revenue of nonnetwork VHF stations and about half of the revenue of nonnetwork UHF stations. Also, cable for the first time began to grow in the big cities where the most profitable stations are found.

In opposing cable, broadcasters employed two strategies: (1) they pressed the FCC for restrictions on cable television and (2) they challenged cable in the courts, on the grounds that distant-signal importatation infringed the copyright of program producers. The FCC first asserted jurisdiction over the microwave relay systems used to import distant signals (1962) and then in 1965–1966 asserted full regulatory jurisdiction over cable television and "froze" all such systems in the largest 100 television markets, forbidding importation of additional

---

* These are terrestrial antennas that retransmit signals, not orbiting communication satellites.

signals. These actions were upheld in the courts. The copyright challenge did not go so well for the broadcasters. In 1968 the Supreme Court held that cable systems had no copyright liability for retransmitted local signals and in 1974 held similarly with respect to distant signals.

The years of the freeze were ones of intense pressure for the industry and for the Commission. Despite the freeze, cable systems grew rapidly. The political strength of the cable industry grew as well, in part because the more spectacular potential services that cable might offer caught the imagination of a number of writers, who produced a growing flood of literature and interest in cable. These "blue sky" services included free public soapbox channels, channels for education, the arts, government, electronic voting, shopping, meter reading, and access to electronic program libraries with limitless possibilities. A major criticism of broadcast TV has been the difficulty of access and the scarcity of channels; cable was called the "medium of abundance."

In 1971, intense negotiations among the trade groups under the auspices of FCC Chairman Dean Burch and Office of Telecommunications Policy Director Clay T. Whitehead resulted in a "compromise" solution to the conflict. This compromise included a formula for payment of royalties for distant signals and a specified limit — varying with market size and other factors — to the number of such signals that could be imported. The compromise was intended to be embodied in a massive set of FCC rules promulgated in 1972. These rules, in addition to regulating the number and type of distant signals that might be imported, imposed a number of requirements on cable systems. Among these were local origination, the provision of free channels for various uses, and technical, capacity, and access rules designed to ensure the more rapid development of the "blue sky" services.

The details of the 1972 rules will be explored below. They were truly a compromise in the sense that the FCC convinced itself and the cable industry that they were the minimum conditions required to get cable moving, while not irreparably harming the broadcasters. The free channels and other requirements imposed on cable systems were designed to ensure that cable lived up to its promise of "abundance," rather than simply existing on the retransmission of broadcast signals. These requirements were on the whole technically and financially unrealistic and were relaxed as their effective dates approached. In an important sense, the public service and capacity requirements were necessary to get the vote of "liberal" commissioners, particularly Nicholas Johnson.

After 1972, the major issues in cable regulation were pay television, copyright, pole rentals, and the question of federal versus state and local jurisdiction over cable. The FCC rules against pay television on cable systems (as well as over-the-air) were gradually relaxed but still remained quite restrictive until 1977, when they were struck down by the courts. One major change came in 1975, when the FCC allowed cable pay-TV systems to use movies between three and four years old (as well as those less than three, the previous rule). In 1976, Congress passed an omnibus copyright bill that included compulsory licenses for distant signals allowed by the FCC, with royalties paid to a central pool for distribution to copyright owners.

In 1974, the Cabinet Committee on Cable Communications issued a report that put forward a new regulatory framework for cable, based on the separation of transmission and content functions. Under the Committee's proposal, cable would be a common carrier with no federal regulation of content. The rationale was that local cable transmission is a natural monopoly, which for competitive and First Amendment reasons ought not to be translated into a monopoly of control over content. If all cable channels were competitively programmed, there would be no scarcity and less need for federal regulations, such as the fairness doctrine, which impinge on freedom of expression. The policy proposals of the Cabinet Committee were endorsed in an influential 1976 House Communications Subcommittee Staff report.

During the Ford Administration, a domestic council regulatory review group headed by Paul MacAvoy considered the problem of cable television and came to the unexpected conclusion that the proponents of cable deregulation had failed to sustain the "burden of proof" necessary to make out a case for abandoning the rules. In fact, a considerable amount of political courage would have been required to overcome broadcast industry opposition to deregulation of cable. Nevertheless, of the half-dozen major attempts to conduct objective reviews of the cable regulations that were undertaken by government committees and private commissions in the 1970s, the MacAvoy effort was the only one that failed to conclude that the rules were unduly restrictive of cable development. By 1979, the FCC itself had gradually abandoned nearly all of its 1972 rules restricting cable growth, except for those limiting distant-signal importation. On April 25, 1979, the Commission issued a massive economic study of the effects of cable regulation, concluded that regulation was not necessary, and released a proposal to abolish its distant-signal restrictions. (Cable systems are, however, still required to carry all local channels.) The Commission adopted these proposals in July 1980, and cable television regulation ended just eighteen years after it began.*

---

* The new order went into effect in November 1980, but it is being appealed in the courts.

CABLE REGULATION
AT FULL FLOOD

The cable regulations adopted by the FCC in 1972, although ending
the five-year absolute freeze on cable growth in the top 100 television
markets, were highly restrictive in a number of respects. After 1972,
these rules were slowly but steadily abandoned, either by voluntary
FCC action or by court order. The FCC's authority to regulate cable
was reinforced in 1968 and 1972 by Supreme Court decisions. After
1972, the tide of judicial endorsement of FCC jurisdiction receded,
most markedly in a 1977 court of appeals decision striking down the
pay-TV rules.

The 1972 rules were enormously complicated, a state of affairs due
at least in part to the technical and legal (and in several cases uninter-
pretable) language employed. What follows is a very summary description.

Certificate of Compliance. Cable systems that retransmit broadcast
signals could not operate legally without what was in effect a license
from the Commission.

Franchising Standards. Licenses were not granted unless the cable system had a franchise meeting certain standards; requirements were imposed on both cable systems and franchising authorities. Franchises
were limited to fifteen years; construction had to begin within one
year; the local authority was required to regulate rates; due process
was required in franchise awards; franchise fees were limited; and local
authorities were preempted on most other matters.

Signals. Cable systems were required to carry local signals and over-the-
air signals that, although nonlocal, were "significantly viewed" in the
market (i.e., had a specified minimum share of the local audience). In
addition, systems might import at least two signals, and as many more
as were necessary, so that after taking account of local signals:

1. Systems in the largest 50 markets had three independents plus three
networks.
2. Systems in the second-largest 50 markets had two independents plus
three networks.
3. Systems in markets smaller than the top 100 had one independent
plus three networks.
4. Systems outside TV markets had no restrictions.

These rules can be illustrated by the following example. Suppose a cable system were in one of the largest 50 markets. First, it must carry all the local stations. Second, it must carry any nearby station that manages to obtain 5 percent or more of the local over-the-air audience. It might then, in addition, import from distant cities two stations and enough more so that it carried at least three network stations and three independent stations. However, the imported signals were subject to two further limitations.

First, the "antileapfrogging" rule (also called the "leapfrogging" rule) required cable systems to import the nearest qualified distant signals. The leapfrogging rule was apparently meant to encourage localism, since the natural tendency of a cable system would be to import the stations that had the best programming, which are likely to be independent VHF stations in the very largest cities. If these stations were widely imported, they might begin to form the basis for regional TV networks, capable of tapping regional advertising markets. To a certain degree this already takes place; Oakland's KTVU, for example, is extensively imported to the intermountain west. The leapfrogging rules discouraged this, often by forcing cable systems to pick up nearby underfinanced independent UHF stations. This policy benefited the imported station and the local broadcasters and hurt viewers and the cable system.

Second, local stations' "exclusivity" rights were protected by blacking out, on any imported signal, program material for which a local station had broadcast rights. The leapfrogging and exclusivity rules both varied by size of market, the latter rules also by type of programming.

Origination. The 1972 rules required cable systems to create their own programming on at least one channel and to make available free channels for, respectively, public free access, local government, and the local school system. Channels not devoted to retransmission of TV stations were subject to the FCC broadcast content regulations, including the fairness doctrine, equal-time provisions, and obscenity rules.

Capacity. The 1972 rules imposed a minimum channel capacity constraint (twenty channels) and a two-way communications requirement. The 1972 regulations also contain the so-called "$n + 1$" rule:

> Whenever all of the channels described in sub-paragraphs (4) through (7) of this paragraph are in use during 80 percent of the weekdays . . . for 80 percent of the time during any consecutive 3-hour period for 6 consecutive weeks, such system shall have 6 months in which to make a new channel available. . . .

This rule, apparently designed to ensure adequate capacity without regulating prices, would perhaps have made sense to one of Lewis Carroll's characters. The FCC made no attempt to enforce it.

Leased Channel Programming. Systems were required to lease available channels to others, relinquishing all control of program content. The FCC asserted jurisdiction to regulate the content and operations of such channel lessees.

Ownership. Cable systems could not be owned by telephone companies, TV stations in the same market, or TV networks.

Pay TV. The FCC required that cable systems carrying per-program or per-channel pay TV meet the following guidelines on the pay channels:

1. No advertising.
2. Maximum of 90 percent combined sports and movies.
3. No sports programs if the event had been broadcast in the market within the past five years; new events could not be shown for five years after their first occurrence.
4. No movies between four and ten years old.

The purpose of these rules was to prevent pay-TV channels from bidding away programs that would otherwise have been shown on "free" over-the-air television. Since they were meant to prevent such siphoning of programs to pay TV, they were called "antisiphoning" rules. For instance, most movies then shown on television were between four and ten years old; pay-TV systems could not bid on such movies, though they could show newer ones, competing with theatrical exhibitors. The practical effect of the FCC's pay-TV rules was to deprive viewers of certain programs and to artificially lower the price that TV stations had to pay for programs, sports, and movies.

The general thrust of the cable rules was to limit the growth of cable by direct constraint and by the imposition of various regulatory taxes. The beneficiaries of this policy were broadcast stations, networks, and those viewers (if any) who might be harmed by cable growth. The costs of cable restraints were borne by cable operators and those viewers who were deprived of the opportunity to subscribe to cable services.

In addition to the FCC's 1972 regulations, various state regulations were and are in effect. These differ from state to state.

Various state governments have created special cable regulatory commissions or awarded such jurisdiction to their Public Utility Commissions. Vermont, Massachusetts, New York, and Connecticut are particularly active in this area. The line between federal and state jurisdiction has not yet been clearly drawn. To the extent that cable systems resemble communication common carriers, state governments may have complete authority over intrastate operations. To the extent cable systems resemble broadcasters, FCC authority is supreme. The telephone company and the local jurisdictions seek to limit federal preemption of cable regulation; the cable industry, broadcasters, and the FCC have favored it.

DISTANT SIGNALS AND COPYRIGHT LIABILITY

A number of studies have looked into the effect of the FCC rules on the growth of cable systems, the profitability of TV stations, and the welfare of viewers. These studies, which are summarized in the FCC's 1979 *Report,* focus on the impact of varying the number and type of distant signals allowed under some assumptions about copyright liability.

Providing distant signals in big cities is probably necessary to cable's economic viability. It increases demand for the system's services at relatively low cost, which may allow the operator to achieve sufficient penetration of the market to make other services profitable, notably pay-TV channels offering movies. More exotic and specialized services, such as alarm systems, meter reading, and electronic shopping, are much talked about. It is argued that these exotic services cannot be offered until cable systems have a high penetration, and that distant signals are a necessary preliminary step. Some studies suggest that in large cities with good over-the-air signals, distant signals may be just enough to make cable systems marginally profitable. The amount of copyright payment and the costs of services required by regulators may make the difference. Thus, although none of the industry groups denied the necessity for copyright liability, it took many years to settle on the particular formula contained in the Copyright Act of 1976.

Similarly, industry groups debated over the extent of exclusivity (geographical and temporal) that copyright owners might grant to stations that buy their programs.

The issue of copyright liability for distant signals is a complex one because it involves what can only be guesses about transactions costs under various policies, the elasticity of program supply, and possible changes in patterns of television advertising. One straightforward approach is to have no copyright liability at all. Cable operators would import an unlimited number of distant signals, paying only the cost of physical transmission. The distant stations being imported would gain additional audiences, additional advertising revenue, and in the end would pay more money to program suppliers.

On the other hand, copyright liability for distant signals may be necessary because otherwise, in the long run, the market for programs would not be able to operate effectively. Program suppliers rent their products to TV stations and networks for "runs" that include geographical and temporal exclusivity provisions; this presumably increases the value of the program to the station (because most of the local audience will not have seen the program before) and therefore increases the revenue that the program supplier can expect. If cable systems had a right to import any distant signals without copyright liability, then a given program would be relatively unproductive to local stations, and the program suppliers might not be able to sell it to more than a few powerful independent VHF stations. But distant local audiences are worth less to the imported station than to the local station in terms of advertising revenue. Therefore the revenues of program suppliers, who are highly competitive, might be decreased. The absence of copyright liability with widespread distant-signal importation might thus result in a decline in the supply of program material, depending on the amount of economic rents in program supply. Ideally, cable systems would bargain with distant stations over the fees to be paid for importation. These payments would then be reflected in the market prices paid for programs by stations. However, stations themselves hold only an exhibition license to the programs, not a copyright. Direct bargaining between cable systems and program suppliers is arguably too expensive because transactions costs are high relative to the value of the material being traded. Giving cable systems a compulsory license to import signals subject to freely negotiated "reasonable" copyright fees might work if stations wishing to be imported were to compete with each other. Then program producers would be able to charge imported stations a price that reflected the royalty payments made to the station by cable systems. Even this approach may be flawed, however, if the physical transmission costs of importation are insufficient to overcome the tendency of competing distant stations to bid down the royalty rate charged to the systems they are serving.

The copyright issue was settled for the time being with the passage of the General Revision of the Copyright Law in 1976. The Act makes retransmissions by cable companies of broadcast programming subject to copyright law. It provides for compulsory licenses for all unaltered retransmissions authorized by the FCC, provided that proper statements of identity and accounts are filed and royalty fees are paid. No royalties need be paid on signals of stations within the local viewing area, but all large cable systems must pay a royalty fee of 0.675 percent of gross revenues, which gives them the right to import such distant signals as the FCC allows. The royalties are accumulated by the Copyright Office and distributed once a year by a newly created Copyright Royalty Tribunal to copyright owners whose programs were retransmitted as distant signals. No claim can be made for local retransmissions or for network programs.

In the context of the FCC's 1979 proposal to abolish the remaining restrictions on distant signals, Assistant Secretary of Commerce Henry Geller proposed that the Commission impose full copyright liability on cable systems. Although adoption of such a proposal seems clearly outside the FCC's jurisdiction, and a matter for Congress, the proposal itself has much to recommend it. Before nonmarket solutions are imposed, we should have a clearer indication that the marketplace will be inefficient. Congress presumably imposed the compulsory license-royalty pool solution on the assumption that transactions costs in a free market would be prohibitive, so that cable systems would be unable to bargain for distant signals. There was and is insufficient empirical evidence to support this assumption.

WHY WAS CABLE DEREGULATED?

Over the course of two decades the FCC has first regulated and then gradually deregulated cable. The FCC's activities generally paralleled those of the federal courts, though it is hard to see which institution, if either, was the leader. Although Congress passed no significant legislation affecting cable other than the Copyright Act, it continually oversaw FCC actions, many of which were heavily influenced by the perceived positions of the communications subcommittees in both houses. In short, the FCC did not act alone.

Two alternative theories explain the phenomenon of cable regulation and deregulation. The first is the FCC's own official version, contained in its 1979 *Report on the Inquiry into the Economic Relationship between Television Broadcasting and Cable Television*. This version holds that, as it became apparent that cable might present a significant economic challenge to TV broadcasting, cable regulation was imposed by the FCC and upheld by the courts in order to protect both broadcasters and their viewers from the risk of harm. As the Commission gradually acquired more information about the nature of the risks and the likely economic effects of cable growth, the regulations were relaxed. The motives of the government were entirely benevolent; so long as any individual members of the viewing public might be disadvantaged by cable, the government was justified in retarding the diffusion of cable among those who might benefit from it. Better information acquired through studies and experience allowed the FCC to increasingly discount the risks of significant harm, and by 1979 the restrictions could be abandoned entirely. In assessing this theory, one might ask not whether the FCC and the courts made minor errors of judgment in timing, but whether the government has a right to protect consumers and corporations from the risks associated with marketplace forces and technological change *by directly retarding the change*. Note that, since few changes benefit everyone, progress will nearly always claim some victims. Sometimes they are impossible to predict or identify so that compensation cannot be arranged; in such cases, delay is the only protection available.

The second theory of the government's behavior is more cynical. Cable television may have been regulated simply to protect the excess profits of TV broadcasters because TV stations have significant political power. According to this theory, claims about the need to protect viewers from the risk of harm are just rhetoric designed to rationalize the government's behavior. This theory is bolstered by the indisputable fact that the most draconian cable restrictions — the freeze and later the distant-signal rules — were imposed in those cities where the most powerful and profitable TV stations were located, and not in the markets where cable posed the greatest threat to TV station viability. Cable television most threatens the economic viability of small-market VHF network affiliates, but large-market VHF affiliates got the most protection.

The cynical theory would presumably explain the gradual deregulation of cable by pointing to the steadily increasing political power of the cable industry and the growing body of public opinion favoring cable development. Alternatively, cable may gradually have been perceived as a less serious economic threat by the broadcast lobby, or the industry may simply have gained all the time it required to make its own adjustments. One such adjustment has been the purchase of cable systems by broadcasters. Under the July 1980 order, TV stations are still prohibited from owning cable systems in their viewing areas, but they can own them elsewhere. A third explanation of deregulation is that "good people" took over control of the FCC and sought to remedy its previous sins.

The "good guys, bad guys" approach to explaining these events is almost certainly fruitless. The FCC is fenced in by congressional and judicial constraints, and these too changed markedly between the period of regulation and the period of deregulation. Perhaps better information and the effects of public opinion affected large numbers of public officials in all three branches.

Which of the two theories is valid? The facts are consistent with both. Perhaps a more general hypothesis would incorporate elements of both theories. Industries proposing to receive government largesse offer public-interest rationales for their proposals; the "protecting viewers from risk" rationale for cable regulation is not absurd in principle, merely in practice. But it certainly was not obvious to every reasonable person in, say, 1968, that cable regulation would in practice be absurd.

THE FUTURE OF CABLE TELEVISION

When the FCC adopted its own proposal to complete the dismantling of cable regulation, a number of restraints remained on the free market in cable services. The Copyright Act of 1976 very likely imposes a significant distortion, but one that will gradually subside as cable operators come to depend more on pay TV and independent program sources such as C-SPAN. Local and state regulatory machinery is in place, and some of it will distort and retard the diffusion of cable services. Each of these policy issues will have to be dealt with in the coming years. Mergers of cable systems and newspapers are also an important policy issue, because electronic delivery of newspapers will probably one day involve cable systems, and because cable program sources may soon begin to compete in local advertising markets.

But the most significant of the potential problems in the future of cable is the possibility that the FCC will come to exercise its continued jurisdiction over cable to regulate the content of programs. This is most likely to come in reaction to a perception that cable operators, with local monopolies of a large number of channels, are abusing their discretion over program content and access by others. The problem will be more acute if the present trend toward concentration of cable system ownership in the hands of a few giant chains continues. Since it is possible that cable systems will carry newspapers as well as "broadcast" programs, the danger of federal regulation of program content is particularly serious. Many of the special committees and task forces set up to study cable in the 1970s recommended that cable systems have a common-carrier access obligation, so that the transmission monopoly would be separated from the programming function. This would avoid both private monopoly and government regulation of programming.

But neither the Congress nor the FCC nor the courts has been willing to impose common-carrier obligations on cable. This issue is likely to arise again over the next two decades.

BIBLIOGRAPHY

Cabinet Committee on Cable Communication, *Cable,* Report to the President, Washington, D.C., 1974.

Federal Communications Commission, *Report on the Inquiry into the Economic Relationship Between Television Broadcasting and Cable Television,* 71 F.C.C.2d 632 (1979).

MacAvoy, Paul W., ed., *Deregulation of Cable Television.* Washington, D.C.: American Enterprise Institute, 1977.

Noll, Roger G., Peck, Merton J., and McGowan, J. J., *Economic Aspects of Television Regulation.* Washington, D.C.: The Brookings Institution, 1973.

Owen, Bruce M., Beebe, Jack, and Manning, W. G., Jr., *Television Economics.* Lexington, Mass.: Lexington Books, 1974.

Subcommittee on Communications, House Committee on Commerce, Staff Report, "Cable Television: Promise versus Regulatory Performance," Committee Print, January 1976.

CASE 4

Equity, Efficiency, and Regulation in the Rail and Trucking Industries

Ann F. Friedlaender
Massachusetts Institute of Technology

INTRODUCTION

The nature and extent of economic regulation in the surface freight industries has been an issue of policy debate for the past twenty years. Critics of regulation have focused on general issues of economic efficiency and resource allocation, arguing that regulatory practices caused traffic to be carried at excessively high rates and distorted shipper choices, so that many goods were carried by truck that could go more cheaply by rail. Thus, according to them, in the absence of regulation, rates would fall, the total freight bill would be reduced, and society as a whole would benefit under the workings of competitively organized transportation industries.[1]

In contrast, defenders of regulation have tended to focus upon distributional considerations, arguing that regulation ensured the orderly provision of service to all shippers by preventing rate wars and carrier instability while protecting small shippers in rural areas, from monopoly exploitation. Thus, according to them, in the absence of regulation, rates would rise and service levels would fall to "captive shippers," who had no effective alternatives to existing transportation services, while rate wars would develop on highly competitive routes, leading to service deterioration and reduction in profits and labor payments; the net result of deregulation would consequently be an increased freight bill, reduced transportation services, and a highly monopolistic freight industry.[2]

Until recently, the lines on each of these sides have been drawn very rigidly. Attacking regulation have been academic economists and policy-makers in recent administrations who were interested primarily in questions of resource allocation and economic efficiency. Defending regulation have been the railroads, the truckers, small shippers in rural areas, and the Interstate Commerce Commission (ICC), which is the governmental agency authorized to oversee economic regulation in the surface freight industries. Since Congress is sensitive to constituents who fear income losses from policy changes, it has tended to accept the regulationist view and therefore has not seriously considered regulatory reform in the surface freight industries.[3]

In the past few years, however, a number of changes have occurred that make significant regulatory reform in the rail and trucking industries a real possibility. The ICC has gradually relaxed its position as a defender of the regulatory status quo and, with the appointment of Darius W. Gaskins as Chairman in January 1980, has increasingly taken an activist role with respect to deregulation. Concurrently, led by Conrail, the railroads have taken the position that their ultimate financial viability requires relaxation of restrictions concerning rates, mergers, and abandonments. Thus, in contrast to their traditional hostility toward deregulation, the railroads as a whole are now encouraging it. Finally, the recent experience of the airlines indicates that deregulation need not be associated with Armageddon. Thus in recent years a significant number of the parties directly affected by regulation have begun to support deregulation in the rail and trucking industries.

Indeed, since January 1980 a regulatory revolution appears to have taken place, as the ICC, the railroads, and the major congressional committees dealing with surface freight transportation have all encouraged the passage of major regulatory reform .The results of these efforts have been the passage of trucking legislation granting considerable easing of existing restrictions and the passage of somewhat similar railroad legislation.* Thus, for the first time since the inception of regulation

---

* A major issue in the railroad bill was the powerful position of railroads hauling low sulfur coal from the high plains of Montana, Wyoming, and the Dakotas to utilities in the south and east. The railroads involved (especially Burlington Northern) probably do have market power in that case, which they seemed likely to exercise as the prices of competitive fuels (oil and gas) rose. At one point the whole regulatory reform legislation in railroads seemed likely to founder on the issue of how such coal freight rates were to be controlled. The bill did ultimately pass with only mild controls of rate increases.

with the passage of the Interstate Commerce Act of 1887, there appears to be a real possibility that transport markets will be shaped by competitive market forces instead of by regulatory restrictions. Consequently, this seems a good time to assess the status of regulation in the rail and trucking industries and to discuss how deregulation might be expected to affect them.*

The first part of this paper provides a brief background on the structure of regulation in the rail and trucking industries and its evolution over the past 90 years. The remainder of the paper discusses how deregulation could be expected to affect these industries. The second part analyzes the nature of rail-truck competition and quantifies the effects of moving from the current regulated equilibrium to a competitive equilibrium, given the existing railroad infrastructure. Since, however, there is considerable evidence that the existing railroad infrastructure is characterized by excessive track and inadequate maintenance, it is likely that substantial economies could be obtained from a rationalization of the railroad infrastructure. Hence the third part analyzes the consequences of changes in the railroad infrastructure and the implications of reaching a long-run equilibrium in which adjustments in both rates and railroad infrastructure are made. The fourth part focuses on the question of the trucking common carriers of general commodities and discusses whether the public interest requires the continued regulation of these carriers. The last part provides a brief summary and conclusion.

THE STRUCTURE OF FREIGHT TRANSPORT REGULATION

Freight transportation has historically been one of the most heavily regulated sectors in the American economy. The Interstate Commerce Act of 1887 introduced economic regulation as a policy tool and brought rail rates under extensive controls to limit discriminatory pricing practices concerning persons, localities, routes, and traffic. This structure was subsequently extended to for-hire motor carriers in 1935 and barge operators in 1940, so that the bulk of intercity freight transportation

---

* It should be pointed out that barge transportation is also regulated by the ICC. However, since the amount of regulated barge transportation is small relative to the total amount of barge traffic, this paper will focus upon the rail and trucking industries.

has been regulated in accordance with the structure of the original Interstate Commerce Act.*

Thus during the past 90 years rates, routes, entry, mergers, and abandonments have been closely monitored in the surface freight industry. Regulation has conferred a common-carrier obligation upon regulated transportation firms to accept all traffic at established rates in exchange for the right to operate transportation services over set routes and among localities. Although the carriers in principle have enjoyed the right to set rates and service levels, in practice these rights are severely circumscribed by regulatory restrictions. Specifically, efforts on the part of a given railroad to make significant departures from existing rate structures or to curtail service through abandonment proceedings are generally not permitted by the ICC.[4] Moreover, railroad merger proceedings must go through lengthy hearings and are often disallowed. Similarly, not only are regulated trucking firms limited to the routes and gateways that they can utilize or the commodities they can carry, but entry into new trucking markets is extremely difficult as well.[5] Finally, since shippers or competing carriers can dispute rates that they feel are unjust or give undue advantage to a particular carrier, rail and trucking firms typically set common rates through rate bureaus, and they concentrate on service instead of rate competition.[6] Consequently, regulated transportation firms have relatively little ability to respond to competitive pressures or to adjust rates or routes serviced without the threat of regulatory intervention. Although substantial regulatory reform appears to have taken place in 1980, until that time the form and intent of regulatory restrictions remained remarkably consistent after the passage of the original Interstate Commerce Act in 1887.

The forces behind the passage of the initial Act of 1887 and its subsequent application have been extensively explored, and there are a number of somewhat contradictory hypotheses concerning them.[7] Perhaps the most appealing of these is the hypothesis that at its initial inception, regulation served on the one hand the interests of the railroads, who were suffering from excess capacity, rate wars, and highly unstable profits, and on the other hand the interests of the expanding agricultural population, which was suffering from discriminatory pricing practices and excessive rates. Consequently, the railroads accepted regulation to ensure stability and orderly growth, while the agricultural interests actively sought regulation to protect them from monopolistic exploitation by the railroads.

* Privately owned intercity carriage and agricultural commodities carried by truck are exempt from regulation. Thus, while all rail shipments are subject to regulation, somewhat less than half of all trucking shipments and one-fourth of all inland waterway shipments are subject to regulation.

The Interstate Commerce Act of 1887 required that rates be "just and reasonable" and specifically prohibited personal price discrimination — that is, charging different rates to different shippers for similar services. Thus the railroads were effectively prohibited from charging isolated shippers with no alternative transportation options higher rates for similar services than shippers who could utilize competing waterways or railroads. However, the Act made no mention of commodity price discrimination, and the so-called value-of-service rate structure soon received official sanction by the ICC,[8] under which systematic rate differentials were established according to the value of the commodity independent of the type of service provided. Thus, for example, if corn were a more valuable commodity than oats, it would be carried at a higher rate, even though the costs of carrying these two commodities any given distance was essentially identical. Thus the rate structure was such that railroads did not practice personal price discrimination and treated shippers more or less equally with respect to their size and location, but did practice commodity price discrimination and received relatively high margins on high-value manufactured commodities and relatively low margins on low-value bulk and agricultural commodities.

At its time of inception, this policy made sense. It served the agricultural and populist interests by ensuring that rates for their commodities would be kept low and thus that farmers and homesteaders would not see any potential economic rent expropriated by the railroads. It served the interests of the railroads by ending the instability caused by the frequent rate wars and by ensuring relatively stable profit levels through the high returns received on high-value manufactured commodities. Indeed, subject to the restriction upon personal price discrimination imposed by the Act, it is likely that the value-of-service rate structure was also the profit-maximizing rate structure for the railroads. Moreover, since the demand for manufactured commodities was quite inelastic at that time, relatively little resource misallocation should have resulted from this pricing structure.

Although many changes have taken place in the structure of the Interstate Commerce Act since its passage in 1887, a concern with the maintenance of rural and agricultural incomes has been a dominant theme. The Hoch-Smith Resolution, passed by Congress in 1925, explicitly required the ICC to give consideration to the relationship between agricultural freight rates and agricultural incomes and has been interpreted as giving clear legislative sanction to the maintenance of the value-of-service rate structure.[9] Consequently, regulation has been extended to the competing modes whenever the railroads have been subjected to competitive pressures that have reduced their profitability and provided incentives to alter the rate structure. Thus, when the railroads were faced with an erosion of their high-value traffic by trucks, regulation was extended to motor carriers in 1935. Similarly, when water competition threatened to reduce the profitability of low-value shipments and put pressures on the railroads to increase rates of the "captive" bulk traffic (that is, traffic with no viable alternative transportation sources), regulation was extended to barges in 1940. Since World War II, the ICC has carefully monitored minimum rate levels on water-competitive traffic in an attempt to ensure that rail profitability is maintained at sufficiently high levels to preclude upward pressures on the rates of captive bulk traffic.*

In the past two decades, however, competitive pressures have not only served to erode railroad profits dramatically, but they have also tended to undermine the historical rate differentials implied by the value-of-service pricing structure. The virtual completion of the Interstate Highway System and the growth of truckload specialized commodity carriers have enabled trucks to compete effectively with railroads for a broad range of manufactured commodities. By offering competitive rates and superior service, trucks have been able to attract much of the high-rated manufactured traffic from railroads, leaving them with the relatively high-cost, low-value manufactured traffic. To compensate for this, the railroads have attempted to raise rates on noncompetitive bulk traffic (that is, traffic that is not subject to intramodal or intermodal competition) and have introduced a number of cost-saving innovations such as unit trains with respect to the carriage of large-volume shipments.[10] Thus there is some evidence, which will be discussed in detail below, that under the current rate structure, bulk commodities may actually enjoy a higher markup relative to marginal cost than manufactured commodities. This implies, of course, that the value-of-service rate structure may no longer be operational, in spite of the ICC's efforts to maintain it.

In view of the high degree of substitutability between rail and full-truckload carriage for manufactured goods and the large amount of noncompetitive bulk traffic hauled by the railroads, this change in the rate structure reflects natural market forces. However, the continuing subsidies of Conrail, the bankruptcies of a number of midwestern railroads, and the continued low rates of return for the rail system as a whole indicate that the current rate structure does not enable the railroads to obtain sufficient funds to maintain their infrastructure and provide effective rail service. However, for the railroads to obtain adequate revenues to maintain their infrastructure and capital stock at sufficiently high levels to provide service that permits effective competition

---

* The formation of Amtrak and the takeover of rail passenger service by the federal government can also be interpreted as an effort to maintain rail profitability and thus foreclose efforts to alter the value-of-service rate structure.

with truck and water carriers, it may be necessary to permit the railroads to raise rates or abandon service on their light-density rural traffic.[11] Thus the maintenance of adequate rail profitability and low rates to light-density rural and agricultural shippers may be fundamentally incompatible. Indeed, much of the current pressure on the part of the railroad industry in favor of deregulation arises from a recognition of this incompatibility and a desire to have the freedom to eliminate noncompensatory traffic or to price it at compensatory levels.

However, it is important to stress that current pressures for deregulation of the surface freight industries arise from forces considerably broader than the railroads' financial plight. Concern with continued inflationary pressures has raised the question of whether increased competition in the rail and trucking industries might not lead to rate reductions and hence lowered production costs for a broad range of commodities. Similarly, concern with energy conservation has raised the question of whether regulation prevents energy-efficient railroads from competing effectively with trucks and limits the backhaul ability of both trucks and rails. Finally, both of these concerns are increasingly generalized into a broad perception that the United States cannot afford resource misallocations and inefficiencies that contribute to its relatively low rate of economic growth and productivity change. Thus in terms of policy-makers' goals, there appears to have been a shift toward increasing emphasis upon the need for improved resource allocation in the transportation industries. Indicative of this are the passage of the airline deregulation bill in 1978, the changing attitude of the ICC toward deregulation, and the increasing receptivity to deregulation on the part of the congressional leadership.

Nevertheless, whether the allocational efficiencies associated with major regulatory reform are sufficiently great to offset the presumed distributional costs that would arise from deregulation is an issue of considerable debate. This suggests that it would be useful to assess the possible consequences of moving from the existing regulated equilibrium in the transportation industries to one that was characterized by competition. The main issues here are (1) whether the structure of technology in the rail and trucking industries is compatible with workable competition, and (2) what the allocational and distributional effects of such a change are likely to be. The remainder of this paper will assess the implications of changing regulatory policies with respect to rates in the rail and truckload trucking markets, railroad abandonments, and the less-than-truckload trucking market to determine if the public interest would be served by substantial relaxation of current regulatory restrictions concerning rates, entry, abandonments, and common-carrier obligations. With a few important caveats, it will argue that the efficiency gains of deregulation could be expected to outweigh the distributional losses to the affected carriers and shippers and hence that society would benefit from deregulation in the transportation industries.

A COMPETITIVE EQUILIBRIUM IN THE RAIL AND TRUCKING INDUSTRIES

Since the value-of-service rate structure is based on a form of commodity price discrimination, rail and trucking rates generally bear relatively little relationship to marginal costs.* It would be interesting, then, to analyze the implications of moving from the present situation to one that was characterized by competitive behavior and marginal-cost pricing. While a full competitive equilibrium would also require adjustments in railroad capital to reflect an efficient amount of infrastructure, focusing on the pricing issue allows us to analyze how a relaxation of rate regulation might affect traffic allocations, income levels of affected shippers and carriers, and aggregate economic efficiency.† Questions of railroad abandonments and infrastructure subsidies will be considered in the next part.

Since each transportation mode carries an enormous range of commodities over an enormous range of origins and destinations, an analysis that incorporates the full complexity of the transportation industries and their interrelationships would be an impossible undertaking. Thus this part summarizes recent work by Friedlaender and Spady (1981) as an initial effort to deal with these general equilibrium effects and to quantify the consequences of moving from the status quo to a competitive equilibrium. Consequently, this part will focus upon the interrelationships between rail and regulated trucking firms that specialize in truckload carriage with respect to modes[12] and between bulk and

---

* In this connection the role of service should be stressed, since with free service competition it is entirely possible that service levels would rise to equate price with marginal costs inclusive of service levels. However, while there is some evidence that service competition plays an important role in the provision of service by trucking carriers of general commodities, there is less evidence that it plays a significant role in the railroads or in trucking specialized commodity carriers.

† Of course, it should be stressed that deregulation need not lead to competitive pricing policies. Moreover, marginal-cost pricing only has normative significance in situations in which prices reflect marginal costs throughout the economy. Nevertheless, by focusing on the competitive equilibrium, a basis of comparison with the status quo can be established.

manufactured commodities with respect to outputs. Although water, pipeline, and exempt and private trucking carriage also transport a considerable portion of freight traffic, data limitations require that the analysis be limited to truck and rail common carriers. Similarly, although manufactured and bulk commodities are aggregates of many different commodities, each having diverse shipment characteristics and transportation requirements, data limitations and analytical tractability require that the analysis be limited to these two generic commodity types. Finally, in keeping with the relatively aggregate framework of the analysis, the regional analysis is limited to two broad regions: the Official Territory, which encompasses the New England, Middle Atlantic, and Great Lakes States, and the South-West Region, which encompasses the rest of the country.

Allocational Effects of Rail-Truck Competition

The value-of-service rate structure has long been held up as an example of the inefficiencies caused by regulation in the surface freight industries.[13] Conventional wisdom contends that rail transportation enjoys a clear cost advantage over truck transportation for all shipments of a carload size (e.g., over 15 tons), except those with short haul (e.g., less than 200 miles) or very high value (e.g., computer parts).[14] Since, however, the value-of-service rate structure has traditionally maintained high rail rates on manufactured goods and has prevented railroads from pricing these goods competitively, shippers have had a clear incentive to use trucks, which provide superior service with respect to transit time, shipment size, and the like. Thus most of the critics of transport regulation feel that the value-of-service rate structure creates a substantial misallocation of resources by encouraging the use of high-cost trucking operations instead of low-cost rail operations. Therefore, according to them, in the absence of regulation, rail rates on manufactured commodities would fall and there would be a shift in freight shipments away from truck and toward rail.

In recent years, however, a revisionist view has evolved, which holds that the inefficiencies caused by value-of-service ratemaking may be considerably less than generally believed. Basically this view holds that in view of the inventory costs of goods in transit and the service advantages offered by trucks, trucking costs of manufactured goods are considerably lower than generally believed, while rail costs are considerably higher. Thus the competitive advantage that rail operations enjoy over trucking operations is actually quite limited, and efficient resource allocation requires increased use of trucks for the carriage of manufactured goods.

Adherents of this view point to two major pieces of evidence. First, Wyckoff (1974) and Wyckoff and Maister (1975) have analyzed the trucking industry extensively and argued that the true source of rail competition comes from full-truckload carriers of specialized commodities instead of from less-than-truckload (LTL) carriers of general freight.* Since truckload carriage does not incur costs of consolidation and terminal handling, and is not subject to specific route restrictions, the costs of truckload trucking operations are considerably lower than the costs of LTL operations and are in fact competitive with rail. Second, the railroads have consistently attempted to raise rates on manufactured goods rather than lower them, arguing that the rates on boxcar operations fail to cover costs. Indeed, the rail industry is presently lobbying for reduced regulation to permit it to raise rates and/or abandon service selectively on a wide range of manufactured commodities.[15] Thus, according to many railroad sources, not only does the value-of-service rate structure fail to permit the railroads to earn sufficient revenue on much of their manufactured traffic and fail to permit them to maintain low rates on bulk and agricultural traffic, but it also may engender losses on much of their manufactured traffic. Consequently, instead of leading to reductions in rates on manufactured commodities, rational pricing may actually require increases in these rates.

Recent analyses by Friedlaender and Spady (1981) strongly support the revisionist view with respect to rail rates and indicate that not only are the price-marginal cost ratios higher for bulk than for manufactured commodities, but also rates on manufactured goods are less than marginal costs. Thus economic efficiency would dictate increases in rail rates on manufactured goods and a reallocation of this traffic in favor of trucks. Nevertheless, it is important to note that because of the wide geographical variation in rail and trucking costs, it is not appropriate to make sweeping generalizations about the economic effects of moving from the present rate structure to one that would reflect competitive pricing.

Table 1 summarizes the rates, marginal costs, output levels, and profits that existed in 1972 and their expected levels under a competitive equilibrium. Although the levels of rates and output have clearly changed since then, the qualitative findings are still valid. With respect

* In particular, in addition to listing fifteen specific truckload commodity categories (e.g., household goods, automobiles, and refrigerated products), the Commission has one category of specific commodities not otherwise grouped. In recent years, trucking firms have expanded their operating rights in this area and can carry a broad range of manufactured commodities under truckload rates. This analysis is based on this latter group of trucking carriers.

to the Official Region,* Table 1 indicates that railroads carry manufactured goods at rates considerably below marginal cost and carry bulk commodities at rates slightly greater than marginal cost. In contrast, trucks carry both types of goods at rates in excess of marginal cost, with the price-marginal cost ratio for bulk commodities considerably higher than that of manufactured goods. Thus, contrary to the conventional wisdom, the rate structure appears to favor manufactured goods rather than bulk commodities on both modes.

Analyzing the price and output changes that would result from moving to a competitive equilibrium is complicated, because changes in rates and traffic mixes cause both the demand and marginal-cost or supply curves to shift. In particular, each mode's demand for each commodity depends on the rate in its own and competing mode, and each mode's marginal cost or supply of any given commodity depends on the traffic mix and volume on that mode. Thus, for example, a fall in the rates of either mode will cause the demand curve of the other mode to decrease. Similarly, if firms are subject to decreasing returns to scale and thus face a rising supply curve, increases in the output of one commodity will shift up the supply curve for the other commodity. Hence the competitive equilibrium cannot be determined by simple movements along the relevant curves.

This is illustrated in Figures 1 and 2.† The curves marked D_0 and S_0 represent the industry demand and supply curves that exist under the present rate structure, while the curves marked D_1 and S_1 represent the demand and supply curves that would exist under a competitive equilibrium. Note that since this analysis focuses on competitive behavior, the supply curves also represent the aggregate marginal-cost curves; hence the intersection of the demand and the supply curves represents a point where price equals marginal cost.[16] Finally, the initial price is denoted by P, the initial marginal cost is denoted by M, and the competitive price-marginal cost equilibrium is denoted by C; Q_0 denotes the initial output and Q_1 the output under a competitive equilibrium.

Before analyzing the nature of the shifts in the relevant demand and supply curves and the shifts in rates and outputs that would occur in moving from the existing to the competitive equilibrium, it is useful to note some significant aspects of the structure of costs and demands. First, the supply curve of rail service is generally upward sloping, indi-

* Official territory includes the northeast through Virginia and West Virginia, and the industrial states of the midwest (Ohio, Indiana, Illinois, the lower peninsula of Michigan, and southeastern Wisconsin). The South-West refers to all the rest of the continental United States.

† These figures are based on the statistical estimates given in Table 1.

Table 1. Market Characteristics, Initial and Competitive Equilibria, Official and South-West Regions, 1972

	1972 Status Quo				Competitive Equilibrium			
	Price (¢/ton-mile)	Marginal Cost (¢/ton-mile)	Output (billion ton-miles)	Profits ($ billion)	Price (¢/ton-mile)	Marginal Cost (¢/ton-mile)	Output (billion ton-miles)	Profits ($ billion)
OFFICIAL								
Rail								
Manufactures	2.41	4.92	83.083	−0.251	4.59	4.59	30.284	1.196
Bulk	2.13	1.93	57.116		1.52	1.52	76.472	
Truck								
Manufactures	6.07	4.92	27.512	0.110	4.51	4.51	49.206	−.609
Bulk	5.90	4.17	13.37		3.69	3.69	22.43	
SOUTH-WEST								
Rail								
Manufactures	2.79	2.93	168.839	2.123	2.98	2.98	148.932	1.627
Bulk	1.66	0.98	134.080		1.0	1.043	237.234	
Truck								
Manufactures	5.45	4.60	31.777	0.145	4.61	4.61	42.122	−0.134
Bulk	3.96	3.97	22.166		3.96	3.96	16.00	

Source: Friedlaender and Spady (1981), Tables 3.1 and 3.2, pp. 85 and 89.

Figure 1. Initial and Competitive Equilibria, Official Territory

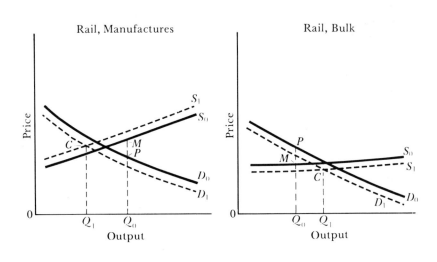

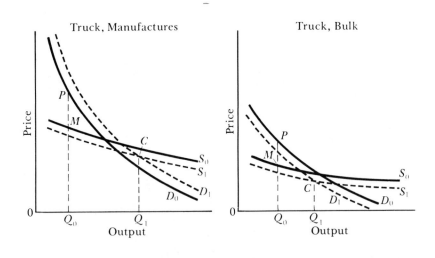

cating that railroads are subject to short-run diseconomies of scale; that is, as output rises, costs rise more than proportionately. However, these diseconomies are more marked for manufactured goods than for bulk commodities. Moreover, railroad costs in the Official Region are generally higher than those in the South-West Region. Second, trucking costs rise slightly in the South-West Region, indicating that these trucking operations appear to be subject to mild diseconomies of scale. However, since the trucking supply curve falls for the relevant range in the Official Region, this indicates that these trucking operations are subject to economies of scale.[17] Finally, there does not appear to be any systematic difference in the structure of the demand curves between modes, commodities, or regions. Nevertheless, under the existing equilibrium, trucking operations appear to be in a less elastic portion of the demand curve than rail operations.

Turning now to a comparison of the initial equilibrium and the competitive equilibrium in the Official Region, Figure 1 indicates that rail rates are initially below marginal cost for manufactured goods, while truck rates are above marginal cost. Thus, under a competitive equilibrium where price equaled marginal cost, rail rates would rise and truck rates would fall, shifting traffic from rail to truck. The rail demand curve would shift in, while the trucking demand curve would shift out. With respect to bulk commodities, prices are initially above marginal costs in both modes, so rates in both modes will be lower in competitive equilibrium. This will lead to a decrease in the demand curves in both modes. Nevertheless, there will be a net increase in bulk output in both modes. Since the supply curve of any one commodity depends upon the total volume of both commodities, an increase in the carriage of one commodity will cause the supply curve of the other commodity to shift up if the mode is subject to decreasing returns to scale, and conversely if the mode is subject to increasing returns to scale. Thus the increase in bulk output will cause the rail supply curve to shift up and the truck supply curve to shift down. Similarly, the reduction in rail manufactures will cause the rail bulk supply curve to shift down, while the increase in truck manufactures will cause the truck bulk supply curve to shift down.

The net result of all of these shifts will be a rise in rail rates for manufactures, a fall in trucking rates for manufactures, and a large shift of manufactured goods away from rail and in favor of truck. In contrast, there will be a fall in both rail and trucking rates for bulk commodities and an increase of bulk carriage in both modes. However, there will be greater increases in rail carriage of bulk commodities than in trucking carriage of these same goods because of the inherent advantage of railroads with respect to shipping bulk commodities.

Within the South-West Region, Table 1 and Figure 2 indicate that

Figure 2. Initial and Competitive Equilibria, South-West Region

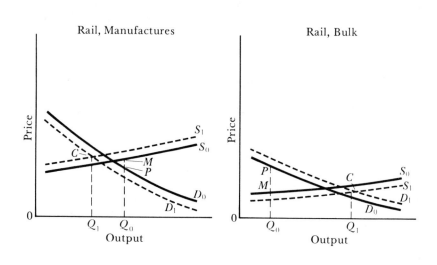

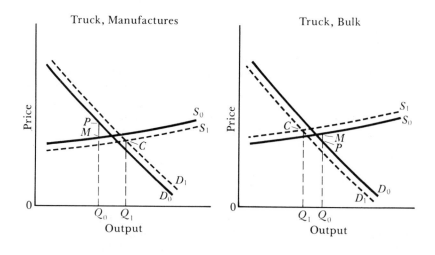

rail rates are slightly below marginal costs for manufactured commodities and considerably in excess of marginal costs for bulk commodities; truck rates are substantially above marginal costs for manufactured commodities, but slightly below marginal costs for bulk commodities. Thus the value-of-service rate structure seems to apply to trucking rates, while the revisionist view of the rate structure seems to apply to rail rates. Consequently a move toward competitive pricing would imply an increase in rail rates and a reduction in trucking rates for manufactured commodities, a reduction in rail rates and an increase in trucking rates for bulk commodities. In terms of modal splits, a competitive pricing structure would lead to a reallocation of manufactured traffic in favor of truck and a reallocation of bulk commodities in favor of rail.

Thus, within both regions a competitive equilibrium in the rail and trucking industries would be characterized by a modal split in favor of truck for manufactured goods and in favor of rail for bulk commodities. In terms of each mode, railroads would carry substantially more bulk commodities than manufactured goods while trucks would carry more manufactured commodities than bulk commodities. Thus this scenario implies that railroads would largely perform a wholesaling function, carrying commodities between major traffic centers, while trucks would largely perform a retailing function, carrying commodities in truckload shipments from these major traffic centers to more geographically dispersed areas.[18]

In assessing these conclusions, it is important to stress that they are based on the assumption of competitive behavior. While the high degree of rail-truck competition should make this a likely result with respect to manufactured commodities, the relative lack of water and truck competition for many bulk commodities make it questionable whether competitive behavior would occur in the rail markets for bulk commodities.[19] Indeed, recent legislation dealing with regulatory reform in the railroad industry has incorporated language aimed at protecting "captive" shippers on rail lines that are not subject to intramodal or intermodal competition.[20] Thus, although these results represent an efficient, competitive allocation of transportation resources, it is problematical whether such an allocation would occur in a deregulated environment. Nevertheless, in view of the increasing efficiency associated with truckload trucking operations, it is unlikely that full monopoly exploitation of "captive" shippers would occur.

Because of the low levels of profitability that the railroad system currently attains, an important policy question is whether a movement toward marginal-cost pricing would enable the railroads to be financially viable. Because of the large amounts of noncompensatory traffic in manufactured goods, rate increases to reach marginal costs should increase rail profits. However, because rates on bulk commodities are currently above marginal cost, marginal-cost pricing should reduce the profitability of these shipments. At a competitive equilibrium, Friedlaender and Spady (1981) have estimated that railroads in the Official Region should have earned a return of 3.34 percent, while those in the South-West Region should have earned a return of 5.36 percent in 1972, figures which were well below the opportunity cost of capital existing at that time. This implies that with their current levels of infrastructure the railroads could not earn a sufficient return to maintain their capital stock. Hence without substantial abandonments or rates in excess of marginal cost, it does not appear that the railroads can be financially self-supporting.

Distributional Effects of a Competitive Equilibrium

Before turning to the question of railroad infrastructure, however, it is important to assess the distributional implications of moving from the status quo to a competitive equilibrium, because if the income losses of such a change are substantial, they must be considered against the efficiency gains.

The preceding analysis indicated that as compared to the status quo, a competitive equilibrium would involve substantial rate increases on rail manufactured goods in the Official Region, substantial rate reductions on rail carriage of bulk commodities in the South-West Region, and reduction in trucking rates on both commodities in both regions.

An analysis of the direct income changes accruing to shippers as a result of competitive pricing indicates that shippers of manufactured goods in the Official Region would suffer direct income losses of approximately $1.2 billion. Counteracting this, however, are the reductions in rates on bulk commodities carried by rail and bulk and manufactured commodities carried by truck in the Official Region. Existing rail shippers of bulk commodities would enjoy income gains of $400 million, while existing shippers using trucks would enjoy gains of $600 million on manufactured goods and $400 million on bulk commodities. Clearly, however, the existing rail shippers of manufactured goods in the Official Region would experience losses of a sufficient magnitude to indicate that they are currently enjoying a substantial subsidy.

In the South-West Region, rail rates are also below marginal cost, and a movement toward competitive pricing would lead to losses to existing shippers of $300 million. In the other markets, prices are generally above marginal costs, and marginal-cost pricing would lead to rate reduction and concomitant gains in consumers' surplus to existing shippers. In this case, the largest gainers are current rail users of bulk commodities, who would receive increases in consumers' surplus of $1.2 billion, followed by current truck users of manufactured commodities, who would receive increases in consumers' surplus of $300 million.

In addition to affecting shippers directly, it is important to realize that moving from the status quo to a competitive equilibrium would have important effects upon carriers. In particular, the railroads in the Official Region would be the largest gainers, while trucking firms in the Official Region would be the largest losers. In addition, both rail and trucking firms in the South-West Region would also lose substantially.

For the railroads in the Official Region, the gains from competitive pricing of manufactured commodities outweigh the losses from competitive pricing of bulk commodities, and total profits would increase by approximately $1.4 billion as a result of competitive pricing. In contrast, for the railroads in the South-West Region, the losses from competitive pricing of bulk commodities are greater than the gains from competitive pricing of manufactured goods, leading to a reduction in profits of $500 million. With respect to trucking, since marginal-cost pricing would remove the economic rents currently enjoyed by these carriers, they would suffer substantial reduction in profits, totaling approximately $700 million for specialized commodity carriers in the Official Region and $300 million for these carriers in the South-West Region. Thus there appears to be substantial foundation for fears of trucking firms that deregulation would lead to reduced profitability. Moreover, to the extent that trucking labor currently shares in the profits conferred by regulation through higher wages, it is possible that reduced trucking profits could also lead to reduction in the returns to trucking labor.[21]

Because freight transportation enters as an input into the production process, it is important to realize that changes in freight rates could affect relative production costs and hence levels of economic activity. In this connection, Friedlaender and Spady (1981) have estimated that additional income losses of approximately $600 million could accrue to workers in the manufacturing industries in the Official Region. This arises from the locational disadvantages accruing to manufacturing activities in the Official Region as a result of the substantial rate increases that would result from marginal-cost pricing.

In conclusion, then, although a movement to competitive pricing in the rail and trucking industries would improve allocative efficiency and rationalize the use of transportation resources, it would also lead to substantial income changes to carriers, shippers, and manufacturing workers in the affected industries. Thus, even though the direct and indirect income gains exceed the comparable losses, unless some means are found to compensate the losers, political pressures will make such a change difficult to achieve.

COMPETITION, INFRASTRUCTURE, AND PROFITABILITY IN THE RAILROAD INDUSTRY

The previous section argued that although a competitive pricing structure would increase rail profitability substantially, it would still not enable the railroads to earn sufficient returns to be financially self-sufficient. This implies that the railroads may suffer from excess capacity and that substantial economies could accrue if the railroads divested themselves of substantial investments in track and structures. Keeler (1974) has recently estimated that cost savings of $2 to $3 billion could result from the elimination of substantial amounts of track. However, the Federal Railway Administration (1978) has recently argued that the railroads suffer from a major capital shortage and that investments of $15 billion are needed if the railroads are to maintain their infrastructure adequately.

While apparently contradictory, these views can be reconciled if we recognize two points: (1) track and capital are not synonymous; (2) investments required to maintain the railroads' common-carrier obligation at some suitable standard may not be consistent with cost minimization at existing output levels.

With respect to the first point, it is important to note that track essentially represents the railroads' common-carrier obligations to transport all traffic at published rates, while capital represents the physical quantity and quality of the steel, ties, roadbed, and so on that comprise the track. Thus railroads with extensive trackage presumably have broad obligations to meet the shippers' needs over their network; however, they can also have relatively low levels of capital embodied in this track if they have let it deteriorate through poor maintenance. Consequently, it is entirely possible for a railroad such as the old Penn-Central to have less infrastructure capital than a railroad with considerably smaller mileage, such as the Southern.

With regard to this second point, traditionally the ICC not only has required the railroads to maintain extensive network to serve shippers in light-density areas as well as those on high-volume corridors but also has monitored the condition of the track to ensure that traffic can be carried safely and reliably. While this approach makes sense in terms of maintaining adequate service standards to meet the railroads' common-carrier obligations, it may make relatively little sense in the presence of the declining rail market that has existed after World War II. Thus, if the railroads were to attempt to minimize costs for existing output levels, they would almost certainly attempt to reduce a significant portion of their trackage and the capital that is embodied in it.

Therefore, although the FRA is doubtless correct in arguing that existing trackage needs massive capital infusions if it is to be maintained at standards sufficient to transport traffic safely and reliably, it is also correct that there is certainly too much track and probably too much infrastructure capital to be consistent with cost minimization by the railroads at existing output levels. Thus it makes sense for the railroads to practice selected deferred maintenance to trim their infrastructure capital to a size that is consistent with their traffic volumes. The policy dilemma, however, is that the excess capacity is primarily centered on light-density branchlines, which are used by the rural and agricultural shippers that regulation has traditionally tried to protect. Hence, while entirely consistent with past regulatory policy, efforts to upgrade the quality of this track would actually move the railroads further away from a position of long-run cost minimization and reduce even further their aggregate return to capital.

This suggests that from the point of view of the financial viability of the railroads, policies aimed at abandonment of track and way-and-structures capital would make sense.[22] Nevertheless, given the existing rate structure, it is unlikely that adjustments in infrastructure alone could yield sufficient economies to make the railroads financially viable. This raises the question of whether there is some combination of rates, output levels, and infrastructure capital that would enable the railroads to be economically viable and self-sustaining.

In analyzing this question, it is useful to review the distinction between the short run and the long run and review the concepts of scale economies and natural monopoly. The short run refers to a time period when a firm is not able to adjust all factors to minimize its costs, while the long run refers to a time period when adjustments in all factors are possible. Capital is typically treated as a fixed factor, since it consists of large and lumpy investments. Thus the firm's short-run cost function represents the least-cost combination of *variable* factors (fuel, equipment, materials, labor, and so on) that can produce a given level of output for any given stock of capital. Similarly, the long-run cost function represents the least-cost combination of *all* factors (including capital) that can produce any given level of output. Since the long-run cost curve represents the least-cost combination of all factors required to produce any given level of output, it must necessarily lie below any short-run cost curve, except at the point where the actual capital stock is optimal for that level of output.

Economies of scale are said to exist if costs rise less than proportionately with output. In this case, marginal costs will lie below average costs, and if firms price at marginal cost, they will fail to generate sufficient revenues to cover their costs. Moreover, if economies of scale exist over the relevant range of output given the size of the market, then the firm is deemed a natural monopoly, since it can supply the market at a lower cost than two or more firms.[23] However, if the firm is a natural monopoly, this implies that marginal costs lie below average costs and that marginal-cost pricing will never yield sufficient revenues to make the firm financially self-sufficient; thus subsidies will be needed to ensure its continued operation. In this case the distinction between the short run and the long run becomes extremely important, because it may be the case that a firm is producing along its short-run cost curve and exhibiting evidence of economies of scale and natural monopoly given its capital stock, but that if optimal adjustments in the capital stock were permitted, the long-run cost curve would not exhibit scale economies throughout its relevant range, and competitive behavior could be self-sustaining over some traffic volumes.

There is considerable evidence that this is precisely the situation facing the railroads. The previous part indicated that if marginal-cost pricing were followed, the railroads would not earn a sufficient return to permit them to be financially viable. Thus, for existing levels of capital and output they appear to exhibit short-run economies of scale. This need not imply, however, that they would exhibit economies of scale for all levels of capital stock and output. To assess the railroads' potential for financial viability it is useful to consider their returns in a long-run competitive equilibrium, where they operate along their long-run marginal-cost curves and their rates reflect long-run marginal costs. In this case, Friedlaender and Spady (1980) have estimated that railroads could earn a net return to capital of 8.2 percent in the Official Region and 7.0 percent in the South-West Region. Although these figures are still somewhat below the opportunity cost of capital,* they do not reflect any abandonment of light-density service. If, in addition to adjusting their rates, output levels, and capital embodied in the track, the railroads also undertook substantial abandonment of low-density lines, it is likely that they could earn rates of return that would compare favorably with those in other industries.

* Note that these figures are based on 1972 data.

These findings should give considerable encouragement to rail policy planners. While there is some evidence of long-run economies of scale at existing levels of output, it appears that they are substantially attenuated at output levels consistent with a long-run competitive equilibrium. Consequently, competition does appear to be a viable alternative to present policies.

Nevertheless, it is important to stress that although a long-run competitive equilibrium may reflect a viable economic solution that requires no government subsidy, it also represents a dramatic shift in government policy regarding the structure of rail rates and rail service. This is particularly true in the Official Region, where its establishment would cause considerable dislocation to shippers of manufactured goods, since rail rates on these goods are projected to rise by more than 100 percent and rail carriage of these goods is projected to fall by approximately 75 percent.

This implies that there may be a fundamental inconsistency between the Commission's and society's goals of an economically viable rail system and income maintenance to certain groups of shippers. While this inconsistency appears throughout the entire rail system, it is greatest in the Northeast, where the maintenance of a long-run competitive equilibrium would apparently result in an economically viable rail system but severe shipper dislocations.

These findings pose a substantial policy dilemma. Conrail has currently received $3.3 billion in direct federal aid, and if existing service levels and rates are maintained, it seems clear that substantial subsidies will have to continue. But if Conrail were to raise rates and abandon track and service to levels that permitted self-sufficiency, it would also be a very different railroad, concentrating its service on a few high-density corridors. Thus the real policy choice is whether society wants financially viable railroads that perform services that meet the standard of private-market profitability or whether it wants railroads to perform public-service activities that require subsidy. In view of the declining nature of the Northeast economy and the historical emphasis on shipper income maintenance, it may well be that subsidies are the appropriate policy. But in this case it is imperative to make clear that the railroads are merely the vehicle through which shipper subsidies are made.*

---

* The recently proposed mergers of the Southern Railroad and the Norfolk and Western and of the Chessie System and the Seaboard Coast Line may provide an opportunity to rationalize the railroad infrastructure in the East. A similarly dramatic merger movement is taking place in the West, which should also facilitate efforts to rationalize the railroad network in that region.

DEREGULATION AND
COMPETITION AMONG
COMMON CARRIERS OF
GENERAL COMMODITIES

The preceding two parts of this paper have focused upon the railroads and the question whether competition is consistent with the historical goals of carrier profitability and income maintenance. This part will focus upon regulated trucking carriers of general commodities, which specialize in less-than-truckload (LTL) shipments, and will ask whether competition provides a viable alternative to present regulatory policies. This part will argue that competition is consistent with a competitive and a financially viable industry and would not lead to any major dislocation among specific shipper groups. Thus, while competitive pricing in the railroad and competing markets posed a policy dilemma between railroad profitability and shipper incomes, such a dilemma does not appear in the markets served by general commodity carriers. This suggests that the public interest would probably be served by deregulation of these carriers.

In analyzing trucking regulation, it is important to note that the regulated trucking market can be segmented into two distinct groups: common carriers of general commodities, which are analyzed in this section, and common carriers of specialized commodities, which were analyzed in the earlier section dealing with rail-truck competition. General commodity carriers tend to specialize in relatively small shipments and hence are characterized by less-than-truckload (LTL) carriage and terminal consolidation. As LTL carriers of general commodities, their traffic encompasses the spectrum of manufactured and related goods that are suitable for truck transport, and their customers tend to be relatively small shippers who do not generate a sufficient volume to support rail or full-truckload operations. Thus there is relatively little competition between railroads and these carriers. In contrast, the carriers of specialized commodities utilize full-truckload operations and perform few, if any, consolidation functions. While their traffic also includes the spectrum of manufactured goods, these carriers tend to compete directly with the railroads and hence concentrate on large-load, long-haul traffic.

Since common carriers of general commodities tend to serve small shippers in rural areas who have few other sources of transportation, the regulatory debate in the trucking industry has tended to focus upon these carriers. In particular, considerable concern has arisen whether the interests and needs of these shippers would be adequately served in an environment in which trucking was deregulated. Particular concern has focused upon the possible existence of economies of scale among these carriers and the possible existence of cross-subsidies between shippers using high-density corridors and those using low-density corridors. If economies of scale exist, in the advent of deregulation shippers might find themselves captives of monopolistic trucking firms who would then attempt to raise rates to their monopoly levels. If a cross-subsidy exists between light-density and high-density traffic, in the advent of deregulation shippers in light-density corridors might find themselves subject to substantial rate increases as carriers attempted to raise their profit margins on low-density traffic to "normal" levels. Thus there is a fundamental concern that deregulation might lead to substantial rate increases to shippers in rural areas and small cities and towns. Indeed, in defending continued trucking regulation, the American Trucking Association has argued that service would deteriorate and rates would increase to small rural shippers as regulatory restrictions on rates and service levels were removed. Hence the likely response of rates and service levels to shippers in rural areas is an issue of considerable debate and relevance for policy.[24]

In analyzing the behavior of the markets for common carriers of general commodities, however, it is important to recognize that substantial differences exist in the nature of trucking firms. In particular, common carriers of general commodities present substantial differences in firm size, age of capital stock, nature of terminal operations, route density, and so forth, not only between geographic regions but also between the relatively localized regional carriers and the geographically dispersed interregional and transcontinental carriers. Thus it makes little sense to regard general commodity carriers as homogeneous entities within homogeneous markets. Indeed, just as wide discrepancies exist in costs among railroads and specialized commodity carriers, similar discrepancies exist among general commodity carriers. Thus this section focuses upon the cost and market structure of three different types of general commodity carriers: regional carriers in the Official Territory, which comprises the New England, Middle Atlantic, and Great Lakes states; all other regional carriers, which comprise carriers in the Southern, Great Plains, and Western regions and which for notational simplicity we refer to as carriers in the South-West Region; and interregional and transcontinental carriers.

In this part we analyze these three different types of carriers and consider whether their deregulation is consistent with a competitive market structure and with rates that are not at variance with historical concerns for rural and agricultural shippers.

Scale Economies, Competition, and Market Structure

Recent econometric evidence indicates that trucking costs depend not only upon factor prices and output levels but also upon the operating characteristics of the firm.[25] Two firms with identical output levels and factor prices could have very different costs if one's traffic was concentrated in short-haul, small-load, LTL traffic while the other's was concentrated on long-haul, large-lot shipments. Since costs rise dramatically as the amount of consolidation increases, firms with large loads, long hauls, and relatively few LTL activities will tend to have substantially lower costs than those whose operations use more short-haul, small-load traffic.

Table 2 summarizes the characteristics of the three types of general commodity carriers and their estimated costs in 1972. This table clearly shows a strong negative correlation between costs, average length of haul, average load, and size of output, with large firms operating with large loads and long hauls having significantly lower costs than small firms operating with small loads and relatively short hauls.

Because carriers in the Official and South-West Regions have considerably smaller output levels than the interregional carriers, the figures in Table 2 might lead one to argue that economies of scale exist among these carriers. In fact, however, each type of carrier has a dis-

Table 2. Mean Values of Selected Characteristics of General Commodity Carriers, by Type of Carrier, 1972

	Type of Carrier		
	Official	*South-West*	*Interregional*
Average length of haul (miles)	120.0	185.0	674.0
Average load (tons)	7.5	10.1	14.7
Proportion of freight in LTL lots	0.48	0.51	0.37
Output (million ton-miles)	21.0	57.2	931.6
Average cost (¢/ton)	14.2	11.8	8.6

Source: Friedlaender and Spady (1981), Chap. 5.

tinctive technology that is specifically adapted to its type of carriage. Thus intercarrier comparisons and cost extrapolations are difficult to make.

This situation is illustrated in Figure 3, which shows the average-cost curve for each type of carrier over its relevant range of operations. This clearly indicates that general commodity carriers in the Official and South-West Regions exhibit rather marked diseconomies of scale at relatively small output levels of under 100 thousand ton-miles. In contrast, the interregional carriers exhibit economies of scale throughout most of their range of output.[26]

Whether general commodity carriers are subject to economies or diseconomies of scale is an issue of considerable importance for policy. If economies of scale are exhausted at low levels of output, as is the case with the Official and South-West carriers, then no cost advantage accrues to firms through expanding their size. Indeed, economic theory suggests that with free entry, in this case the long-run industry supply curve will be horizontal, reflecting the minimum average costs of the

Figure 3. Average Cost of Trucking Firms with Mean Characteristics, by Type of Carrier

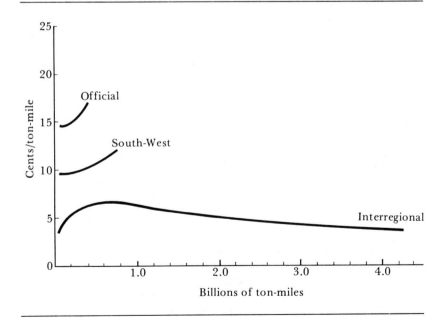

carriers in the industry. For the Official Region carriers this would be at approximately 14 cents/ton-mile while for the South-West Region carriers it would be at approximately 10 cents/ton-mile. In contrast, the interregional carriers exhibit increasing returns to scale throughout the relevant range of output, indicating that large firms could obtain a cost advantage over small firms. This suggests that in the absence of regulation, large, efficient interregional carriers could monopolize this market. Figure 3 also indicates that beyond 1 billion ton-miles the relative cost advantage diminishes substantially. Given the variability of average costs of these firms, this suggests that their industry long-run supply curve should be roughly horizontal at approximately 8.5 cents/ton-mile. However, while the size of the "typical" Official carrier would be 20 million ton-miles and the size of the "typical" South-West carrier would be 50 million ton-miles, the size of the "typical" interregional carrier would be at least 1 billion ton-miles. Given the size of the relevant markets, this implies that the Official and South-West markets would be highly competitive with a large number of carriers operating at the minimum scale, while the interregional market would be relatively concentrated with only a few carriers operating at scales that imply low cost. Nevertheless, the scale of the market is probably sufficiently large to permit workable competition to be established in the interregional market.[27]

A striking aspect of Figure 3 is the disparity of costs among the three types of general commodity carriers. While the costs of South-West carriers approach those of the Official Region carriers at high output levels, the costs of the interregional carriers appear to be below those of the other two carriers at all levels of output. This suggests that in a deregulated environment these large interregional carriers could encroach upon the traffic of the small regional carriers. If, however, these differences in costs are due primarily to differences in factor prices and operating characteristics rather than size per se, then as the interregional carriers undertook operations similar to those undertaken by the regional carriers their costs should rise accordingly, and the incentives for encroachment would be reduced.

To analyze the source of the cost differentials among the various types of carriers, hypothetical costs were analyzed that the interregional carriers would have experienced if they had had the factor prices and operating characteristics of firms in the other two regions. This analysis indicated that the cost differential arises primarily from differences in operating characteristics rather than from technology per se. Thus if the interregional carriers were to take over the traffic of regional carriers in the Official or the South-West Region, their costs would rise as their operating characteristics approached those of the regional carriers. Similarly, if the carriers in the South-West Region used the same operating characteristics as those of the Official Region, the costs of carriers in the two regions would become comparable.

Consequently, fears of significant encroachment under deregulation appear to be unfounded. The mass of evidence indicates that each carrier type has "adapted" to its environment, in that each class generally attains lowest average costs for the type of traffic it most often handles. In the event of deregulation, current inefficient firms will face their greatest competition from firms that will essentially replicate the current modes of operation, following a policy of simultaneous route consolidation *and* route "fill-ins," as opposed to "superlarge" firms that will attempt to usurp existing route patterns and carrier operations. Thus, short-haul, small-shipment traffic will remain in the hands of small firms specializing in such traffic, while long-haul, large-shipment traffic will remain the domain of the large, interregional carriers.

Marginal Costs and the Cross-Subsidy Hypothesis

Conventional wisdom holds that a cross-subsidy exists between traffic in high-density corridors between large urban centers and traffic in low-density corridors between rural areas. Similarly, cross-subsidies are believed to exist between long-haul, large-load shipments (the "cream" of the traffic) and short-haul, small-load shipments. Thus, it is generally believed that short-haul, small-load shipments in low-density corridors fail to cover costs and are subsidized by long-haul, large-load shipments on high-density corridors. If so, then under current regulatory policies we would expect to find the price-marginal cost ratios of long-haul, large-load, high-density traffic to be significantly higher than those associated with short-haul, small-load, low-density traffic. Similarly, in the absence of regulation, we would also expect the rates on this "subsidized" low-density traffic to rise as firms attempted to restore their profit margins on it. Indeed, precisely this spectre of untrammeled rate increases to small, low-density shippers has proved to be one of the most effective arguments presented by the interests supporting regulation, such as the American Trucking Association.

To answer this question, Friedlaender and Spady (1981) analyzed the relationship between the price-marginal cost differentials and the operating characteristics of the different types of general commodity carriers. On balance, the relationships between prices and marginal costs associated with the various operating characteristics appear to give little support to the cross-subsidy hypothesis. While certain types of shipments appear to be favored by the rate structure for certain types of carriers in that they received a relatively high price-marginal cost markup, no consistent pattern emerges that implies that traffic associated with light-density rural traffic is subsidized by the rate structure and receives relatively low price-marginal cost markups. Indeed, there is some evidence that this traffic is actually favored by the rate structure in that it receives relatively high price-marginal cost markups and is therefore relatively more profitable than traffic associated with high-density corridors. However, the econometric evidence on this question is sufficiently inconclusive that no single pattern of subsidy emerges. We are thus led to conclude that although operating and shipment characteristics affect the price-marginal cost ratios, they do not do so in a consistent or systematic fashion that would imply a pattern of cross-subsidization from high-density, urban traffic to low-density, rural traffic. Consequently, fears that rates would rise dramatically on small shipments, short-haul traffic, or low-density traffic in the absence of regulation do not appear to be substantiated by the available econometric evidence.[28]

In conclusion, then, the evidence generally supports deregulation of trucking general commodity carriers. Although the econometric evidence concerning the existence of economies of scale within the interregional carriers is somewhat mixed, there is no evidence that these carriers are characterized by marked and persistent economies of scale. Thus, in the event of a relaxation of regulation concerning rates, routes, and entry, it is likely that these carriers would be characterized by workable competition, under which no carrier or group of carriers would be able to dominate the industry. Moreover, because different types of general commodity carriers appear to have adapted to specific market environments, it appears unlikely that smaller, high-cost carriers would suffer from encroachment from larger, lower-cost carriers. Thus the market segmentation and structure that are currently observed under regulation would remain essentially unchanged in a deregulated environment.

However, because prices now deviate from marginal costs, a competitive rate structure would differ from the existing rate structure, and shippers would generally experience rate reductions. Indeed, since the rate structure currently provides somewhat higher markups on light-density traffic, it is possible that rural and agricultural shippers could experience rate reductions rather than rate increases in the advent of deregulation. Thus, deregulation of general commodity carriers appears consistent not only with a competitive market structure but also with the Commission's historical concern with rural and agricultural shippers.

Of course, as in all policy changes, a movement to deregulation would not be entirely costless, since trucking firms would doubtless suffer some reduction in profitability. Similarly, to the extent that unionized labor has shared in these economic rents, they may expect smaller wage increases in a deregulated environment than they have enjoyed under current regulatory practices.[29] Because, however, the bulk of these carriers operate under conditions of increasing or constant costs, they could still be expected to earn a return to capital that is competitive with other sectors of the economy. Consequently, although these carriers might receive a reduced economic rent as a result of deregulation, they should still remain strong and viable entities. Thus, on balance, the public interest should be served by deregulation of the general commodity carriers.

DEREGULATION VERSUS COMPETITION IN THE RAIL AND TRUCKING INDUSTRIES

The "public interest" is inherently difficult to define, depending as it does upon subtle trade-offs between considerations of economic efficiency and income maintenance to affected groups. Rarely are major policy changes unambiguously in the public interest, since they necessarily involve changes in the income levels of the affected groups as well as changes in the allocation of resources. Consequently, even if a policy change may lead to a clear gain in economic efficiency and income levels to certain groups, insofar as it may impose costs on other groups, the losses must be considered against the gains before it can be decided that such a change is in the public interest.

In this connection, deregulation of the rail and trucking industries poses a particularly difficult policy dilemma, since associated with its substantial efficiency gains would also be substantial income transfers among the various carriers and shippers.

This suggests that an effort at piecemeal deregulation might be fruitful if an area could be found in which the income transfers would be relatively small and the efficiency gains relatively high. In this regard, trucking general commodity carriers look particularly promising. Current restrictions on operating authorities prescribe the routes and gateways over which these carriers can operate. This means that loads are generally smaller and hauls generally shorter than they would be in a deregulated environment. Since costs are particularly sensitive to these two operating characteristics, it is likely that deregulation would lead to lower costs as firms were able to achieve fuller backhauls and greater efficiencies in the use of equipment. Moreover, since a competitive market structure should not substantially reduce firm profitability while leading to reduced rates, this appears to be a case in which the efficiency gains may dominate the income losses.

However, because general commodity carriers do not operate independently of special commodity carriers, it does not seem possible to deregulate one segment of the trucking industry without deregulating the other. Indeed, once route and commodity restrictions were removed from general commodity carriers, there is no reason why they could not perform the same function as specialized commodity carriers. Besides placing these carriers at an unfair advantage, this arrangement would also appear unworkable. If one segment of the trucking industry is to be deregulated, then it would make little sense not to deregulate the remaining segments. Therefore, if general commodity carriers are to be deregulated, special commodity carriers should also be deregulated.

But, if the entire trucking industry were deregulated while leaving the railroad industry regulated, the current inefficiencies would be exacerbated. Trucks would be able to compete not only with service levels but also with rates. They would consequently tend to skim off whatever profitable manufacturing traffic the railroads still carry and increase the weakness of an already financially fragile industry. The result would be increased rail bankruptcies and requirements of subsidies for the railroads to meet their common-carrier obligation at existing rate levels.

Thus the choice appears to be between broad deregulation, which would permit competitive ratemaking and the free entry and abandonment of service, and the maintenance of the status quo. The benefits of deregulation are considerable. Not only would it enable the railroads to be financially viable, but by permitting rate flexibility and seasonal rate changes it would improve the allocation of freight cars and eliminate the chronic car shortage that currently plagues the industry.[30] In addition, by permitting a rationalization of the railroad infrastructure and a more efficient allocation of resources among the various modes, it would lead to reduced resource costs and substantial cost savings. Furthermore, by giving all the modes the chance to price to meet demand, it would enable fuller utilization of backhauls and thus lead to better equipment utilization and thus substantial energy savings. A competitive equilibrium would result in which the various modes were earning a return on capital that was competitive with other sectors of the economy and in which the private market provided adequate transportation services.*

---

* If, in fact, the specialized commodity carriers are subject to technological increasing returns to scale, competitive pricing would cause them to suffer losses. However, to the extent that the observed scale economies are of a regulatory nature, they could be expected to disappear in a deregulated environment.

However, such a scenario implies a substantially reduced rail network, an end to noncompensatory rail services, and the elimination of many public-service activities that the railroads now perform in the guise of their common-carrier obligations. Many small rural shippers who currently are the beneficiaries of noncompensatory rates would find themselves subject to substantial rate increases. Hence deregulation would undoubtedly impose a considerable hardship on a number of shippers.

Whether the efficiency gains associated with deregulation are sufficiently great to offset these shipper losses is, of course, the fundamental question in assessing whether deregulation is in the public interest. On balance, however, the answer should probably be in the affirmative, since the freight rate structure and common-carrier obligation are a particularly clumsy way to satisfy these distributional goals. If noncompensatory service is thought to be in the public interest, let it be stated so explicitly and a direct subsidy paid. This has worked well in Canada and England,[31] and there seems little reason why such a plan could not work in the United States. But to maintain the existing inefficiencies for fear of the income losses that their correction would impose upon certain favored shippers seems to be poor policy. If they are deemed sufficiently important that the public interest requires support of their income, let that support be made explicit.

In conclusion, then, it appears that the public interest would best be served by general deregulation and policies aimed at maintaining the income of shippers adversely affected by such a change. In this case, the losers would be compensated and the efficiency gains would accrue to the public at large. Thus, instead of focusing upon the question of *whether* the rail and trucking industries should be deregulated, the debate should focus on the question of *how* they could be deregulated to minimize the transitional costs to the shippers of moving from the current situation of implicit subsidies to one of explicit subsidies or perhaps of their abandonment.

THE 1980 LEGISLATION

In Trucking

Things moved fast in freight regulation in 1980. By the end of June, Congress had passed and the president had signed the Motor Carrier Act of 1980. Trucks were not wholly deregulated, but the regulatory environment was basically changed.

New entrants or truckers trying to enter new routes should find it much easier to get certificates. They must still be "fit, willing, and able" to perform the proposed service. The ICC can still turn them down if it finds that their application is inconsistent with the public interest, but the burden of proof is shifted from the applicants to those opposing the new certificates. Moreover, diversion of revenue from existing carriers may not be the basis for denying a certificate.

The new act expands the exemption from regulation enjoyed by agricultural products to all processed foods. It eliminates ICC regulations that impose circuitous routes, "narrow gateways," and backhaul or intermediate stop restrictions. These provisions should result in a much more efficient trucking industry.

The new act permits truckers to increase or decrease rates by up to 10 percent per year without specific approval from the ICC. The commission may widen this "zone of reasonableness" beyond 10 percent, and it is automatically escalated for inflation. Moreover, it is cumulative. A firm can raise or lower any rate by 10 percent this year, and it will be free to make a further 10 percent change next year.

Altogether, the trucking industry should be much more efficient and competitive under the new legislation.

On the Railroads

At the end of the same session Congress also passed the Staggers Rail Act, which lessened ICC control of railroad rates. Like the truckers, the railroads got some rate flexibility — they can raise or lower their rates by 6 percent per year up to an 18 percent total by 1984 and 4 percent more per year after that. Outside of that range the ICC or outsiders have the burden of proof unless the railroads have market dominance and the rate exceeds 160 percent (1981) to 180 percent (1984) of average variable cost. So long as rates are less than these upper limits and more than "going concern value," the ICC cannot suspend them. "Going concern value" would permit any rate reduction that exceeds short-run incremented cost — roughly marginal cost. For instance, very low rates for backhauls that fill what would otherwise be empty cars meet the test. The standards for abandonments are still the quite liberal ones passed by Congress four years earlier, but the procedure for their approval was expedited.

The Act covers a multitude of other issues: limits on rate bureau practices where in the past the railroads discussed, negotiated and voted on individual rates; extensive provisions to help or protect railroad workers affected by abandonments; and procedures for the sale of branch lines to interested parties when abandonment is approved. The interested parties are apt to be affected shippers or state or local governments.

The new legislation is certainly not deregulation of the railroads, but it does move a few steps in that direction.

NOTES

1 John Meyer and his associates (1959) were the first to make this argument. Their analysis was subsequently extended by Friedlaender (1969), Moore (1972, 1975), and Harbeson (1969). For a good review of the debate see Nelson (1978).

2 For a defense of regulation see ICC (1976), Flott (1973), and O'Neal (1975).

3 In recent years there have been a number of hearings on transport deregulation in both the House and Senate. Of these, probably the following are the most important: Senate (1975a), Senate (1975b), Senate (1977–1978), Senate (1978), Senate (1979), House (1975).

4 For example, during the early 1960s, when the Southern Railroad introduced large-sized hopper cars to carry grain and attempted to reduce rates accordingly, the new rates were disallowed by the ICC. Only after extensive litigation, which went all the way to the Supreme Court, were these rates allowed, some four years after their service was first introduced. Similarly, the introduction of unit-train operations from Appalachian mines to inland utilities was delayed by several years in the 1960s because of regulatory concern with the unit-train rate structure. More recently, efforts of the Burlington Northern to raise rates on unit-train coal traffic from the Wyoming coal fields to utilities in San Antonio have met with litigation and their initial disapproval by the ICC. For a full discussion of these and related issues see Friedlaender (1969), Mac-Avoy and Sloss (1967), and Sloss (1979).

5 See, for example, Fulda (1961), Nelson (1965), Williams (1958), and Moore (1975).

6 The role of rate bureaus in the trucking industry has come under increasing attack and was the subject of extensive hearings by the Senate Judiciary Committee in 1979. Under the recently passed trucking legislation, single-line rates will be subject to the antitrust laws in 1984, presumably ending collective ratemaking through rate bureaus for all shipments that go by a single carrier. However, rate bureaus will continue to function for interlined shipments that use two or more carriers.

7 See, for example, Buck (1965), Kolko (1965), Benson (1955), Tarbell (1904), MacAvoy (1965), Friedlaender (1969).

8 For example, the first annual report of the ICC stated "the public interest is best served when the rates are so apportioned . . . by making value an important consideration and by placing upon the higher classes of freight some

share of the burden that on a relatively equal apportionment . . . would fall upon those of less value" [ICC (1887, p. 36)].

[9] For a good discussion of the Hoch-Smith Resolution see Nelson and Greiner (1965).

[10] Unit-train operations use full trainloads to haul a specific commodity between a given point of origin and of destination. As such, they are able to avoid the costs of consolidation and switching that characterize most rail operations and consequently provide rail service at costs well under those associated with conventional boxcar operations. Although the use of unit trains was pioneered in coal hauled between a given mine and a given electrical utility, they are now used to haul a broad range of bulk commodities. For a good discussion of unit trains see MacAvoy and Sloss (1967).

[11] As a third alternative, the railroads could raise rates on their "captive" traffic. This alternative, however, would permit the monopoly exploitation of these shippers and is both politically and socially unacceptable. For an interesting discussion of an alleged recent example of potential monopoly exploitation see Sloss's (1979) discussion of the so-called San Antonio case, which involves the rates at which coal will be hauled from the coal fields of Wyoming to San Antonio.

[12] Wyckoff and Maister (1975) have argued persuasively that the main source of railroad competition from regulated trucking firms comes from the specialized commodity carriers, which use full-truckload shipments and carry a broad range of manufactured goods. Thus general commodity carriers, which perform consolidation functions and use a large percentage of less-than-truckload (LTL) operations, do not generally compete with railroads. The competitive structure of the LTL trucking market is considered in detail in the fourth part of this paper.

[13] This argument was first put forth by John Meyer and his associates (1959) and has been extended in recent years by Harbeson (1969), Friedlaender (1969), and Moore (1972).

[14] However, it should be noted that the full costs of transport not only include the carrier costs but also the shippers' inventory costs associated with the goods in transit. The greater time in transit of rail shipments, and the greater probability of damage en route, increase rail shippers' costs over and above freight rate differences. Thus, even though the direct carrier costs of rail transport may be considerably less than the direct carrier trucking costs, the full costs of shipment by rail to the shipper may be substantially greater when all of the inventory and damage costs are included. Recent analyses by Levin (1978) and Boyer (1977) on the costs of misallocation in the rail and trucking industries, which attempt to consider these service cost differentials more fully than previous analyses, indicate that the present extent of misallocation is less than generally believed.

[15] For a discussion of this point, see *Traffic World*, October 23, 1978, p. 19.

[16] For a specific discussion of the derivation of the supply and demand curves see Friedlaender and Spady (1981), Chapter 2 and Appendix E.

[17] The finding of increasing returns to scale in the trucking carriers of specialized commodities is surprising, since the capital requirements in this industry are relatively small. Nevertheless, this result was quite robust to dif-

ferent specifications and different samples [Furchtgott (1978), Friedlaender and Chiang (1980)]. It is likely, however, that these observed scale economies are of a regulatory, rather than a technological, nature. That is, since regulation requires these carriers to have very specific operating authorities with respect to commodities, large firms are able to have more operating authorities and thus obtain better equipment utilization and lower costs. Hence it is likely that these observed scale economies would disappear in a competitive environment.

18 The notion that railroads should concentrate upon wholesale or line-haul operations that require relatively little switching and consolidation is not new and is widely held by transportation analysts. See, for example, Meyer et al. (1959), Meyer and Morton (1974), and National Council on Productivity (1973).

19 For an interesting analysis of the potential degree of monopoly exploitation in the rail industry, see Levin (1980).

20 For example, the Railroad Revitalization and Regulatory Reform Act of 1976 (4-R Act) limits the ability of the railroads to raise rates in situations where "market dominance" prevails. For a discussion of this see ICC (1977).

21 Annable (1973), Moore (1976a), and Winston (1980) have analyzed the question of the extent to which trucking labor has benefited from regulation, and all found that trucking wages of union labor are higher than they would be in the absence of regulation. However, in assessing this question, it is important to note that owner-operators are typically not unionized and receive returns that are considerably below teamster labor. Since special commodity carriers use a preponderance of owner-operators, it is less likely that the returns accruing to their labor would fall in the presence of deregulation than the returns to unionized labor. For a good discussion of the structure of the trucking industry and the use of owner-operators see Wyckoff (1974) and Wyckoff and Maister (1975, 1977).

22 Friedlaender and Spady (1981) have estimated that elimination of low-density track would lead to cost savings of approximately $120,000 per mile of track in the Official Region and of $90,000 in the South-West Region. In contrast, elimination of mainline track would lead to cost savings of only $11,000 per mile in the Official Region and $4,500 in the South-West Region. Harris (1977) has estimated that similar savings could accrue from abandonment of light-density lines.

23 Actually, for a firm such as a railroad that produces many different outputs, the definition of a natural monopoly is considerably more complex. For a full discussion of these and related issues see Baumol (1977) and Baumol, Bailey, and Willig (1977).

24 For a good summary of the debate concerning the desirability of trucking regulation, see National Research Council (1978).

25 See Spady and Friedlaender (1978), Friedlaender, Spady, and Chiang (1980), and Friedlaender and Spady (1981).

26 Since factor prices, operating characteristics, and output levels are all interrelated in the cost function, the nature of each carrier's average-cost function will vary with factor prices and operating characteristics. Nevertheless, the general shape of the average-cost curve for the Official and South-

West carriers appears to be relatively insensitive to the levels of factor prices or operating characteristics experienced by these carriers. In contrast, the behavior of average costs of the interregional carriers appears to be quite sensitive to their operating characteristics, making generalization about scale economies difficult for these carriers. Thus the illustrated average-cost curve for the interregional carriers is representative only of a limited number of interregional carriers that have characteristics similar to the mean characteristics of the interregional firms in the sample. For a full discussion of this point see Friedlaender, Spady, and Chiang (1980).

[27] While the overall market is doubtless sufficiently large to support workable competition, there is considerable concern whether the size of the market on any given city-pair corridor is sufficiently large to support workable competition. These concerns were exacerbated by recent evidence developed by the Senate Judiciary Committee that the concentration ratios on many corridors are extremely high, with the four largest firms in any given city-pair corridor carrying 60 to 80 percent of the market [Senate (1980b)]. Whether these high levels of market concentration represent pure market forces or regulatory forces is an issue of intense debate.

[28] For a discussion of trucking service to small rural shippers see U.S. Senate (1978).

[29] For evidence of this see Moore (1976), Annable (1973), and Winston (1980).

[30] For a discussion of this see Felton (1979).

[31] See, for example, Moore (1976b) and Heaver and Nelson (1977).

BIBLIOGRAPHY

Annable, J. E., Jr., "The ICC, the IBT, and the Cartelization of the American Trucking Industry," *Quarterly Review of Economics and Business,* 13:2 (Summer 1973), 33–48.

Baumol, W. J., "On the Proper Cost Tests for a Natural Monopoly in a Multiproduct Industry," *American Economic Review,* 67:5 (December 1977), 809–822.

———, Bailey, E., and Willig, R., "Weak Invisible Hand Theorems on Pricing and Entry in a Multiproduct Natural Monopoly," *American Economic Review,* 67:3 (June 1977), 350–365.

Benson, L., *Merchants, Farms and Railroads: Railroad Regulation and New York Politics, 1850–1887,* Cambridge: Harvard University Press, 1955.

Boyer, K. D., "Minimum Rate Regulation, Modal Split Sensitivities and the Railroad Problem," *Journal of Political Economy,* 85:3 (1977), 493–512.

Buck, S. J., *The Granger Movement, 1870–1880.* Cambridge: Harvard University Press, 1965.

Federal Railway Administration, *A Prospectus for Change in the Railroad Industry,* Preliminary Report to the Secretary of Transportation, October 1978.

Felton, J. R., *The Economics of Freight Car Supply*. Lincoln: The University of Nebraska Press, 1978.

Flott, A. C., "The Case against the Case against Regulation," *ICC Practitioners' Journal*, 40 (March–April 1973).

Friedlaender, Ann F., *The Dilemma of Freight Transport Regulation*. Washington, D.C.: The Brookings Institution, 1969.

—— and Spady, Richard H., *Freight Transport Regulation: Equity, Efficiency, and Competition*. Cambridge: MIT Press, 1981.

—— and Chiang, J. S. Wang, "Technology and Productivity in Regulated Carriers of Special Commodities, 1972–1975," Massachusetts Institute of Technology, Center for Transportation Studies (mimeo), 1980.

——, Spady, Richard H., and Chiang, J. S. Wang, "Regulation and the Structure of Technology in the Regulated Trucking Industry," in T. Cowing and R. Stevenson (eds.), *Productivity Measurement in Regulated Industries*. New York: Academic Press, 1980.

Fulda, C., *Competition in the Regulated Industries: Transportation*. Boston: Little, Brown and Company, 1961.

Furchtgott, Harold, "A Comparison of Technology within the Regulated Trucking Industry between Carriers of General Freight and Carriers of Other Specialized Commodities," B.S. Thesis, Massachusetts Institute of Technology, Department of Economics, 1978.

Harbeson, R. W., "Toward Better Resource Allocation in Transport," *Journal of Law and Economics*, 12:2 (1969), 321–338.

Harris, R. G., "Rationalizing the Rail Freight Industry: A Case Study in Institutional Failure and Proposal for Reform." Berkeley: University of California Working Paper SL-7705 (Department of Economics), 1977.

Heaver, T. D., and Nelson, J. C., *Railway Pricing under Commercial Freedom: The Canadian Experience*. Centre for Transportation Studies, University of British Columbia, 1977.

Interstate Commerce Commission, "The Impact of the 4-R Act Ratemaking Provisions," October 5, 1977.

——, *The Costs and Benefits of Transport Regulation*, 1976.

——, *First Annual Report*, 1887.

Keeler, T. E., "Railroad Costs, Returns to Scale, and Excess Capacity," *Review of Economics and Statistics*, 56:2 (May 1974), 201–208.

Kolko, G., *Railroads and Regulation*. Princeton, N.J.: Princeton University Press, 1965.

Levin, R. C., "Railroad Regulation and Workable Competition," Paper presented at the meeting of the American Economic Association, September 1980.

——, (1978), "Allocation in Surface Freight Transportation: Does Rate Regulation Matter?" *Bell Journal of Economics* 9:1 (Spring 1978), 18–45.

MacAvoy, P. W., *The Economic Effects of Regulation: The Trunk-Line Railroad Cartels and the Interstate Commerce Commission before 1900*. Cambridge: MIT Press, 1965.

—— and Sloss, J., *Regulation and Transport Innovation: The ICC and Unit Coal Trains to the East Coast*. New York: Random House, 1967.

Meyer, John R., and Morton, Alexander, "A Better Way to Run the Railroads," *Harvard Business Review*, 52:4 (July–August 1974), 141–148.

———, Peck, M. J., Stenason, J., and Zwick, C., *The Economics of Competition in the Transportation Industries*. Cambridge: MIT Press, 1959.

Moore, T. G., "The Beneficiaries of Trucking Regulation." Stanford, Calif.: Hoover Institution on War, Revolution and Peace, 1976a (mimeo).

———, *Trucking Regulation: Lessons from Europe*. American Enterprise Institute — Hoover Institution, 1976b.

———, "Deregulating Surface Freight Transportation," in A. Philips (ed.), *Promoting Competition in Regulated Markets*. Washington, D.C.: The Brookings Institution, 1975.

———, *Freight Transportation Regulation*. Washington, D.C.: American Enterprise Institute, 1972.

National Research Council, *Motor Carrier Regulation,* Proceedings of a workshop conducted by the NRC, Committee on Transportation, in cooperation with the Transportation Center, Northwestern University, 1978.

Nelson, James C., "Regulation of Overland Movements of Freight," in Study on Federal Regulation, U.S. Senate, Committee on Governmental Affairs, 96th Congress, 1st Session, Senate Document No. 96-14. Washington, D.C.: Government Printing Office, 1978.

———, "The Effects of Entry Control in Surface Transport," in *Transportation Economics*. New York: Columbia University Press, 1965.

Nelson, R. A., and Greiner, W. R., "The Relevance of the Common Carrier under Modern Economic Conditions," in *Transportation Economics*. New York: Columbia University Press, 1965.

O'Neal, A. D., "No Clamor for Deregulation: Should There Be?," in James C. Miller, III (ed.), *Perspectives on Federal Transportation Policy*. Washington, D.C.: American Enterprise Institute, 1975.

Sloss, James, "Railroad Volume Coal Rates: A Prolific Source of Regulatory Intervention," *Transportation Research Forum 20 (1)*. Oxford, Ind.: R. B. Cross Co., 1979.

Spady, R. H., and Friedlaender, A. F., "Hedonic Cost Functions for the Regulated Trucking Industry," *Bell Journal of Economics,* 9:1 (Spring 1978), 159–179.

Tarbell, I., *The History of the Standard Oil Company*. New York: Macmillan & Co., 1904.

U.S. House of Representatives, "Railroad Revitalization," Hearings before the Subcommittee on Transportation and Commerce of the Committee on Interstate and Foreign Commerce, 94th Congress, 1st Session, H.R. 6351 and H.R. 7681, 1975.

U.S. National Council on Productivity, *Improving Railroad Productivity*. Washington, D.C., 1973.

U.S. Senate, *Federal Restraints on Competition in the Trucking Industry: Antitrust Immunity and Economic Regulation,* Draft Report of the Committee on the Judiciary, 96th Congress, 2d Session, 1980.

———, "Economic Regulation of the Trucking Industry," Hearings before the Senate Committee on Commerce, Science, and Transportation, 96th Congress, 1st Session, 1979.

————, "Hearings, the Impact on Small Communities of Motor Carrier Regulatory Revision," Committee on Commerce, Science and Transportation, 95th Congress, 2d Session, 1978.

————, "Hearings, Oversight of Freight Competition in the Motor Carrier Industry," Subcommittee on Antitrust and Monopoly of the Senate Committee on the Judiciary, 95th Congress, 1st and 2d Sessions, 1977–1978.

————, "Hearings," Subcommittee on Surface Transportation, 94th Congress, 1st Session, 1975a.

————, "Hearings Pursuant to S. Resolution 71," 94th Congress, 1st Session, 1975b.

Williams, E. W., Jr., *The Regulation of Rail-Motor Rate Competition.* New York: Harper & Row, 1958.

Winston, Clifford, "Regulation, Wages, and Economic Rent: The Case of the Trucking Industry," Massachusetts Institute of Technology, Center for Transportation Studies (mimeo), 1980.

Wyckoff, D. D., *Organizational Formality and Performance in the Motor Carrier Industry.* Lexington, Mass.: D. C. Heath & Co., 1974 .

———— and Maister, D., *The Motor Carrier Industry.* Lexington, Mass.: D. C. Heath & Co., 1975.

———— and ————, *The Owner-Operator: Independent Trucker.* Lexington, Mass.: D. C. Heath & Co., 1975.

CASE 5

The Deregulation of Natural Gas

Ronald R. Braeutigam
Northwestern University

INTRODUCTION

One of the important recent pieces of legislation dealing with deregulation in American industry is The Natural Gas Policy Act of 1978.*
This legislation marked the culmination of an extended debate over the regulation of the price of natural gas at the wellhead (the point at which natural gas comes out of the ground to be sold to pipeline delivery systems). This chapter begins by examining the history of the natural gas industry, including the origin, evolution, and economic consequences of regulation. It then focuses on the forces that led to deregulation, particularly on the changing market conditions of the 1970s that made it impossible for regulators simultaneously to hold down wellhead prices and avoid shortages of gas. Finally, it describes the Natural Gas Policy Act (NGPA) and indicates some of the consequences to be expected as it takes force during the 1980s.

The contemporary gas industry may be characterized as having three segments: production, pipeline delivery, and local distribution. Natural gas is produced either from fields that primarily yield natural

Copyright © 1981 by Ronald R. Braeutigam. The author is an Associate Professor of Economics at Northwestern. This case is based on an earlier paper, "An Examination of Regulation in the Natural Gas Industry," in *Study on Federal Regulation*, United States Committee on Government Operations, Appendix to Volume VI, December 1978. The author would like to thank Leonard Weiss, Michael Klass, and F. M. Scherer for their comments on earlier drafts of this work. Portions of this chapter are reprinted with permission from *The Regulation Game*, copyright 1978, Ballinger Publishing Company.

* This legislation became effective in November 1978.

Table 1. Percentage of Total Energy Produced by Type[a]

Source	1948	1963	1978
Coal	48	26	25
Natural gas (dry)	14	31	32
Petroleum	33	35	30
Natural gas plant liquids	2	4	4
Hydropower	4	4	5
Nuclear power	0	1	5
Geothermal and other	0	0	—[b]
Total gross energy produced (quadrillion BTU)	35.99	46.15	61.00

Source: *Annual Report to Congress,* 1978, Vol. II, Energy Information Administration, Department of Energy, p. 5.

[a] Totals do not equal 100 percent because of independent rounding.

[b] Less than 0.5 percent.

gas or from fields that produce oil and gas together.* Producers gather the gas at the wellhead and sell it under contract to pipelines, which deliver the gas to various markets. A pipeline may sell the gas directly to a large end user (such as an industry) or to a local distribution company, which in turn delivers it to an end user (typically a residential or commercial customer). The focus of this chapter and the NGPA is on the regulation of the price at which a producer sells gas to a pipeline at the wellhead. Both pipelines and local distribution companies will remain regulated, even under the NGPA, especially since both appear to be characterized by economies of scale.

Natural gas is a vital part of America's total energy supply. A clean-burning fuel, it has grown from supplying only 14 percent of our total energy in 1948 to about 32 percent in 1978 (see Table 1). Approximately a quarter of the yearly gas supply is used by residential consumers, and nearly half is used by American industry (see Table 2).

Before beginning an analysis of the industry, let us examine some of the signals that pushed the debate over natural gas to the national forefront during the 1970s. Until 1970 the amount of gas produced nationally was sufficient to meet the contractual demands for shipment by pipelines. However, during the 1970s production began to fall short of these contractual demands by increasing amounts each year. Pipeline shipments were curtailed.[1] For the period from September 1976 to

* Gas found in conjunction with oil is termed associated gas.

Table 2. Consumption of Natural Gas by Sector (Tcf)

Year	Residential	Commercial	Industrial	Electric Utilities	Transportation	Other	Total
1950	1.20	0.39	3.43	0.63	0.13	—	5.77
1960	3.10	1.02	5.77	1.73	0.35	—	11.97
1970	4.84	2.06	9.25	3.93	0.72	0.34	21.14
1978	4.97	2.31	8.14	3.22	0.52	0.26	19.41

Source: Annual Report to Congress, 1978, Energy Information Administration, Department of Energy, p. 77.

August 1977 net curtailments of contracted .interstate gas deliveries amounted to 3.77 trillion cubic feet (Tcf), a significant amount considering that the total supply of natural gas was about 19 Tcf for that period.[2] Consequently, some industries cut back production, some users went without service, and many people temporarily lost jobs.

Among other major concerns was the continual decline in proven reserves. Gas reserves include all of the gas that actual drilling has proven to exist and that is therefore potentially available for production. As Table 3 shows, proven reserves declined from 291 Tcf in 1970 to 209 Tcf in 1977. Thus, throughout the 1970s the rate of extraction of natural gas exceeded the rate of discovery of new reserves.

Before we can understand how regulation may have contributed to these trends and what the effects of the NGPA are likely to be, we must examine the development of the natural gas industry in a historical context. This is the subject of the first part of this chapter.

HISTORICAL BACKGROUND

The use of gas in the United States dates back to the early nineteenth century. The first gas companies were formed primarily to operate gas lighting systems in major cities, since gas lighting was superior to the available alternatives, including candles and whale oil lamps. By the time of the Civil War there were gas lights in the streets of many major cities, although they were not prevalent inside most city homes and not available in rural areas.

In the last half of the century gas became more widely used. The primary source of gas was not hydrocarbon-bearing wells (from which natural gas is produced); instead it was manufactured by passing steam through hot coke to yield "water gas." As the nineteenth century drew to a close, and after the development of the incandescent lamp by Edison in 1878, electricity replaced gas as the dominant energy source for artificial lighting. The gas industry was successful in its search for a new market after the loss of predominance in lighting. The new market it found at the turn of the century was domestic cooking, where gas replaced coal as the main fuel.

More important in revitalizing the gas industry was the transition from manufactured gas to natural gas, which contains approximately twice the potential energy per Mcf. This transition was made possible with the construction of pipeline systems to carry gas under high pressure from wells in the field to major cities. By 1931 a pipeline connected

Table 3. Natural Gas Supply, Average Wellhead Price, and Consumption

Year	Total Energy Production, Quadrillion BTU [a]	Natural Gas (Dry) Produced		Proved Reserves (Dry Gas), Tcf [a,c]	Average Wellhead Value, ¢/Mcf [d]	Total Consumption, Tcf [a]
		Quadrillion BTU [a]	Tcf [a]			
1948	36	5.1	4.9	173	6.5	4.7
1949	31	5.4	5.2	180	6.3	5.0
1950	35	6.2	6.0	185	6.5	5.8
1951	38	7.4	7.2	193	7.3	6.8
1952	37	8.0	7.7	193	7.3	6.8
1953	37	8.4	8.1	210	9.2	7.6
1954	36	8.7	8.4	211	10.1	8.1
1955	39	9.3	9.0	223	10.4	8.7
1956	42	10.0	15.2	237	10.8	9.3
1957	42	10.6	10.3	245	11.3	9.9
1958	39	11.0	10.6	253	11.9	10.3
1959	41	12.0	11.6	261	12.9	11.3
1960	42	12.7	12.2	262	14.0	12.0
1961	42	13.1	12.7	266	15.1	12.5
1962	44	13.7	13.3	272	15.5	13.3
1963	46	14.5	14.1	276	15.8	14.0
1964	48	15.3	14.8	281	15.4	14.8
1965	50	15.8	15.3	287	15.6	15.3
1966	53	17.0	16.5	290	15.7	16.5
1967	55	18.0	17.4	293	16.0	17.4
1968	57	19.1	18.5	287	16.4	18.6
1969	59	20.5	19.9	275	16.7	20.1
1970	63	21.7	21.0	291	17.1	21.1
1971	62	22.3	21.6	279	18.2	21.8
1972	63	22.2	21.6	266	18.6	22.1
1973	62	22.2	21.7	250	21.6	22.1
1974	61	21.2	20.7	237	30.4	21.2
1975	60	19.6	19.2	228	44.5	19.5
1976	60	19.5	19.1	216	58.0	20.0
1977	60	19.6	19.1	209	79.0	19.5
1978	61	19.3	18.9	—	91.9	19.4
1979	37 [b]	11.3 [b]	—	—	102.0 [e]	—

Table footnotes at bottom of page 147.

the gas fields of Texas with Chicago, and more long-distance construction followed. After World War II the network of natural gas pipelines grew rapidly as gas became the preferred means of space heating.

The Natural Gas Act of 1938

Several factors led to the federal regulation of natural gas. In the 1930s many new large oil and gas fields were found in regions far from the large city markets, particularly in the Southwest. Improved drilling and exploration techniques aided in the discovery of fields. At the same time, other technological improvements made it possible to transport the natural gas produced in these remote fields to large markets. Among those improvements was the development of seamless pipe, which greatly reduced the problems of leakage posed by the high pressures required in the transport of gas. The consequences of the new fields of high-quality gas and better pipelines were predictable. Natural gas transmitted across state lines became an important source of energy.

Until 1938 state and local regulators had no power to control the price distributors paid for gas imported from other states. The Supreme Court had held that the interstate pipelines were beyond their reach.[3] Alfred Kahn points to this as the major reason for the regulatory legislation of the time:

For example, as the progress of technology in the 1920's and 1930's made increasingly feasible the interstate transmission of electricity and natural gas, local and state commissions found an increasingly large component of the cost of service of the companies under their jurisdiction — namely, the electric current or the gas imported from out of state — falling outside their reach. This growing gap was filled by the Federal Power Act of 1935 and the Natural Gas Act of 1938, which conferred on the Federal Power Commission regulatory authority over those wholesale rates.[4]

---

a Source: *Annual Report to Congress,* 1978, Energy Information Administration, Department of Energy, Vol. 2, pp. 5, 33, 77.

b Source: *Monthly Energy Review,* Department of Energy, October 1979, p. 4, includes data through July.

c Proved reserves are defined to be "the estimated quantities of natural gas, which geological and engineering data demonstrate, with reasonable certainty, to be recoverable in the future from known natural oil and gas reservoirs, under existing economic and operating conditions." See *Annual Report to Congress* (note *a* above), p. 169.

d This column is generated "by dividing the sum of total values of natural gas produced in all States by the sum of total quantities of natural gas produced in all States." See *Annual Report,* (note *a* above), p. 85.

e Figure for March 1979. Source: *Monthly Energy Review,* Department of Energy, October 1979, p. 92.

In 1928 Congress directed the Federal Trade Commission to investigate electric and gas utilities. The considerations just described were reported in a 1935 summary of more than 70 volumes of hearings and exhibits. On the basis of this report, Congress declared "that the business of transporting and selling natural gas for ultimate distribution to the public is affected with a public interest, and that Federal regulation in matters relating to the transportation of natural gas and the sale thereof in interstate and foreign commerce is necessary in the public interest." [5]

The Natural Gas Act brought the interstate transmission of natural gas and its sale for resale under the control of the Federal Power Commission. The Act exempted the gathering of gas and its retail distribution. The rates for transmission and sale were to be "just and reasonable" and without "undue" preferences.[6] Pipelines were required to publish and adhere to published tariff schedules and to give advance notice of proposed tariff changes.[7] The Commission was empowered to suspend proposed changes, conduct hearings, order refunds to consumers when warranted, and issue orders to insure that reasonable rates would be in effect.[8]

The Act also authorized the Commission to prescribe and enforce methods of accounting and to "investigate and ascertain the actual legitimate cost" of pipeline company properties.[9] As amended in 1942, the Act required the companies to obtain certificates from the Commission for the construction of interstate facilities and for acquisitions, extensions, and abandonments. The law differed from the earlier similar legislation for electricity in one important respect: it did not authorize the FPC to order interconnections among pipelines.

As we shall see, the passage of the Act was surrounded by less controversy than its interpretations and extensions over later years. An interesting journalistic account of the conditions at the time of the Act is provided by Kohlmeier. He notes that "Congress attempted to help consumers by placing under regulation the interstate pipelines.... The Federal Government did not attempt to regulate wholly intrastate local utilities and thus it did not directly control the consumer price of natural gas. But the *theory* [emphasis added] in 1938 was that the FPC indirectly could control the consumer price by regulating the interstate pipeline companies and the prices at which they sold gas to the local distribution systems." [10]

After World War II the federal regulation of wellhead prices became an increasingly important issue. Before pipeline networks were established, gas was often produced as a worthless byproduct of oil production. Often it was burned (flared) at the wellhead. With the advent of pipelines its value went up rapidly. Prices negotiated in new contracts rose. Prices for gas already in production at that time increased as a result of "favored nation" clauses, which required a purchasing pipeline to pay the producer a price equal to the highest price paid to any other producer within a given area by that pipeline, or in some cases by any pipeline in the area. The pipelines responded by submitting proposals for increases in the prices that they in turn charged to local gas distributors.

Until 1954 the FPC had assumed (amid spirited debate) that it did not have jurisdiction over the price at which gas was sold to pipelines by producers. This belief was based on a clause of the Natural Gas Act stating that the Act "shall not apply . . . to the production or gathering of natural gas," even though these were sales to pipelines for resale.[11]

Several states in the gas-consuming areas in the North felt that the Commission should indeed regulate wellhead prices, while the gas-producing states in the Southwest opposed this view. The problem came to a head in 1954 in a famous case, *Phillips Petroleum Company* v. *Wisconsin et al.*[12] Phillips at the time was the largest of the independent gas producers. After Phillips raised the price of its natural gas, the State of Wisconsin, along with the cities of Milwaukee, Detroit, and Kansas City, complained before the FPC. When the Commission declined to act, the case went to court.

During the testimony in the *Phillips* case, the Wisconsin consumer representatives stated that they felt that Phillips had monopoly power in the market for natural gas sales to pipelines, and they were concerned that this power led to excessively high gas prices at the wellhead and, in turn, for the consumer. The Phillips position was to deny strongly the existence of the alleged monopoly power. Phillips pointed out that in 1946 and 1947 approximately 2,300 independent producers or gatherers supplied gas directly to pipelines, so that the supply of natural gas was in fact quite competitive. Phillips contended that federal regulation was therefore not necessary to protect consumers against excessive prices.[13]

Ultimately the Supreme Court ruled that, while the production activities of Phillips were not regulated within the scope of the Natural Gas Act, the sales of Phillips to pipelines intending resale did fall under the provision of the Act. This declaration assigned to the Commission the duty to adjudge the reasonableness of prices for gas sold by Phillips. In making this decision the Court noted that the protection of consumers from exploitation by natural gas companies was the primary aim of the Natural Gas Act.

The controversy surrounding this ruling has arisen for two very important reasons. First, as already described, it is certainly not clear that Congress intended that the law be interpreted to include regulation of wellhead prices. Second, the nature of any market imperfection that one might cite as a basis for regulating wellhead prices was never made clear. Did producers of natural gas have sufficient monopoly power to warrant the extension of regulation to them? Kahn points out by analogy that in the electric power industry the assumption has been that suppliers of fuel oil or coal to electricity generating companies have been sufficiently competitive to protect the consumer, and "that as long as they remained financially independent, the regulated monopolists had no incentive to pay more than the competitive price." [14] There is some debate as to whether the same is true for the natural gas wellhead market. (The structure of wellhead gas markets in recent years will be examined later in this chapter.)

Some Consequences of the *Phillips* Decision

Following the Court's *Phillips* decision, the FPC began to regulate wellhead prices. Between 1954 and 1960 "the Commission had accumulated some 11,091 rate schedules and 33,231 supplements to those schedules from 3,372 independent producers," and by 1960 "there were 3,278 producer rate increase filings under suspension and awaiting hearings and decisions." [15] The Commission was confronted with the impossible task of making thousands of individual rate determinations using the methods traditionally employed in rate cases for public utilities. The Commission estimated that it would not finish its 1960 caseload until the year 2043. [16]

Among the problems that the FPC faced in its case-by-case approach was the fact that the costs of production and exploration are often shared between oil and gas. First, both oil and associated gas are produced from some wells. Second, even if only gas is produced from a well, the exploration activities leading to the development of that well almost always lead to the development of other wells, some of which may produce both oil and gas. As a result, virtually all exploration costs are common. It is not unusual to find production fields in which at least one-third of the total costs of production and exploration cannot be directly attributed to either oil or gas, but instead are common costs.

A traditional approach to the regulation of gas prices would require not only that the common production and exploration costs be allocated to define a rate base, but also that a proper allowance be made for depletion of the resource and for the risk incurred in developing producing fields. These kinds of problems and a rapidly growing caseload made the Commission's tasks overwhelmingly difficult. A more pragmatic procedure became necessary.

Area Ratemaking

The Commission decided in 1960 to divide the country's gas wells into 23 geographic areas and then set uniform ceiling prices for each of them, based on prices observed during the 1956–1958 period. In 1965 the Commission set its first ceiling for the Permian Basin, including parts of New Mexico and Texas. There were really two ceiling prices, one for gas already being produced ("old gas") and for gas associated with oil, and the second (higher) price for gas not associated with oil, which was classified as "new gas." New gas refers to gas that was either discovered or first committed to interstate commerce after a date specified by the FPC. The justification for this two-level system of prices was that it "was both undesirable and unnecessary to extend that higher price to old gas, undesirable because to do so would confer windfalls on the owners of reserves discovered and developed at lower costs in the past (a noneconomic argument), and unnecessary because the investments in the old gas had already been made (an economic consideration)." [17]

The first (old-gas) ceiling was based on average costs and investment data available for all producers in the area for gas wells already in production. This ceiling applied to all gas extracted from properties whose reserves were committed to interstate commerce before the date specified by the FPC, even though some of the gas might be extracted from wells drilled after that date. There was no special calculation made for associated gas in the area. The second (new-gas) ceiling was determined from industry averages of costs arising from the production of new unassociated gas.

The procedure established by the Commission was soon taken to court, and in 1968 in the Permian Basin Area Rate Cases, the Supreme Court upheld the FPC order.[18] In later area determinations the Commission continued its system of multiple ceilings for each area, although with some variation. For example, in certain areas there was a ceiling price for old gas committed to interstate commerce before one time, another ceiling price for gas committed between the first date and a later one, and a third price for gas committed thereafter.

As the first years of the 1970s passed it became apparent that the area ratemaking approach was simply too cumbersome to permit the Commission to react promptly and responsively to changing conditions in wellhead markets. By 1974 the Commission had completed ratemaking proceedings in less than half of the 23 geographic areas. In addition, as the demand for gas increased rapidly over this period, it became apparent that area rates already established were too low and would have to be reviewed. These prospects, together with an increasing gas shortage, led the Commission to reassess its ratemaking practices. Instead of setting rates by areas, the FPC moved to a policy of establishing nationwide price ceilings.

Nationwide Ratemaking

On June 21, 1974, the FPC extended the concept of area rate regulation to establish "a uniform just and reasonable national base rate of 42 cents per thousand cubic feet [Mcf] at 14.73 psia [pounds per square inch, absolute pressure], for interstate sales of natural gas." [19] This rate was designed to apply to gas from wells completed after January 1, 1973. The Commission also announced that it would begin a similar nationwide ratemaking procedure for gas whose sales commenced before 1973.

In determining the uniform nationwide rate, the Commission took into account the following components of the costs of nonassociated gas exploration and production: drilling and completion costs for successful wells, recompletion and deeper drilling, lease acquisition, other production facilities, dry hole costs, risk, exploration overhead, operating expenses, return on investment, regulatory expenses, and royalties paid.[20] A special additional allowance of 1 cent per thousand cubic feet was to be allowed for gas produced offshore and transported to an onshore delivery point. The Commission also set up procedures by which exceptions to the nationwide rate could be made when circumstances warranted (for example, where extraordinarily deep drilling was required, where gas quality was exceptional, or where other allowances seemed appropriate). Following a rehearing the Commission raised the nationwide base rate for new gas from 42 cents to 50 cents per thousand cubic feet on December 4, 1974. The nationwide rate was to be reviewed every two years, with adjustments made for changes in the current cost of exploration and production of new gas.

In July and November of 1976 the Commission increased gas prices once again in an effort to combat the gas shortage. At that time there were five tiers of gas, ranging from 29.5 cents per Mcf for gas whose production commenced prior to January 1, 1973, to $1.42 per Mcf for gas whose production commenced after January 1, 1975.

This basic price structure remained in force until the NGPA of 1978. The control of wellhead price regulation was transferred to the Federal Energy Regulatory Commission of the Department of Energy with the signing of the Department of Energy Reorganization Act of 1977.

THE SHORTAGE IN
INTERSTATE MARKETS

The basic forces at work in production and consumption of natural gas can be illustrated using the framework of supply and demand in the wellhead market, assuming that market to be competitive. In Figure 1, S represents a supply schedule, D a demand schedule, and E a market-clearing equilibrium. Throughout the 1970s — at least until the passage of the NGPA in 1978 — the wellhead prices of gas in intrastate markets were unregulated. Thus, in each intrastate market, one might expect that sales were taking place at a price near the market-clearing level (P_E) at each point in time.

Figure 1. Wellhead Market: Supply and Demand

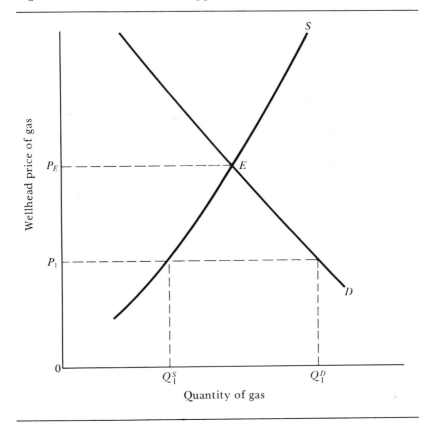

Quantity of gas

In interstate markets, on the other hand, especially after 1970 when shortages began to occur, one would have expected that the wellhead prices would have been held below P_E, at some level such as P_1 in Figure 1. If P_1 were the regulated price, then the quantity demanded at P_1 would exceed the quantity supplied by the amount $(Q_1^D - Q_1^s)$.

As suggested earlier, there can be little doubt that changing economic conditions, including a higher demand for energy, rising oil prices, and increasing shortages, generated pressure on regulators to raise wellhead prices during the 1970s. The average prices paid by interstate pipelines at the wellhead have indeed risen over time, as shown in the last column of Table 4. The weighted average price in a given year is determined as the price that, if multiplied by the volume of all interstate sales, would yield the same revenue as did the sum of all the individual transactions at their respective actual prices. So, for example, while some gas may have been sold at $0.50 per Mcf in 1974, much old gas was sold to pipelines at prices below the weighted average.

Table 4 also shows how the average prices paid to the pipelines by intrastate gas companies (the local distributors) have risen over time (see column 2). This is not surprising, since pipelines typically pass through the increased wellhead prices to their own customers.

Table 4. Average Prices of Gas Bought and Sold by Natural Gas Interstate Pipeline Companies ($/Mcf)

Year	Sales to Local Gas Companies (under FPC Rate Schedules)	Firm Sales to Industrial Users	Purchases from Domestic Producers
1969 [a]	$0.37	$0.26	$0.18
1970 [a]	0.38	0.30	0.18
1971 [a]	0.43	0.32	0.19
1972 [a]	0.46	0.35	0.20
1973 [a]	0.50	0.44	0.22
1974 [a]	0.61	0.55	0.27
May 1974 [a]	0.59	0.54	0.27
May 1975 [a]	0.83	0.60	0.40
July 1976 [b]	1.03	0.95	0.44
July 1977 [b]	1.36	1.34	0.72
July 1978 [b]	1.56	1.50	0.84
July 1979 [b]	1.90	1.99	1.19

[a] Source: *FPC News*, 8:35 (week ending August 29, 1975), 1, 5. The numbers are rounded to the nearest cent.

[b] Source: *Monthly Energy Review*, Department of Energy, October 1979, p. 90.

Intrastate Wellhead Prices

Before 1970 no shortages of gas were observed in either interstate or intrastate markets. Since producers of natural gas often had the option of selling into either market, one would have expected sales to occur in these two markets so that the prices observed were about equal. Table 5 shows that this did happen. (In fact, the table suggests that intrastate prices may have actually been less than interstate prices before 1970, although they were virtually the same.) However, the table indicates that at least by 1972 regulators were holding interstate wellhead prices below the levels observed in the unregulated intrastate markets, and increasingly so over time. This trend toward diverging wellhead prices is even more easily observed if one examines the prices in new gas contracts over the period (instead of weighted average prices). "During the period 1969–1975, interstate natural gas prices for new contracts rose by 158 percent, from approximately $0.198 per Mcf to over $0.51 per Mcf. However, during the same period, intrastate natural gas prices rose at an even greater rate, from approximately $0.18 per Mcf in 1969 to in excess of $1.35 per Mcf in 1975, a 650 percent increase." [21]

As the difference between prices of new gas sold in the two markets increased over the first half of the 1970s, producers were given incen-

Table 5. Comparison of Intrastate and Jurisdictional
Weighted Average Prices ($/Mcf)

Date of Contract	Intrastate	Jurisdictional (Interstate)
1966 [a]	$0.168	$0.185
1967 [a]	0.173	0.191
1968 [a]	0.175	0.192
1969 [a]	0.180	0.198
First half, 1970 [a]	0.207	0.202
July 1, 1970, to Sept. 14, 1971 [a]	0.241	0.284
Sept. 15, 1971, to Sept. 14, 1972 [a]	0.316	0.286
1975	0.60 (est.)[b]	0.40 [c]

[a] Source: FPC data as presented in Report No. 94-732 (House of Representatives, 94th Congress, first session), p. 6.

[b] Source: No hard data are available, but this figure was named as a consensus estimate by Chip Schroeder of the House Energy and Power Subcommittee Staff. See L. Kumins, "Cost of S. 3422's Pricing Provisions," Senate Report 94-907.

[c] Source: Table 4.

tives to commit newly found reserves to an intrastate (rather than the interstate) market. This shift to the intrastate markets is apparent from Table 6. In the 1964–1969 period, producers dedicated 67 percent of their new reserves to the interstate market, but this figure fell to less than 8 percent over the 1970–1973 period.

Intrastate prices continued to be higher than interstate prices over the last half of the 1970s. Table 7 displays average intrastate natural gas prices for new contracts and for renegotiated (or amended) contracts in three major gas producing states for selected months from 1976 to 1978. Many of these prices have exceeded $2 per Mcf.

Curtailment Priorities

As the shortage increased during the early 1970s, the FPC was confronted with an inevitable problem: how to allocate whatever gas was available. Since interstate prices were held below the market-clearing level, the FPC designed a system of curtailment priorities to specify those categories of users who would get gas first. These categories are listed below, ordered from highest to lowest priority:[22]

1. Residential, small commercial (less than 50 Mcf on a peak day).
2. Large commercial requirements (50 Mcf or more on a peak day), firm industrial requirements for plant protection, feedstock and process needs, and pipeline customer storage injection requirements.
3. All industrial requirements not specified in items 2, 4, 5, 6, 7, 8, or 9.
4. Firm industrial requirements for boiler fuel use at less than 3,000

Table 6. Natural Gas: Average Annual Net Reserve Additions
to Interstate and Intrastate Pipelines

Time Period	Additions to Interstate Reserves (Tcf)	Additions to Intrastate Reserves (Tcf)
1964–1969	11.4	5.6
1970–1973	0.7	8.4

Source: House of Representatives, Report No. 94-732 (94th Congress, 1st Session), p. 56.

Table 7. Average Intrastate Natural Gas Prices for Selected States by Type of Contract ($/Mcf)

Month	Louisiana		Oklahoma		Texas	
	New Contracts	Renegotiated or Amended	New Contracts	Renegotiated or Amended	New Contracts	Renegotiated or Amended
January 1976	1.39	1.31	1.50	1.09	1.81	1.93
July 1976	1.28	1.42	1.48	0.95	1.51	1.76
January 1977	1.56	1.38	1.72	1.67	1.93	2.04
July 1977	1.75	1.70	1.73	1.68	2.07	2.02
January 1978	1.94	2.03	1.69	1.81	1.69	2.12
July 1978	2.04	2.02	1.64	1.54	2.04	2.09

Source: Monthly Energy Review, Department of Energy, October 1979, p. 91. Prices are for FERC jurisdictional natural gas companies selling more than 1 Bcf per year in intrastate commerce.

Mcf per day, but more than 1,500 Mcf per day, where alternate fuel capabilities can meet such requirements.
5. Firm industrial requirements for large volume (3,000 Mcf or more per day) boiler fuel use where alternate fuel capabilities can meet such requirements.
6. Interruptible requirements of less than 3,000 Mcf per day, but more than 1,500 Mcf per day, where alternate fuel capabilities can meet such requirements.
7. Interruptible requirements of intermediate volumes (from 1,500 Mcf per day through 3,000 Mcf per day), where alternate fuel capabilities can meet such requirements.
8. Interruptible requirements of more than 3,000 Mcf per day, but less than 10,000 Mcf per day, where alternate fuel capabilities can meet such requirements.
9. Interruptible requirements of more than 10,000 Mcf per day, where alternate fuel capabilities can meet such requirements.

The nine categories represent an attempt by the FPC to rank the value of gas by the user categories. To some extent the ranking makes sense. Users with available alternatives would probably not value gas as highly as they would if no alternative were available. Also, users with interruptible clauses in their contracts could probably absorb some curtailment with only minimal effects.

However, this approach to rationing gas also raises many problems. Are the categories really "correctly" defined and ordered? Is the gas rationed to uses where its value is greatest? Even if this is thought to be the case at a coarse level, there are obvious problems at finer levels. For example, a residential user would have a top priority under this scheme to get additional gas to heat his home from 68°F to, say, 75°F. But is the gas used in that way really more valuable than any use for that gas in, for example, a plant classified in category 9? It would seem highly unlikely. Even the procedures that allow parties to seek relief in special cases would not be adequate to make the many such adjustments that probably ought to be made.

OTHER CONSEQUENCES OF REGULATION

Regulation typically affects the distribution of income and the economic efficiency with which resources are allocated. We consider each of these in turn.

Income Redistribution

Like Figure 1, Figure 2 depicts a supply schedule for producers and a demand schedule for consumers of natural gas in the interstate well-head market. The regulated price, P_R, is below the unregulated market-clearing price, P_E. As a result, only Q_R^s is actually supplied to customers, while the demand for $(Q_R^D - Q_R^s)$ remains unsatisfied. Under these conditions, producers realize dollar revenues corresponding to the area *DCHO*, and incur cost of *OECH*, leaving them with dollar profits represented by the area *CDE*. If those consumers who were successful in obtaining the quantity Q_R^s had paid the unregulated price, P_E, then producer profits would be increased by the amount *ABCD*, and consumer expenditures would be increased by the same amount. In short, regulation effectively transfers *ABCD* from producers to consumers. (In discussing the empirical results, however, we will see that there is some doubt that income redistribution is adequately measured by *ABCD* alone.)

As Table 5 indicates, the wellhead prices in interstate and intrastate prices were approximately the same until the 1970s. It would seem reasonable to take the observed intrastate prices as an approximation of the market-clearing prices over time. If we do so, then we can infer that the size of the rectangle *ABCD* was very small before the 1970s. In other words there was probably only a very small effect, if any, in terms of income redistribution resulting from regulation during that period.*

However, since interstate and intrastate prices diverged significantly by the mid-1970s, the effects of income redistribution became quite large. Several studies were performed to measure these effects. In one such study MacAvoy and Pindyck (1975) concluded that if regulation of wellhead prices were continued for the rest of the decade at 1974 prices, regulation would redistribute more than $1 billion from producers to consumers in 1975, and more than $4.8 billion in 1980.

Of course, the FPC did raise interstate prices significantly in 1976, as discussed earlier. This might have made the redistribution effects less pronounced than MacAvoy and Pindyck predicted, since they assumed no such increase would occur. However, intrastate gas prices increased more rapidly than anticipated during the last part of the 1970s, providing a reason to believe that perhaps MacAvoy and

---

* As noted earlier, Table 5 shows that intrastate prices were even a bit lower than interstate prices before the 1970s, suggesting that regulation may not have held prices down at all. In any case, even though the direction of the redistribution is not clear, the main point is that the magnitude of the redistribution was quite small.

Figure 2. The Interstate Wellhead Market

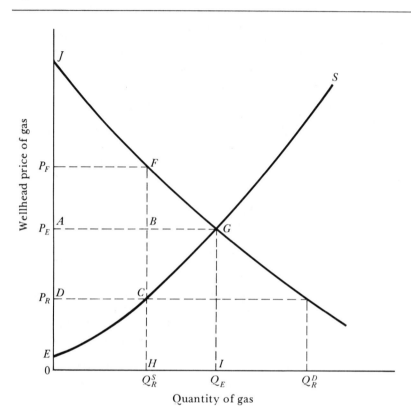

Pindyck underestimated the amount of the redistribution. Just how these two unanticipated effects would have affected the MacAvoy and Pindyck calculations is not clear. Nevertheless, the study was important in pointing out that the redistribution effects were probably in the billions of dollars.

In another study, Helms (1974) suggested an additional aspect of income redistribution occurring under regulation. He noted that, while some consumers have been "fortunate" enough to be able to purchase gas, other consumers who desire it have not been able to acquire it at all. Those consumers have been forced to seek alternative sources of energy, including imported gas, at much higher prices. Helms's conclusion is that while regulation may redistribute income from producers to those fortunate consumers, income has also been redistributed away from other consumers, in many cases to foreign instead of domestic suppliers.

Data from the last half of the 1970s would appear to support Helms's contention. Major interstate pipeline companies were paying a weighted average wellhead price of $0.43 per Mcf purchased from domestic producers in July 1976 and $1.19 per Mcf in July 1979. When these same pipelines purchased gas from foreign sources, they paid an average price of $1.68 per Mcf in July 1976 and $2.32 per Mcf in July 1979.[23]

A very simple method allows us to approximate the amount of income redistributed from producers to consumers who are able to get interstate gas. Table 3 shows that approximately 19 Tcf were produced in 1975. About two-thirds of this (say, 13 Tcf) was sold into interstate commerce. Table 5 shows that the weighted average price was thought to be about $0.20 per Mcf higher in intrastate than in interstate markets. It is not unreasonable to believe that virtually all of this difference in average prices resulted from regulation. Thus the amount of income redistribution can be approximated as the product of 13 Tcf and $0.20 per Mcf, or about $2.6 billion for the year. While this is only an approximation, it serves to emphasize that the redistribution may well have been in the billions of dollars annually during the mid-1970s.

Economic Efficiency

Since a demand schedule shows how much gas buyers would like to purchase at any announced price in the market, it can be used to determine the value of a given quantity of gas to consumers. For example, in Figure 2, suppose that Q_R^s were provided to all consumers willing to pay at least P_F. Then the gross value of that gas can be represented in dollars by the area $OHFJ$.[24] However, since it costs producers an amount $OHCE$ to produce the gas, then the net economic benefit of producing Q_R^s is the area $ECFJ$. How this net economic benefit (or, as it is often called, surplus) is divided between consumers and producers depends on the price charged. If the regulated price P_R is in effect, then the consumer surplus is $DCFJ$, and the producer surplus is ECD.

Now suppose that regulation were removed, so that the price in the market could move to P_E (at which the market clears). The quantity of gas offered for sale would increase by the amount $(Q_E - Q_R^s)$.

A measure of the gross value of this additional gas for consumers is provided by the area $HFGI$. The costs to producers of providing this additional gas would be $HCGI$. Note that $HFGI$ is larger than $HCGI$. Therefore, a net benefit increase would be realized if regulation were removed, where the size of the net value is represented by the triangular area CFG. In other words, regulation may prevent the market from allocating $(Q_E - Q_R^S)$ to consumers even though the benefits they attach to the additional gas exceed the cost of production. Economists therefore say that gas is not being produced or allocated efficiently under regulation, and they call the net benefit loss CFG an "efficiency loss."

Under the system of regulation now used in the natural gas industry, there is strong reason to suspect that the efficiency loss is even larger than CFG. To see this, recall that at the regulated price, P_R, only Q_R^S will be supplied to customers. There is no guarantee that the customers who actually get the gas value it the most. Restated, gas may not be allocated so that consumers get the most benefit from it. It may very well be that some people valuing gas less than P_E — indeed, as low as P_R — are receiving gas under regulation. At the same time, there may be others willing to pay very high prices (even higher than P_E) who are rationed out of the market. All that one can say is that CFG places a lower bound on the efficiency loss due to regulation.

MacAvoy (1975) proposes a slightly different way of looking at efficiency losses to define a better lower bound on them. It is worthwhile developing this notion here, since he has provided some empirical estimates using this method.

MacAvoy notes that the demand for gas can be considered in two parts, as depicted in Figure 3. There is one set of consumers who are able to purchase gas at regulated prices. Typically those consumers who have had access to gas in one year will continue to have access in the next year. One could represent the demand schedule for this group of consumers by D' in Figure 3.

As time has passed, many new would-be consumers have not been able to purchase gas because of the shortage. If the demand of this unfortunate group were added to D', the actual demand for gas could be represented by D. (In Figure 3 it is assumed that neither existing nor potential consumers would purchase any gas at a price higher than that represented by point J.) Most of the burden of the shortage will be borne by new would-be consumers and industrial users who cannot get gas at all, since existing customers will be served first.

Thus, in addition to the efficiency loss CFG (see Figure 3), there is an additional loss of CFJ. The loss CFJ arises because some prospective consumers who are not able to get gas value it more than some of

Figure 3. Efficiency Loss: Two Consumer Groups

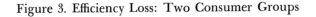

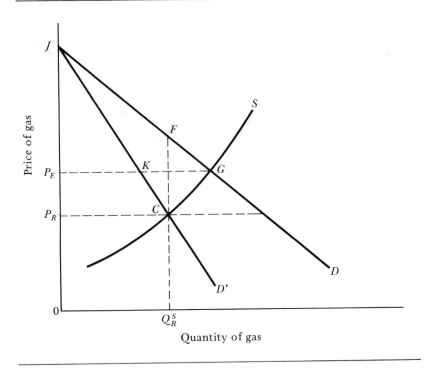

Quantity of gas

those who are able to purchase it. Thus, gas is not being allocated to users who place the highest values on it.

The Importance of the Slope of the Supply Schedule

So far we have identified two important consequences of regulation. If policymakers do use regulation to effect an income transfer ($ABCD$ in Figure 2) from producers to consumers, they should realize that a real net loss in efficiency (of CGJ in Figure 3) occurs at the same time.

The slope of the supply curve will be important in determining the relative magnitudes of these two effects. If the quantity produced is not very responsive to price changes, the supply schedule will be nearly vertical. If this were the case, one would expect higher prices to yield no more advanced technology, and no new production from reserves from which extraction is more costly. (Economists would characterize this as an "inelastic" supply.)

The efficiency loss caused by regulation tends to be smaller with an inelastic supply schedule, and at the same time the redistribution of income from producers to consumers may be quite large. Stated another way, if regulation were removed, the primary results could be a large increase in producer profits, a large increase in consumer expenditures on gas, a small increase in the quantity of gas produced, and a smaller increase in efficiency than one would have observed with a less steeply sloped supply curve.

The last point mentioned is worth a final word. Economists often say that price regulation does not cause an efficiency loss in a market if the supply schedule is totally inelastic (i.e., vertical). If old and new customers of gas could not be distinguished from one another, and if everyone who received gas valued gas more highly than anyone who did not receive it, then this statement would be true. In Figure 3 note that the area CFG would become zero if S is vertical. However, if new and old customers are treated differently in the allocation of existing supplies of gas, there is an efficiency loss with regulation. Suppose that S were vertical through points C and F. Then the amount of the loss occurring because of regulation would be represented by the area CFJ.

Not many estimates of the size of the efficiency loss resulting from regulation have appeared in the literature. Since regulated interstate prices were probably not far from their unregulated levels before 1970, the size of the efficiency loss was most likely quite small. However, since intrastate wellhead prices (a proxy for the prices that would have been observed in interstate markets without regulation) rose rapidly during the 1970s, the size of the efficiency loss may have become substantial, even in the billions of dollars annually.

The most systematic examination was by MacAvoy and Pindyck (1975). They estimated that if regulation were to continue at the 1974 prices for the rest of the decade, then the efficiency loss would be more than $2.5 billion in 1978 and more than $5.8 billion in 1980. To this author's knowledge no one has attempted to reestimate the size of the loss, given that the increases in regulated prices and intrastate prices were more rapid than MacAvoy and Pindyck estimated. Furthermore, the MacAvoy and Pindyck procedure requires extensive knowledge of the nature of the demand for natural gas in order to calculate the size of the area CGJ in Figure 3. MacAvoy and Pindyck assumed in their study that the demand schedule was linear — a procedure that may introduce significant error, since the difference between regulated and unregulated prices is quite large.[25]

STRUCTURE OF
WELLHEAD MARKETS

In order to assess the likely impacts of the Natural Gas Policy Act of 1978, it is necessary to understand the structure of the wellhead markets that are being deregulated. Over the last three decades several of the arguments against deregulation have in fact been structural arguments, including monopoly power by producers and monopsony power on the part of pipeline buyers. Both of these possibilities have received special attention because of the vertical integration among many producers and pipelines. Since deregulation can be expected to work well only if the market structure appears to be conducive to competition rather than collusion, we must examine that structure.

Monopoly Power by Producers

The issue of producer monopoly power has been important ever since the *Phillips* case in 1954. Subsequent analyses have cast doubt on the proposition that the industry is essentially monopolistic.

As a beginning, note that the largest producer of natural gas sold in the interstate market in 1971 served less than 10 percent of the national market, with the largest 4, 8, and 20 firms supplying 26.7, 45.4, and 69.6 percent, respectively (see Table 8). These figures do not by themselves say very much about the degree of competition or monopoly power, so to put them in perspective we consider the following items.

First, the concentration figures are somewhat higher if we look at major gas-producing regions instead of the national market. In Table 8 the concentration figures are shown by region for gas sold under new sales contracts during 1969. No single producer approaches domination in any regional market, although by some standards the concentration ratios are high enough in the Texas Gulf Coast and Permian Basin areas to appear oligopolistic. It should be noted that if concentration ratios are taken as an indicator of market power, there is an argument that the relevant market is national rather than regional. Many gas-consuming regions receive gas from more than one major producing area. This would limit the extent to which producers in any single area could control the price of gas, even if they attempted to collude in doing so.

Since most gas supply contracts are for a long term, the ranking of firms by market shares does not vary much year by year. However, the ranking of firms by percentage of annual volume under new sales contracts does change more rapidly from year to year. "In 1964 only

Table 8. Selected Concentration Ratios for Producers

Concentration Ratio, Including This Number of Largest Firms	Percentage of Annual Volume under New Sales Contract, 1969				National Sales of Natural Gas to Interstate Pipelines, 1971 Percentage of Total Sales
	Southern Louisiana	Permian Basin		Texas Gulf Coast	
1	11.1	21.1		21.9	9.8
4	38.4	57.8		62.6	26.7
8	63.7	71.5		71.5	45.4
20	—	—		—	69.6

Source: *National Gas Survey*, Vol. I, pages 57–58.

one of the eight top sellers [new contracts] in Southern Louisiana was among the top eight in 1965, while in 1966 the top eight sellers comprised completely different companies from those in 1964 or 1968." [26] This kind of turnover has existed in other years and in other producing areas, and tends to make the higher concentration ratio observed in any year for new sales look less important than if the same producers regularly dominated the new-sales markets.

The concentration measures of Table 8 can be compared with concentration ratios for selected unregulated industries. It is apparent that the national concentration of gas producers is less than in many other industries that have functioned for years without price regulation of the sort imposed on the natural gas industry after the *Phillips* decision. Unregulated industries less concentrated than natural gas, measured by the four- and eight-firm concentration indices in 1972, include the following with the appropriate four-digit S.I.C. codes in parentheses: turbines and turbine generators (3511), electric lamps (3641), household refrigerators and freezers (3632), tires and inner tubes (3011), metal cans (3411), synthetic rubber (2822), soap and detergents (2841), storage batteries (3691), glass containers (3221), and a host of others.[27]

Some aspects of wellhead market structure might stand to qualify the extent of competition. Producers do often enter into joint ventures in production, and particularly so in costly and risky operations offshore. Larger companies have an advantage in being able to pool their risks so that they can better withstand any single drilling or leasing failure. Also, in obtaining leases for drilling offshore, small firms may not be able to bid, since large financial resources are required under present government leasing policies.

It is not clear how large a company must be in order to make joint ventures unnecessary from a risk-sharing perspective. Neither is it clear at what size the advantages of risk sharing become outweighed by the prospects of collusion and excessive market power. To some extent this is no doubt a function of government leasing policy for offshore activities. For both offshore and onshore activities, it will remain an important task to encourage competition as much as practical, given the risks of production. This is obviously important where wellhead price regulation is discontinued. But it is also important where wellhead prices continue to be regulated, since competitive bidding for leases is expected to continue under the Natural Gas Policy Act.

There is also concern over the fact that in many cases pipelines and producers are affiliated with one another; that is, they are vertically integrated. Even if pipelines continue to be regulated as they presently are (except for wellhead price regulation), and even if a producer delivering gas to an affiliated pipeline is surrounded by other competing producers, there is reason to be wary. If regulators of the pipeline were not very observant, the affiliated producer could conceivably charge a higher-than-competitive wellhead price to the pipeline, thereby making excessive profits, and the pipeline might in turn try to pass the excessive prices it paid for gas through to its customers as a cost it had incurred. Note that even competitive wellhead markets would not eliminate these incentives.

Although one possible solution would be to prohibit pipelines and producer affiliates in the same wellhead markets, one should not leap from this warning to a proposal for disintegration. After all, there are a number of potential economic efficiencies that may be gained by vertical integration, including possibly the opportunity for affiliated firms to share risks and negotiate contracts in a less costly fashion. The point of the argument is simply to indicate that at the minimum, some problems of a regulatory nature may remain under the Natural Gas Policy Act. In particular, the incentives for inefficiency we have described under vertical integration might be controlled if the pipeline regulator could recognize and disallow any excessively high prices charged by a producer affiliate — prices exceeding those charged by nonaffiliated producers. The drawback here is evident: the regulator would have to be very watchful, and the task would not be easy, since gas delivery contracts can be quite complicated.

Monopsony Power by Pipelines

One possible justification for the regulation of wellhead prices would be the existence of substantial monopsony power by pipelines. If, for example, only one pipeline were buying the gas from a given field, it might recognize that the field price of gas varied directly with the amount of gas it purchased. It would be able to force producers to sell their gas at a lower price than that which would efficiently allocate resources. Efficient allocation means that at higher wellhead prices additional gas would be produced, and the value of that additional gas to society would be higher than the production costs. By interfering with pricing, monopsony power could promote a wasteful allocation of resources. Thus monopsony power could be a problem that would justify regulation where it was substantial.[28]

Monopsony power was not cited as a reason for natural gas regulation either in the Natural Gas Act or as a part of the subsequent judicial interpretations extending regulation to the wellhead. To the extent that regulation is found necessary to correct for this problem, it would *raise* wellhead prices to their efficient levels rather than lowering them.

There are about 33 major interstate pipeline companies and 74 others.[29] The concentration ratios for pipelines as buyers in the national interstate market as of 1971 are displayed in Table 9. These concentration ratios are higher than those for producers in the national market (see Table 8). This relationship holds in most producing areas as well as for the national market. Table 10 displays concentration ratios for pipelines as buyers in four of the major gas-producing areas. Concentration is higher by area than in the national market (compare this table with Table 9). The concentration of buyers by area is also higher than for sellers by area (compare with Table 8). All of this suggests that monopsony power could be a problem and leads us to look at other available evidence.

The main empirical work on the subject of monopsony is reported in studies by MacAvoy (1962, 1970a). These studies differ from the relatively simplistic perspective offered by looking at concentration ratios alone. Rather, MacAvoy constructed statistical tests designed to see if the observed variations in wellhead prices across field markets significantly depended on the number of pipeline buyers in the market. He concluded that monopsony power was not pervasive, although in a few cases there was some evidence of its existence. The following excerpts summarize his assessment:

In the last years of the 1950's more of the new fields were in competitive markets. There was buyers' competition for new reserves throughout the Gulf Coast and Louisiana. The entry of Transwestern Pipeline into West Texas-New Mexico provided extensive potential competition in demand there. The Panhandle-Hugoton region of the Mid-Continent long had been competitive in supply and demand. Only the isolated central fields of

Table 9. Natural Gas Purchases by Interstate Pipelines: Concentration Ratios for National Market, 1971

Number of Largest Firms Included	Cumulative Percentage of Volume Purchased
1	11.2
4	35.8
8	58.2
12	73.7
16	86.1
20	93.1

Source: FPC, Sales by Producers of Natural Gas to Interstate Pipeline Companies, 1971, as reported in the Natural Gas Survey (1975), Vol. 1, p. 62.

Table 10. Natural Gas Purchases by Interstate Pipelines:
Concentration Ratios for Selected Gas Areas, 1972

Number of Largest Firms Included	Cumulative Percentage of Gas Purchases by Area			
	Southern Louisiana (Onshore)	Permian Basin	Texas Gulf Coast	Hugoton-Anadarko
1	24.1	45.1	18.6	21.2
4	60.7	88.2	59.2	70.4
8	88.0	≅100%	90.1	94.1

Source: Sales by Producers of Natural Gas to Interstate Pipeline Companies, 1972, extracted from Table D, p. XV, and Table 6, pp. 633–642.

Kansas and Oklahoma each had one pipeline buyer. . . . The question remaining is what should be the nature of Federal [Power] Commission regulation in this diverse group of markets.[30]

As suggested by price formation in the 1950's, gas markets are diverse in structure and behavior, but are generally competitive or changing from monopsony toward competition. Markets with such characteristics need not be regulated by the Federal Power Commission to prevent monopoly pricing. Nor, at present, is it easy to justify regulation on other grounds, given the undesirable effects on consumers and the rate of discovery and sale of reserves. By and large, the strongest suggestion arising from this study of competition, monopsony, and regulations in the 1950's is that there should be more of the first.[31]

Empirical testing of monopoly and monopsony in the period after regulation was implemented will be difficult for at least two reasons. First, interstate market prices were fixed, so variations in prices over regions result from the many factors dealt with in regulatory proceedings rather than from monopoly or monopsony behavior; thus statistical tests of the sort performed by MacAvoy cannot be made. Second, the only remaining markets in which price has fluctuated without regulation are the intrastate markets, and data have only recently been recorded at the Department of Energy on a consistent reporting basis. This is indeed unfortunate, since it is reasonable to suppose that markets that were to some extent monopsonistic in the past would be less so now than just before regulation, as natural gas markets have grown and new entrants have appeared.

In summary, from its inception the regulation of wellhead prices has raised perplexing questions. Many reasons for regulation have been cited at one time or another. It has been claimed that monopoly power on the part of producers provided justification, because producers are highly concentrated and the largest ten of them control a majority of known reserves. Yet empirical work designed to test for monopolistic tendencies in pricing before regulation has rejected that hypothesis (i.e., statistical tests have shown it to be highly improbable that well-head market prices were determined as a result of monopolistic behavior before regulation).

A comparison of measures of concentration of gas production with similar measures of other American industries shows that many unregulated industries are much more concentrated than natural gas producers. If deregulation is to work well, then, it would seem important to keep joint ventures from proliferating without limit, particularly where production risks are not great. It will also be necessary to deal with the pipeline-producer affiliation problem in the same wellhead market.

THE NGPA: PROVISIONS AND EXPECTED CONSEQUENCES

The Natural Gas Policy Act of 1978 represents a major change in the structure and direction of regulation in the natural gas industry. In three areas the Act entails significant changes from the past. First, the FERC is granted regulatory control over intrastate as well as interstate wellhead prices. Second, the Act contains a time schedule for the deregulation of new gas and of gas produced from "high-cost" sources, and it indicates a set of wellhead prices to be in effect during the transition to deregulation. Old-gas prices will remain regulated indefinitely. Third, the Act provides a set of rules under which the interstate pipelines must pass along the higher costs incurred with the purchase of "high-cost" gas to selected large industrial customers. This is known as the incremental pricing provision of the Act. These three areas will be discussed in detail below.

In addition, the NGPA empowers the President to declare a natural gas supply emergency if a shortage that would endanger supplies to certain high-priority users exists or is imminent. In such an emergency the President can authorize pipelines and local distributors to purchase gas at any price he believes appropriate. If these emergency purchases are insufficient to meet designated high-priority needs, the President can reallocate gas supplies as necessary under some circumstances.[32]

The Act also provides guidelines for a system of curtailments during times of shortage. We have discussed the system of priorities implemented by the FPC in 1973. Under the Department of Energy Organization Act, the Secretary of Energy was charged with reviewing and establishing those procedures, and the FERC implements them. The basic tenor of the curtailment priorities has not changed over time, and they will not be reviewed in detail here, since they were discussed earlier in connection with the procedures of the FPC.

Wellhead Price Ceilings Under the NGPA

As noted earlier, the NGPA extends the hand of regulation to include intrastate markets. Together with the already numerous categories of interstate gas as defined by regulators before the Act, there now exists an even more complicated set of categories. In fact, during the first year following the Act there were a number of debates as to just how many categories there actually were (with numbers ranging all the way from eleven to thirty-three).[33]

A convenient summary of the price ceilings set by the NGPA has been provided by the FERC and appears in Table 11. Of particular interest is the definition of new natural gas produced from onshore wells. The concept of a marker well is important in delineating what is new gas. As footnote e of Table 11 shows, a "marker well is any well from which natural gas was produced in commercial quantities after January 1, 1970, and before April 20, 1977, with the exception of wells the surface drilling of which began after February 19, 1977." According to Section 102 of the NGPA, new gas must come from wells at least 2.5 miles from the nearest marker well, or from a production zone at least 1,000 feet deeper than gas-producing zones from any marker well closer than 2.5 miles.

New gas receives a price that rises over time. The value at any particular time is determined by a price of $1.75, inflated to reflect the difference in the GNP deflator at the current time relative to May 1977, plus an additional escalation factor of 3.5 or 4.0 percent annually (see footnote c in Table 11). Thus, the price of new gas in October 1978 was $2.07 per Mcf. Note that all gas categorized as new under Section 102, except for some gas discovered offshore, will be deregulated by 1985.

Gas produced from new onshore wells, but not far enough away from established operations to qualify as new gas, will be priced in much the same way as new gas, but without the additional escalation factor. According to Section 103 of the Act this gas will be deregulated by 1985 or 1987, depending on the depth of the well.

Gas previously dedicated to interstate commerce and regulated by the FPC will be priced in tiers under Section 104 of the NGPA. Some of this old gas is presently being sold for less than 40 cents per Mcf, as the table shows. It will not be deregulated under the NGPA.

In between the higher new-gas prices and the lower old interstate gas prices are other ceilings. Included here are gas produced from the Prudhoe Bay in Alaska (Section 109), and sales of gas made under expired contracts that have been renegotiated (Section 106). Gas sold under existing intrastate contracts will have a ceiling of the contract price plus an inflation allowance, or the price of new gas as defined in Section 102, whichever is higher. Note that some, but not all, of these categories are destined for deregulation. Finally, certain high-cost sources of gas (very deep wells, geopressurized brine, Devonian shale, and so on) were deregulated on November 1, 1979, as provided in Section 107 of the NGPA.

Incremental Pricing

As the description of wellhead pricing has indicated, pipelines will be purchasing gas at a wide variety of prices under the NGPA. Before the passage of the Act, it was most often the case that pipelines charged all customers for the transportation of the gas plus a weighted average of the pipeline's own gas purchase costs. This method of averaging is usually referred to as rolled-in pricing.

However, under the incremental pricing provision of the NGPA, interstate pipeline and local distribution companies must pass along the costs of selected "high-cost" gas to "nonexempt" users, primarily large industrial customers who use gas as a boiler fuel to generate steam or electricity. The practice of charging these users for the high-cost gas (to the benefit of the other users) will continue until the price of the high-cost gas rises to the BTU equivalent price of alternative fuel, where the alternative fuel will in most cases be distillate fuel oil.* If the price charged to nonexempt customers reaches this level, then the exempt users begin to pay for high-cost gas in whatever amount is necessary to keep the nonexempt prices at the BTU equivalent price of distillate fuel oil.

---

* This method of pricing at a BTU equivalent means that the price per BTU contained in the natural gas stream is set equal to the price of a BTU contained in distillate fuel oil.

Table 11. Maximum Gas Price Ceilings Set by the Natural Gas Policy Act

Section of the Act	Price per Million BTU's[a]	Category of Gas	Date of Deregulation
102	$1.75 + inflation[b] and escalation[c] ($2.07)[d]	NEW NATURAL GAS	
		New outer Continental Shelf (offshore) leases (on or after 4/20/77)	1/1/85
		New onshore wells	
		1) 2.5 miles from the nearest marker well [e]	
		2) If closer than 2.5 miles to a marker well, 1000 feet deeper than the deepest completion location of each marker well within 2.5 miles	
		New onshore reservoirs	
		Gas from reservoirs discovered after 7/27/76 on old (pre–4/20/77) Offshore Continental Shelf	Not deregulated
103	$1.75 + inflation ($1.97)[d]	NEW ONSHORE PRODUCTION WELLS (Wells, the surface drilling of which began after 2/19/77, that are within 2.5 miles of a marker well and not 1000 feet deeper than the deepest completion location in each marker well within 2.5 miles)	
		Gas produced above 5000-foot depth	7/1/87
		Gas produced from below 5000-foot depth	1/1/85

		Price	Deregulation
104	**GAS DEDICATED TO INTERSTATE COMMERCE BEFORE THE DATE OF ENACTMENT** (Rates previously set by FPC)		Not deregulated
	From wells commenced from 1/1/75–2/18/77	$1.45 + inflation ($1.68)[a]	
	From wells commenced from 1/1/73–12/31/74	$.94 + inflation ($1.06)[a]	
	From wells commenced prior to 1/1/73	$.295 + inflation ($.33)[a]	
	Other gas (gas produced by small producers, gas qualifying for special relief rates, etc.)	Applicable FERC rate + inflation	
105	**GAS SOLD UNDER EXISTING INTRASTATE CONTRACTS**	Contract price[f]	1/1/85 — if contract price exceeds $1.00 by 12/31/84; if lower, not deregulated
	If contract price is less than Section 102 price it may escalate, as called for by contract, up to Section 102 price		
	If contract price exceeds Section 102 price then contract price plus annual inflation factor or Section 102 price plus escalation applies, whichever is higher		
106	**SALES OF GAS MADE UNDER "ROLLOVER" CONTRACTS** (An expired contract which has been renegotiated)		
	Interstate	$.54 or other applicable FERC price + inflation ($.61)[a]	Not deregulated
	Intrastate	The higher of expired contract price or $1.00 + inflation ($1.13)[a]	1/1/85 if more than $1.00

Table 11. Maximum Gas Price Ceilings Set by the Natural Gas Policy Act (*cont.*)

Section of the Act	Price per Million BTU's[a]	Category of Gas	Date of Deregulation
		HIGH-COST NATURAL GAS	
107	$1.75 + inflation + escalation[c] ($2.07)[d]	Production from below 15,000 feet from wells drilled after 2/19/77	Deregulated on effective date of FERC incremental pricing rule called for by the Act (approximately one year after enactment)
	Applicable rate under the Act or higher incentive rate as set by FERC	Gas produced from geopressurized brine, coal seams, Devonian shale	
		Gas produced under other conditions the FERC determines to present "extraordinary risks or costs"	Not deregulated
		STRIPPER WELL NATURAL GAS	
108	$2.09 + inflation (after 5/78) + escalation[c] ($2.21)[d]	(Natural gas not produced in association with crude oil, which is produced at an average rate less than or equal to 60,000 cubic feet per day over a 90-day period)	Not deregulated

	OTHER CATEGORIES OF NATURAL GAS	
$1.45, or other "just and reasonable" rate set by FERC, + inflation ($1.63)[a]		Not deregulated
	Any natural gas not covered under any other section of the bill	
	Natural gas produced from the Prudhoe Bay area of Alaska	

Source: FERC Fact Sheet, November 1978.

[a] Under the NGPA, if natural gas qualifies under more than one price category the seller may be permitted to collect the higher price. The ceiling prices set by the NGPA do not include state severance taxes.

[b] These prices include an "annual inflation adjustment factor" in order to adjust prices for inflation. The price for a given month is arrived at by multiplying the price for the previous month by the monthly equivalent of the annual inflation factor. Since most of the prices set by the NGPA are as of April 20, 1977, the adjustment for inflation begins in May 1977.

[c] These prices will escalate monthly, in addition to the inflation adjustment factor, by an annual rate of 3.5 percent until April 1981, after which they will escalate by 4 percent.

[d] The estimated maximum ceiling price as of October 1978, due to operation of inflation and escalation adjusters.

[e] A marker well is any well from which natural gas was produced in commercial quantities after January 1, 1970, and before April 20, 1977, with the exception of wells the surface drilling of which began after February 19, 1977.

[f] The average price reported to the FERC for intrastate gas sales contracted for during the second quarter of 1978 was approximately $1.90.

The customers who are protected (or "exempt") under the provisions of the Act include institutions such as schools and hospitals, some electric utilities, and agricultural users who have no alternative fuel available. The FERC is empowered to exempt other categories of customers where appropriate.

The First Year Under the NGPA

As the brief summary of the major provisions of the Act suggests, the NGPA is a complex piece of legislation. Many of the aspects of implementation were left to the FERC. During the first year a major task has been the determination of the type of gas produced from approximately 30,000 wells. All of the major gas-producing states decided to participate in the NGPA well-determination process. The states made the initial determination of the categories of gas from those 30,000 wells. The FERC has found that only about five percent of those determinations required further review, and in fact "only a handful of determinations have actually been reversed by the FERC." [34]

The Commission has also been forced to deal with the particularly difficult issue of gas that was "behind the pipe" at the time the NGPA was passed. This refers to gas in reservoirs and wells that, with relatively little additional effort in well completion, could have been produced early enough not to qualify as new gas under Section 102 of the Act.

Throughout the 1970s some members of Congress were concerned that producers were holding back production in the expectation of realizing higher prices later, an issue that received much attention as gas shortages increased toward the middle of the decade. There can be little doubt that such an incentive did exist, given the pattern of regulation adapted by the FPC. The FPC periodically reclassified what was new gas at one time as old gas at some later time. Further, at any given time, the price allowed for new gas exceeded the price of old gas.

As producers became accustomed to this pattern of regulation, they were confronted with a decision as to when to initiate production from a gas reservoir whose reserves had not previously been classified as new or old. Producers could begin production at some time (say, t_1) or wait until a later time (t_2). If they began production at t_1, they received revenues earlier. However, they often expected that when t_2 arrived, the gas would be reclassified as old gas if production had started at t_1. By waiting until t_2, they would postpone the receipt of revenues but receive a higher price for each Mcf produced. The basic nature of the trade-off was clear: the producer could expect lower revenues earlier, or higher revenues later.

If producers delayed production because of this incentive, it is hard to say by how much. However, the FERC has been forced to decide whether gas that could have been, but was not, produced before 1977 should be allowed the status of new gas. The current trend in FERC rulings appears to be that some sort of economic test, rather than a straightforward determination of technological capability, should be used to determine the status of gas behind the pipe, although the exact nature of that trend is not yet well established.

Some Expected Consequences of the NGPA

While many of the details of implementation remain to be worked out, the basic patterns of regulation and deregulation in the NGPA are now quite clear. We can now state several of the consequences that can be expected under the Act.

First, we address the potential impact on gas shortages. Before the passage of the NGPA, many people (economists and otherwise) had urged that a law be passed to provide incentives sufficient to eliminate shortages in the long run. Past measures, including curtailment and emergency procedures, are clearly not the answer in the long run. The basic economic analysis of this chapter has indicated that a shortage will prevail whenever the price of natural gas is below the marginal cost of producing gas. If we are concerned about eliminating shortages over a long period, the appropriate marginal cost includes not only the fairly small cost of extracting additional gas from an existing well, but also the costs of exploration, development, and maintenance that will go into the long-run calculations for producing additional gas.

A first observation is that the new law will indeed help to reduce the shortage as the weighted average price of gas as well as the price of new gas at the wellhead rises closer to marginal production cost. It should surprise no one that shortages will exist during the interim; indeed, the point of having an interim is to moderate price increases relative to immediate deregulation, with full recognition that some (though declining) shortages will occur.

However, a second observation is in order here, one dealing with the period after 1985. It may come as a surprise to some that the present law provides incentives to a shortage even then. While new-gas prices can be expected to approximate marginal costs after 1985, old-gas prices will not. Thus, the weighted average price of gas at the wellhead will be below marginal cost.

The extent of the post-1985 shortage will diminish over time as new gas comprises a larger and larger part of gas production streams. It will also diminish if rollover contract prices on old gas rise more rapidly than marginal production costs as time passes, although the provisions of Section 106 of the NGPA (see Table 9) indicate that this is not likely for old gas dedicated to interstate commerce before the Act was passed.

A third observation, and one that affects income redistribution, economic efficiency, and the smoothness of transition, is that the price of new natural gas may be well below the world market price of natural gas as we approach the deregulation date of 1985. World oil prices have risen even more rapidly than expected during 1979 and early 1980. If this trend continues, then the price schedule embedded in Section 102 of the Act will almost surely lag behind the market-clearing level of gas prices. Thus it is altogether possible that a significant jump in new-gas prices will occur on the date of deregulation. To the extent that this is true, consumers fortunate enough to be able to purchase gas will benefit in the interim, since weighted average wellhead prices will be held down relative to the unregulated price levels.

If the third observation does in fact develop, there will remain some incentives for producers to hold back production until the date of deregulation arrives. The story here is similar to the one discussed earlier in connection with incentives to hold back production during the 1970s. Producers can decide to supply new gas before 1985 at the lower regulated prices, or wait until deregulation when they can obtain higher prices.

With respect to economic efficiency, two basic kinds of questions can be asked. First, will the new law lead to a more efficient use of our natural gas resources? And second, what kinds of incentives remain for inefficient uses of natural gas under the law?

The analysis given earlier in this chapter suggests that the economic efficiency of resource allocation will be improved when the price charged for the resource moves closer to the marginal cost of production. Thus, in a broad sense, since we expect the weighted average wellhead price to be closer to marginal cost under the NGPA than under the former system of regulation, the new law will indeed lead to a more efficient use of our natural gas resources.

Regarding the second question, it should be obvious that between now and 1985, both old and new gas prices will, for the most part, be held down below marginal costs. Thus the weighted average price at the wellhead will also be less than marginal cost. This is no surprise, again because the purpose of the transition is to "phase in" deregulation. Thus, the conclusion that resource allocation will remain inefficient during the transition, although less so than under a continuation of the old policies, is valid.

What may be surprising to some is that the new law will also provide incentives for inefficiency in the long term, after 1985. The reason is the same one given earlier to show why some shortages will prevail after 1985. The weighted average price of gas at the wellhead will be below marginal cost, even after new gas is deregulated, because old-gas prices will be below marginal cost. The extent of this inefficiency will depend on the rate at which the FERC permits old-gas prices to rise after 1985.

Two other sources of inefficiency are present in the NGPA. First, under the incremental pricing provision of the Act, the burden of high-cost gas is placed on certain large industrial (nonexempt) users. To understand the nature of the inefficiency, suppose that the incremental pricing provision leads to a price for nonexempt users equal to the BTU equivalent of oil, P_o. Suppose also that the price of gas for exempt users is $(P_o - 50\text{¢})$ per Mcf. It may be that some nonexempt users value the gas at $(P_o - 10\text{¢})$ and some exempt users value the gas at $(P_o - 40\text{¢})$. The exempt users would desire to purchase the gas, whereas the nonexempt users would not, at the respective prices charged to each group. In this example some gas would be allocated to (exempt) users who placed a lower value on the gas than the deprived (nonexempt) users. This kind of inefficiency can be expected to exist as long as exempt and nonexempt users pay different prices under the incremental pricing provision of the NGPA.

A second potentially important source of inefficiency is the NGPA specification of ceiling prices that differ by the type of well. Let us construct an example to illustrate this type of inefficiency. Suppose that regulation imposes a ceiling of 40 cents per Mcf on gas produced for well A and $1.80 per Mcf on gas from well B. Possibly a substantial increase in the rate of production could be obtained from well A by any of a number of technological processes (such as water flooding, fracturing the formation to improve the rate of flow, and chemical treatment) that might raise the marginal cost of production to, say, 50 cents per Mcf. These improvements will not be made, however, since regulation allows only 40 cents per Mcf. At the same time, well B is producing gas that costs as much as $1.80 per Mcf. Thus it is quite likely that the total cost of producing any given amount of gas is much higher under the NGPA than it would be if differential price ceilings were not in force.[35]

CONCLUSION

The natural gas industry has never been either completely regulated or deregulated at the wellhead since 1938. Between the Natural Gas Act of 1938 and the *Phillips* decision of 1954, the statutory basis for such regulation was evidently in place, but it was not until the *Phillips* decision that regulation was enforced. Even then intrastate wellhead prices were uncontrolled, and there were serious administrative problems in regulating interstate prices. The best evidence available suggests that regulators had no real effect in holding interstate wellhead prices down below the levels that would have prevailed absent regulation, at least until about 1970. During the 1960s no shortages were evident, and wellhead prices in interstate markets were approximately the same as the prices in the uncontrolled intrastate markets.

When the 1970s arrived, however, with a rising demand for energy and increased world oil prices, the FPC did hold interstate wellhead prices below the levels that would have been observed absent regulation. Shortages occurred. Natural gas reserves declined. The FPC was forced to let new-gas prices rise to avert worse shortages. The clamor for deregulation of wellhead prices led to many proposals that were rejected amidst intense debate before the passage of the Natural Gas Policy Act of 1978.

This new Act forms the framework for the deregulation of certain categories of natural gas at the wellhead. But deregulation is not complete. Previously unregulated intrastate markets are now regulated, at least until 1985. Old gas in interstate markets will not be deregulated, even after 1985. Neither will gas from stripper wells, from the Prudhoe Bay in Alaska, or from certain offshore areas.

It is not an easy task to analyze a piece of legislation that appears to have as many objectives as the Natural Gas Policy Act of 1978. In one rather lengthy fell swoop it apparently seeks to promote efficiency in the use of energy resources, to provide at least a partial solution to the problem of gas shortages, to remove the incentives to dedicate new reserves only to intrastate markets wherever possible, to decrease reliance on imported energy, to distribute much of the burden of high-cost gas to large industrial users, and to do all these things without large inflationary consequences.

We have concluded that the Act will lead to reduced shortages, both in the interim period and after 1985. However, it will not totally eliminate shortages either in the interim or after 1985.[36]

The Act will lead to substantial improvements in the efficiency with which natural gas is used. However, it will not totally eliminate the old incentives for inefficiency, and it has introduced some new incentives for inefficiency, including incremental pricing and differentiated price ceilings for a large number of types of gas.

The NGPA does eliminate the incentive for producers to dedicate new reserves only to intrastate markets wherever possible. However, it does not include provisions to strongly reverse the historical dedications of gas reserves, so that areas that desperately need clean-burning natural gas, such as the Southern California Air Basin, will not receive very large amounts, especially in the near term.

Finally, there is some doubt as to whether the pricing schedules for new natural gas and new onshore wells, as described in Sections 102 and 103 of the Act, will lead to a price as high as the unregulated price that will prevail at the end of the transition period. Thus, at the end of transition one might expect a jump in gas prices as deregulation occurs. Further, this may create incentives for producers to hold back production to some extent, particularly in the years immediately preceding deregulation.

Finally, we have described a potentially serious problem of extranormal transfer payments between affiliated producers and pipelines, even though the supply of gas at the wellhead is quite competitive. At the minimum, close scrutiny by regulators of pipelines will be required.

NOTES

[1] "The Economics of the Natural Gas Controversy," staff study of the Subcommittee on Energy of the Joint Economic Committee, Congress of the United States, September 19, 1977, p. 16.

[2] See, for example, "An Analysis of the Impact of the Projected Natural Gas Curtailments for the Winter of 1975–76," a report of the Office of Technology Assessment, November 4, 1975.

[3] See, for example, *Barrett* v. *Kansas Natural Gas Co.,* 265 U.S. 298 (1924).

[4] Kahn (1971), Vol. 1, p. 30.

[5] Natural Gas Act, 52 Stat. 821 (1938), 15 U.S.C.A. 717 et seq., Section 1(a).

[6] *Ibid.,* Sections 4(a) and 4(b).

[7] *Ibid.,* Section 4(c) and 4(d).

[8] *Ibid.,* Section 4(e).

[9] *Ibid.,* Section 6(a).

[10] Kohlmeier (1969), p. 193.

[11] See Section 1(c) of the Natural Gas Act.

[12] *Phillips Petroleum Company* v. *Wisconsin et al.,* 342 U.S. 672 (1954).

[13] See MacAvoy (1970a), p. 154.

[14] Kahn (1971), Vol. II, p. 31.

[15] National Gas Survey (1975), Vol. 1, p. 85.

[16] See *In re Phillips Petroleum Company,* 24 FPC 537 (1960).

[17] This justification was suggested by Kahn (1970), Vol. 1, p. 43.

[18] *Permian Basin Area Rate Cases,* 390 U.S. 747 (1968).

[19] Federal Power Commission Annual Report for 1974, p. 41.

[20] *Ibid.* p. 41. An existing well, producing from one set of reservoirs, may be redesigned (or recompleted) to produce from other reservoirs that can be reached by that well. This may be accomplished by deeper drilling, or by perforating the casing in the well to allow for production from a different reservoir.

[21] House of Representatives, Report No. 94-732, p. 6.

[22] FPC Order No. 467-B in Docket No. R-469, March 2, 1973.

[23] These data were drawn from the *Monthly Energy Review,* Department of Energy, October 1979, p. 90.

[24] As a technical point, the use of consumer surplus exactly measures the welfare change for an individual if there are zero income effects associated with the demand schedule. However, Willig (1973) has shown that even if there are nonzero income effects, the measure may serve to approximate the actual welfare change.

[25] For a more detailed critique of the MacAvoy and Pindyck approach, see Braeutigam (1978).

[26] Natural Gas Survey (1975), Vol. I, p. 57.

[27] See Scherer (1980), p. 62.

[28] If the pipeline were regulated by rate of return with no regulation of the wellhead price, the pipeline might have an incentive to act to some extent as a monopsonist.

[29] National Gas Survey, Vol. I, p. 57.

[30] MacAvoy (1970a), p. 160.

[31] *Ibid.,* p. 168.

[32] NGPA, Title III.

[33] See the comments of Commissioner Charles B. Curtis, "The NGPA: One Year Later," remarks delivered before the Interstate Oil Compact Commission, Los Angeles, California, December 3, 1979, p. 2.

[34] *Ibid.,* p. 4.

[35] For more on this point, see *Pricing Provisions of the Natural Gas Policy Act of 1978,* Energy Policy Study, Vol. 3, Energy Information Administration of the Department of Energy, pp. 15–17.

[36] There is evidence that the supply of gas will continue to increase at higher gas prices. In its 1978 Annual Report to Congress, the Energy Information Administration of the Department of Energy reported that the "1977 drilling footage rate more than doubled the low 1971 rate" (p. 166 of Vol. 3). The monthly energy reports of that agency indicate that the number of exploratory wells drilled has increased substantially throughout the 1970s.

BIBLIOGRAPHY

An Analysis of the Impacts of the Projected Natural Gas Curtailments for the Winter 1975–76, report of the Office of Technology Assessments, November 4, 1975.

Annual Report of The Federal Power Commission, 1974.

Balestra, P., *The Demand for Natural Gas in the United States*. Amsterdam: North Holland Publishing Company, 1967.

―――― and Nerlove, M., "Pooling Cross-Section and Time Series Data in the Estimation of a Dynamic Model: The Demand for Natural Gas," *Econometrica*, 34:3 (July 1966), 585–612.

Braeutigam, Ronald R., "An Examination of Regulation in the Natural Gas Industry," *Study on Federal Regulation*, appendix to Vol. VI, United States Senate Committee on Government Operations, December 1978.

Breyer, S. G., and MacAvoy, P. W., *Energy Regulation by the Federal Power Commission*. Washington, D.C.: The Brookings Institution, 1973.

―――― and ――――, "The Natural Gas Shortage and the Regulation of Natural Gas Producers," *Harvard Law Review*, 86:6 (April 1973), 941–987.

Demsetz, H., "Why Regulate Utilities," *Journal of Law and Economics*, April 1968.

Erickson, E. W., and Spann, R. M., "Supply Price in a Regulated Industry, The Case of Natural Gas," *The Bell Journal of Economics and Management Science*, 2:1 (Spring 1971), 94–121.

FPC News (Federal Power Commission), 8:35 (August 29, 1975).

Gas Facts. American Gas Association, Inc., Department of Statistics, annual.

Hausman, J. A., "*Project Independence Report:* An Appraisal of U.S. Energy Needs Up to 1985," *Bell Journal of Economics*, Autumn 1975.

Helms, Robert B., *Natural Gas Regulation, An Evaluation of FPC Price Controls*. American Enterprise Institute for Public Policy Research, 1974.

Jones, William K., *Cases and Materials on Regulated Industries*, 2d ed., and Statutory Supplement. La Habra, Calif.: The Foundation Press, Inc., 1976.

Kahn, Alfred E., *The Economics of Regulation: Principles and Institutions*, Vols. I and II. New York: John Wiley & Sons, 1971.

Khazoom, "The FPC Staff's Econometric Model of Natural Gas Supply in the U.S.," *Bell Journal of Economics and Management Science*, 1971.

Kitch, E. W., "Regulation of the Field Market for Natural Gas by the Federal Power Commission," in Paul W. MacAvoy (ed.), *The Crisis of the Regulatory Commissions*. New York: W. W. Norton & Co., Inc., 1970.

Kohlmeier, Louis M., Jr., *Watchdog Agencies and The Public Interest: The Regulators*. New York: Harper & Row, 1969.

MacAvoy, Paul W., "The Regulation-Induced Shortage of Natural Gas," *Journal of Law and Economics*, 14:1 (April 1971), 167–199.

――――, *Price Formation in Natural Gas Fields*. New Haven: Yale University Press, 1962.

――――, "The Reasons and Results in Natural Gas Field Price Regulation," in Paul W. MacAvoy (ed.), *The Crisis of the Regulatory Commissions*. New York: W. W. Norton & Co., Inc., 1970 (reference 1970a).

――――, *Price Formulation in Natural Gas Fields*. New Haven: Yale University Press, 1962.

――――, "The Effectiveness of the Federal Power Commission," *Bell Journal of Economics*, Spring 1970 (reference 1970b).

―――― and Pindyck, Robert S., "Alternative Regulatory Policies for Dealing with the Natural Gas Shortage," *The Bell Journal of Economics and Management Science*, Autumn 1973.

MacAvoy, Paul W., and Pindyck, Robert S., *Price Controls and the Natural Gas Shortage.* American Enterprise Institute for Public Policy Research, 1975.

Natural Gas Curtailments, 1975–76 Heating Season. National Gas Task Force, Federal Energy Administration, October 1975.

"Natural Gas Policy Act of 1978: Interim Regulations," Federal Energy Regulatory Commission, *Federal Register,* December 1, 1978, part VIII.

National Gas Survey, United States Federal Power Commission, 1975.

National Petroleum Council, *United States Energy Outlook.* Washington, D.C., December 1972.

Owen, B., and Braeutigam, R., *The Regulation Game: Strategic Use of the Administrative Process.* Cambridge, Mass.: Ballinger Publishing Co., 1978.

Pricing Provisions of the Natural Gas Policy Act of 1978, Energy Information Administration, United States Department of Energy, Energy Policy Study, Vol. 3, October 1979.

Sales by Producers of Natural Gas to Interstate Pipeline Companies, Federal Power Commission, annual.

Scherer, F. M., *Industrial Market Structure and Economic Performance.* New York: Rand McNally & Co., 1980.

Smith, V. L., "Economics of Production from Natural Resources," *American Economic Review,* June 1968.

The Natural Gas Industry, Hearing before The Subcommittee on Antitrust and Monopoly of The Committee on The Judiciary, United States Senate, June 26–28, 1973.

U.S. Federal Power Commission, *Annual Report.* Washington, D.C.: U.S. Government Printing Office, annual.

Weiss, Leonard W., and Strickland, Allyn D., *Regulation: A Case Approach.* New York: McGraw-Hill Book Company, 1976.

Wellicz, S. H., "Regulation of Natural Gas Pipeline Companies: An Economic Analysis," *Journal of Political Economy* 71:30 (1969) 30–43.

Wilcox, Clair, and Shepherd, William G., *Public Policies Toward Business,* 5th ed. Homewood, Ill.: Richard D. Irwin, Inc., 1975.

Willig, R. D., "Consumer's Surplus Without Apology," *American Economic Review,* 66:4 (September 1976), 589–97.

CASE 6

Decontrol of Crude Oil Prices

W. David Montgomery
United States Department of Energy

INTRODUCTION

In 1971 crude oil produced in the United States was placed under federal price controls. Through the seventies those controls, supplemented by an allocation program and regulation of refined-product prices, evolved into a complex system including multiple pricing tiers and an ingenious system of cross payments among refiners that rolled in the high cost of imported oil with the lower cost of domestic oil. The price at which crude oil could be sold depended on numerous factors including the date on which production of oil from a particular property began, the amount of oil produced, the kind of recovery method employed, and the location and viscosity of the oil itself. The price charged consumers for refined products was also held below market levels. Increased oil imports prevented a shortage of crude oil from developing.

Throughout its history, the system of petroleum price controls imposed two clear and direct net economic costs on the nation. By holding the prices that could be charged for some categories of oil below the cost of imports, price controls discouraged production of domestic oil that could have been produced at a cost less than the price of imported oil. The difference in cost was a net loss to the economy. Petroleum pricing and allocation regulations also held the prices of petroleum products in the United States below the level they would have reached if all crude oil had been priced at the cost of the marginal source of supply — imported oil. As a result, petroleum products were used in applications in which they had a value less than the cost of importing and refining oil. The difference again represented a net loss to the economy.

The magnitude of these efficiency losses varied a great deal during the seventies, as the structure of crude oil price controls and the relation between average crude oil prices in the United States and world oil prices changed. The subsidy to oil consumption ranged from a low of $2 to a high of $5 per barrel. In percentage terms, the subsidy ranged from 15 to 30 percent. Assuming a medium-term demand elasticity of −0.2 to −0.4, those subsidies could have stimulated demand by anything from 400,000 to 800,000 barrels per day.

Generalizing about the size of the disincentive to domestic production throughout the history of controls is impossible because of continual changes in the definition of the pricing tiers. In some cases, incremental oil produced from a domestic property could receive the world oil price, so that virtually no disincentive existed. In other cases incremental production received prices much below the world oil prices. To complicate matters further, producers' expectations about the future of price controls undoubtedly affected current production incentives.

The difference between the price of oil in the lowest tier of production and the world oil price grew from virtually nothing in 1973 to over $20 per barrel by 1979, and the difference in the ceiling price for the upper tier of controlled oil and the world oil price became as large as $15 per barrel. Throughout the period some oil was exempt from controls.

The price regulations in effect at the end of 1979 would have created a major disincentive to domestic oil production if they had been continued indefinitely. The Department of Energy forecast that continued controls would have reduced domestic oil production by at least 800,000 to 1,200,000 barrels per day in 1985 and 1,200,000 to 1,800,000 barrels per day in 1990 — a 10 to 15 percent decrease in 1985 and a 15 to 25 percent decrease in 1990 below the levels forecast with decontrol.

In addition, more subtle costs were imposed. Congress required a "small-refiner bias" in the operation of the pricing regulations that provided small refiners with a subsidy on purchases of crude oil. It led to the construction or continued operation of numerous small, inefficient refineries and, together with the general crude oil cost advantage enjoyed by domestic refiners, led to excessive costs of refining oil in the United States. Those costs could have been avoided by some importing of finished products instead of crude oil. Finally, the excessive oil imports stimulated by price controls helped to shore up world oil prices and to increase the nation's vulnerability to disruptions in world oil markets.

These efficiency losses were suffered in order to prevent very large wealth transfers within the economy. In some conditions, the income redistributed by oil price controls could have exceeded the net efficiency losses by an order of magnitude. Working away from price controls required a delicate compromise between efficiency and equity.

There have been two major decision points in the history of price controls. In late 1975, the law authorizing controls on petroleum prices — the Emergency Petroleum Allocation Act of 1973 (EPAA) — was due to expire. At that time Congress extended the life of controls and, indeed, required a rollback of crude oil prices. Two factors weighed heavily in that decision: one was the fear that another increase in energy prices would drop the economy back into recession, and the other was the unwillingness to transfer wealth from consumers to energy producers. If oil prices had been decontrolled in 1975, consumer expenditures on oil and oil-related products would have risen by over $13 billion, as would revenues of oil producers. Something under half of those producer revenues would have in turn been collected by the U.S. Treasury as corporate income taxes.

The mandatory price controls established by Congress in 1975 were scheduled to convert to discretionary controls in May 1979, facing the President with the choice of whether to continue oil price controls. In April 1979, President Carter announced his intention of phasing out crude oil price controls by October 1981, the date on which all price-control authority would expire. In order to limit the wealth transfers that would accompany decontrol, the President also proposed legislation to establish an excise tax on crude oil produced in the United States. The resulting "Windfall Profit Tax Act" was signed into law on April 2, 1980. With passage of that tax, the compromise necessary to dismantle the apparatus of economic regulation of the oil industry was achieved.

THE ORIGINS OF PRICE CONTROLS

Price controls were first placed on crude oil produced in the United States on August 15, 1971, when President Nixon announced the wage-price freeze that inaugurated his Economic Stabilization Program. As part of an economywide attempt to control inflation, those controls were not directed toward any particular characteristics of the oil industry. However, rising prices of oil in the world market and the crisis of the Arab oil embargo of 1973 quickly led to the development of a special system of oil price controls.

The Cost of Living Council created a sophisticated two-tier system of price controls for crude oil just before the Arab oil embargo. While the embargo was in effect, Congress passed the Emergency Petroleum Allocation Act (EPAA), which gave the President specific authority to regulate the price and allocation of crude oil and petroleum products. From passage of the EPAA on, crude oil price controls changed continually, as congressional, administrative, and executive actions followed — and indeed trod — on each other's heels.

The primary purpose of the EPAA was to create an allocation program that would mitigate the effects of petroleum shortages caused by the 1973 embargo. Price controls were authorized as an adjunct to the allocation program, but with the clear purpose of preventing windfall profits to energy producers that would result from a rise of domestic oil prices to the price of imported oil, and of transferring those potential profits into the hands of consumers as low energy prices. Coping with inflation was not mentioned as a purpose of price controls, and only terse mention was made of "economic efficiency" and "minimization of economic distortion, inflexibility, and unnecessary interference with market mechanism."

THE INSTITUTIONALIZATION
OF PRICE CONTROLS

The system of crude oil price controls created by the CLC was continued by the Federal Energy Administration (FEA) under the authority granted by the EPAA. Consequently, crude oil price controls continued after termination of the Economic Stabilization Program removed price controls from other sectors of the economy. Under the EPAA, imported crude oil was exempt from controls. All domestic oil was classified in two tiers, only one of which ("old oil") was subject to price controls.

"Old" oil was defined as oil produced at a specific location in quantities less than 1972 production levels at that location. The price of old oil was set at the posted price in effect at that field on May 15, 1973, plus $1.35 per barrel. That rule resulted in an average price of old oil of about $5 per barrel.

Crude oil produced in excess of 1972 production levels from the same location ("new oil") and oil from properties that averaged less than ten barrels per well per day was exempt from controls. In addition, each barrel of new oil produced "released" one barrel of old oil from controls. By December 1975, uncontrolled oil was selling at a price of $13 per barrel, about equal to the world oil price. Because of "released" oil, the additional revenue generated by producing a barrel of new oil was about $21 — the price of new oil plus the increase in the price at which old oil could be sold.

When this two-tier system of controls was introduced, there was little difference between old oil and new oil prices. However, the price of imported oil, and with it the price of oil exempt from controls, quadrupled between August 1973 and June 1974. As a result, problems of preventing increases in the price of refined products became intractable. In addition, the access to price-controlled crude oil tended to be politically unpopular major oil companies, leading to demands for protection of small and independent refiners.

To rectify these problems, an ingenious "entitlements" system was devised. Each refiner was required to possess one entitlement for every barrel of price-controlled oil refined. Refiners who were issued fewer entitlements than barrels of oil refined were required to purchase an entitlement from some refiner with an excess of entitlements over barrels of crude oil refined.

Entitlements were given to each refiner monthly; each received a number of entitlements equal to the number of barrels of price-controlled oil it would run if the percentage of controlled oil in its total crude oil input were the same as the national average. If the percentage of controlled oil exceeded the national average, the refiner had to purchase additional entitlements from some other refiner that was given more entitlements than needed for the amount of controlled oil in its refinery runs. For example, in December 1974 the national average percentage of controlled oil in refinery inputs was 40 percent. A refiner that ran 1 million barrels of oil in that month would receive 400,000 entitlements. If it were in fact using only 200,000 barrels of controlled oil, it would have 200,000 entitlements to sell, whereas if it were using 800,000 barrels of controlled oil, it would have to buy 400,000 entitlements.

The number of entitlements that refiners were required to sell in every month equalled the number that must be purchased. Ideally, the price of an entitlement would have been set so that the cost advantage that would be created by greater access to controlled crude was exactly removed. Such a price would equal the difference between the cost of controlled oil and the cost of uncontrolled oil. In September 1975 the average cost of controlled oil was $5 and the average cost of imported and uncontrolled oil was $12.50. If an entitlement was worth $7.50, any refiner who substituted a barrel of imported oil for a barrel of controlled domestic oil (raising crude costs by $7.50) would have available an unused entitlement that could be sold to recoup that $7.50.

Entitlements also made the marginal cost of crude oil to any refinery equal to its average cost. Consider the case of a refiner deciding to increase refinery runs by one barrel. Suppose that the refiner must choose between a barrel of controlled oil at $5 per barrel and a barrel of imported oil at $12.50 per barrel. If the controlled oil were purchased, the refiner would need an additional entitlement, but would automatically receive four-tenths of an entitlement (because total crude oil input would increase by one barrel). When an entitlement was worth $7.50, purchasing the controlled oil would actually cost $9.50 per barrel [$5.00 + (0.6 × 7.50)], because the refiner would gain the $3 value of the additional four-tenths of an entitlement.

Similarly, if one additional barrel of imported oil were purchased, the refiner would need one less entitlement and would receive an additional four-tenths of an entitlement worth $3. The net cost of a barrel of imported oil would thus be reduced to $9.50 per barrel. Consequently, no matter whether the refiner bought a barrel of oil at the average uncontrolled (import) price or at the average controlled price, its costs after entitlements would be the same. That cost would in turn equal the national average cost of all crude oil inputs — in this case (0.4 × $5) + (0.6 × $12.50) = $9.50.

Because refiners faced a marginal cost of crude oil less than the world oil price, competition held the prices of refined products below the level they would have reached in the absence of price controls. Consequently, the entitlements system made refined product price controls largely unnecessary.

There is some controversy about whether the entitlements system held refined-product prices down by the full difference between world oil prices and average crude oil costs. In the absence of any price controls, domestic crude oil prices would have risen to world levels and refined product prices would have equalled the world crude oil price plus refining costs and normal profits. With price controls and entitlements, refined product prices would equal the lower *average* cost of crude oil plus refining costs and normal profits. Apparently, the price of refined products would be held down by exactly the difference between world oil prices and average crude oil cost. Refining capacity in the United States was limited, however, and the United States has always had to import some refined products. Competition between imported and domestic refined products may have bid up the price of domestic products, leading refiners in turn to overutilize domestic refining capacity. As a result, some potential cost savings would go into increased refining costs and profits. Exactly how much difference the competition with imported products made in domestic product prices has never been decided.

Entitlements were also used to redistribute revenues among refiners. Early on, small refiners were granted an additional allocation of entitlements each month, in inverse ratio to their size, and as a result enjoyed lower average crude oil costs than large refiners. As the system matured administratively, more and more adjustments were made to the entitlements system to provide special incentives or to redistribute revenues among refiners.

ECONOMIC LOSSES FROM PRICE CONTROLS

The price control system in effect under EPAA created inefficiencies in the production and in the use of oil. With a given level of energy demand, efficient production of crude oil implies keeping the total cost of oil — the total resources used to produce oil domestically and to pay for imported oil — as low as possible. In order to achieve the most efficient allocation of resources in oil production, domestic oil production should include all oil that can be produced at a unit cost less than the price of imported oil. This efficient use of resource requires that production rates for all domestic oil fields be adjusted so that marginal cost — the cost of increasing output by one unit — is equal everywhere. Marginal cost of domestic production should also equal the price of imported oil. If marginal cost of domestic production were greater than the cost of imported oil, it would be possible to save resources by decreasing domestic output and increasing imports. Alternatively, if marginal cost of any domestic energy production were less than the cost of imports, it would be possible to save resources by increasing domestic production and reducing imports. In the absence of crude oil price controls, domestic crude oil would sell at a price approximately equal to the landed cost of imported crude oil of similar characteristics, thus satisfying the conditions for economic efficiency.

An efficient level of demand for crude oil would be one in which oil was used only in ways that had an economic value no less, per unit of oil consumed, than the price of imported oil. This result could be achieved if each consumer paid a price for refined products that was based on the cost of imported oil. As long as demand exceeds domestic supply, every change in demand changes the level of imports in a like amount, increasing or decreasing the energy bill by the cost of imports. Unless consumers pay the full price of oil that they cause to be imported, consumption decisions will not be based on the real trade-offs involved in energy use. Consequently, a system that charges consumers less than the cost of imports can create a loss in efficiency.

The legislative history of oil price controls makes it clear that an additional criterion for evaluating crude oil programs has to do with the distribution of wealth. Congress intended that price controls should prevent the transfer of income from oil consumers to oil producers and owners of oil properties. The magnitude of that transfer can be estimated by subtracting the revenues that crude oil producers actually receive from selling domestic crude oil under price controls from the amount they would have earned on that quantity of crude oil in the absence of price controls. The transfer of income is a cost to one sector of the economy, but a gain to another. The cost and the gain cancel each other out from the point of view of economic efficiency.

Another criterion by which oil price controls may be judged is their impact on oil imports. The efficiency criterion specifies a level of imports at which the cost of obtaining oil is a minimum. Because of the potential damage that reduction in supplies or increases in the price of imported oil could cause, a case can be made that imports should be lower than the level at which the cost of increasing domestic production equals the price of imports.

Because oil price ceilings are set on a property-by-property basis, evaluation of those controls requires shifting perspective from a domestic supply curve to an individual property marginal-cost curve (Figure 1). The area above the marginal-cost curve and below a horizontal line at the selling price of crude oil equals producers' profits. A multipart pricing system can, in principle, transfer some of those profits to consumers without changing crude oil production. A two-tier system of prices for domestic crude oil can be superimposed on the marginal-cost curve as a step function. So long as the price function is entirely above the marginal-cost curve, it should have no effect on production decisions. If the price function offers market-level prices at an output level less than that at which marginal cost equals market price, there will be no marginal effect on output. However, if the price function crosses the marginal-cost curve, a producer may be unwilling to produce up to the point at which marginal cost equals the world oil price.

Price function A, for example, lies entirely above the marginal-cost curve. The profit-maximizing choice is to produce at Q_3, just as it would be if all output could be sold at the world price, but with price function B that need not be the case. Profits are the difference between the triangle labeled $(+)$ and those labeled $(-)$. Even though marginal cost equals price at Q_3, total profits may be negative when Q_3 is produced, or they may be positive but smaller than profits from producing Q_1 or Q_2 (where marginal cost also equals price).

The more tiers there are, the closer the price function can come to approximating the marginal-cost curve. Putting the price function closer to the marginal-cost curve makes it possible to reduce profits and

Figure 1. Price Ceilings and Oil Production

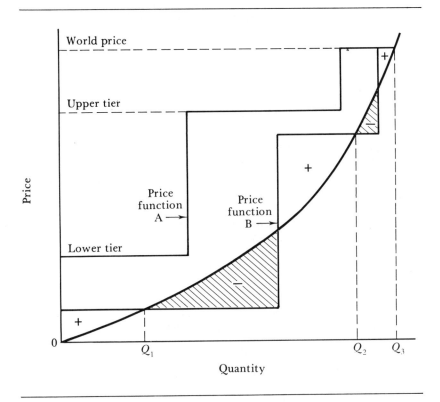

the average price of domestic crude oil without affecting production incentives.

Under the EPAA many producers found themselves in a situation where, because of the depletion of oil deposits on given properties, their actual production rates had fallen significantly below the level at which additional production became exempt from controls. Production at rates below the base level created a "cumulative deficiency" in production, which must be paid back, under EPAA regulations, before any production above the base level qualified for exempt prices. As a result, producers were discouraged from increasing production, even though the world oil price was available on the margin.

Producers who did maintain production above the base level received an excessive price for additional oil production because of the released-oil provision. The substantial increase in drilling of additional wells from old fields that occurred while EPAA rules were in effect may have resulted from this provision. This "infill" drilling increased the depletion of existing reserves at the expense of the exploratory drilling that would have added new reserves.

THE CONTINUATION
OF CONTROLS

The price control and allocation authorities granted in the EPAA were scheduled to expire on August 30, 1975. During the summer and fall of 1975, when Congress faced a decision regarding extension of controls, attention had shifted from dealing with an acute shortage to dealing with the consequences of the high price of imported oil. Despite price controls on domestic crude oil, the precipitate increase in the average cost of crude oil during 1974 caused substantial increases in the cost of petroleum products to consumers. Those price increases were in turn seen by many economists as partially responsible for plunging the economy into a deep recession during 1974 and 1975.

Congress and President Ford took different positions on the extension of price controls, with Congress generally favoring slower removal of controls than was proposed by the President. The Energy Policy and Conservation Act (EPCA) passed in December 1975 was a compromise between those two positions. It made two important changes in oil price regulation: it rolled back the prices of some domestic crude oil and it provided for gradual easing of price controls over 39 months beginning in February 1976. In all other respects, EPCA left the prior regulatory program in effect. The price rollback mandated in EPCA was accompanied by a set of energy conservation programs designed to substitute for higher prices in controlling demand and some nonprice measures to increase production.

The legislative history of the EPCA reveals that Congress intended continued price controls to prevent the macroeconomic disturbances and increased cost of living that would result from a precipitate increase in energy prices. Despite the provision for easing of price controls, the legislative history establishes no clear intent to achieve ultimate decontrol. Indeed the committee report that accompanied the House version of EPCA made a strong case for continued controls.

The EPCA required the President to develop a system of crude oil price controls that would result in an average price of domestic crude, at its first sale, of $7.66 per barrel. At the time EPCA was passed, that average price was $8.63. Consequently, the Federal Energy Administration faced the task of revising the structure of price controls to reduce the weighted average price.

The EPCA also allowed the average price of domestic crude oil to rise at an annual rate not to exceed the rate of inflation plus 3 percent.

In August 1976 Congress amended the EPCA to allow average crude oil prices to increase at a rate of 10 percent per year and to revise the structure of price controls. The conference report on these amendments stated that "the dramatic change in the inflation rate (to 3 percent in mid-1976) itself evidences the ability of the economy to absorb more substantial real dollar price increases." Because of this change, Congress amended the EPCA to allow greater increases in crude oil prices, and directed FEA to use some of the newly allowable price increases to give additional incentives to the use of exotic methods to increase production from existing fields ("tertiary recovery"), to remove some regional crude oil price differences, and to exempt stripper wells from price controls.

The system of price controls created under authority of the EPCA, as amended, was based on the classification of all domestic crude oil into three tiers. The third tier, including imported oil, stripper-well lease oil, and some categories of oil eligible for special incentives, was exempt from controls. The definition of the two lower tiers hinged on the concept of a "base production control level" (BPCL) of oil production. In the initial stage of implementation of EPCA, the base production control level for any property was set "equal to that property's average monthly production and sale of *old* crude oil during calendar year 1975." "Old oil" is synonymous with oil subject to price controls under the system that existed until February 1976.

If the quantity of oil produced on a property did not exceed the base production control level, all oil from that property fell in the *lower tier* of price controls. If production from a property exceeded the base production control level, the difference between actual production and the base production control level went into the *upper tier,* and the remainder (equal to the base production control level) went into the lower tier. The upper tier also included all oil from properties that began production after December 1972.

During the first month of the new price regulations (February 1976), ceiling prices on lower tier oil were identical to those that existed under the previous control program. The price ceiling on upper tier oil was below the level at which uncontrolled oil sold before enactment of the EPCS, providing a new disincentive to domestic exploration and production. The new price ceiling was set equal to the highest posted price for a particular grade on a particular field on September 30, 1975, less $1.32 per barrel.

The changes in the definition of the base production control level and in domestic oil price ceilings constituted the first stage of implementation of EPCA. The initial stage of implementation of EPCA set the base production control level for each property at or below the rate of production at which the per barrel cost of increasing output equalled the lower tier ceiling price, except for some properties producing released oil during 1975. It did so by revising the base production control level to equal actual production in 1975. In theory, producers without released oil set their 1975 production at the level at which marginal cost equaled the price ceiling. The second stage, announced in April 1976, provided for gradual increases in ceiling prices and gradual reduction in the BPCL for all properties that continued to produce only lower tier oil.

The adjustment in the base production control level was intended to prevent the increasing disincentive to increasing production observed under the previous set of price controls, which specified a *fixed* base production control level. By eliminating this disincentive, the adjustment eliminated much of the efficiency loss associated with price controls on fields producing only old oil under EPAA.

Whereas the adjustment in the BPCL was intended to compensate for the effects of naturally declining production rates, the ceiling price adjustment was intended to compensate for the effects of inflation on costs of production. Inflation could, by shifting the marginal-cost curve up, have an effect similar and additional to the effect of reservoir decline. The two adjustments resulted in a situation in which any increment to production that could be obtained through investment in enhanced recovery would be sold at upper tier prices.

The initial schedule of price increases announced by FEA was based on FEA's estimates of the average price of domestic crude oil in January 1976. New data collection methods revealed after several months that FEA had underestimated the average domestic price. To bring its regulations into compliance with EPCA, FEA "froze" all oil prices, delaying the schedule of increases. The first such delay of two months was announced on June 30, 1976. As additional price data became available, they revealed that average prices were remaining above the levels allowed under EPCA. During 1976 the price "freeze" was extended two more times, and it remained in effect on December 31, 1976.

Amendments to the EPCA and changes originated by FEA in the definitions of oil that could be sold at upper tier prices also took effect during 1976. Their effect was to make the rate of decline in the proportion of lower tier oil in total domestic production greater than forecast. As a result actual prices exceeded forecast prices. In January 1977, FEA acted to remove "excess receipts" by reducing upper tier price ceilings by $0.20, and in March it reduced price ceilings by a further $0.45.

On September 9, 1977, FEA announced its final system of crude oil price ceilings. Because excess receipts had been eliminated, crude oil prices could again be allowed to rise. FEA announced that upper tier prices would be returned to their February 1976 level. Thereafter upper and lower tier prices would be increased at a rate equal to the rate of inflation. Reclassification of lower tier oil into the upper tier through operation of the automatic BPCL adjustment and incentives to expensive production techniques would continue. FEA estimated that reclassification plus scheduled ceiling price increases would just use up the statutory 10 percent annual rate of increase in the average price of domestic crude oil. Sufficient slack was, however, believed to exist that incentive prices for tertiary and newly discovered oil would be possible.

Under the EPCA, the entitlements system continued to flow low costs of price-controlled oil through to consumers, leading to inefficient use of refined products.

DECONTROL

The EPCA gave the President discretion as to whether to continue price controls after May of 1979 — all authority for price controls was to lapse in October 1981.

On April 5, 1979, the President announced his intention to phase out crude oil price controls at the wellhead between June 1, 1979, and September 30, 1981. DOE then adopted a series of rules to carry out the President's direction. Effective June 1, 1979, DOE allowed certain low-volume, deep-production properties ("marginal" properties) to release 80 percent of their lower tier production to upper tier levels. The same rulemaking allowed all other lower tier production to be released to upper tier levels at the rate of 1.5 percent per month from June 1 to December 31, 1979, and at the rate of 3 percent per month thereafter. Effective January 1, 1980, upper tier production was released to uncontrolled levels at the rate of 4.6 percent per month. These schedules would result in the phasing out of all crude oil from controls by September 30, 1980.

In addition, action was taken to release entirely certain types of crude oils from price controls. Effective June 1, 1979, all newly discovered crude oil (oil produced from a property that was not producing in 1978) was released from controls. Incremental production from certain qualified tertiary enhanced production projects was exempted from controls in a rulemaking effective September 1, 1978, and effective October 1, 1979, DOE adopted a rule under which producers could release from controls a specified portion of their current production in order to provide revenues for the "up front" financing of high-cost, high-risk tertiary projects. Finally, effective August 17, 1979, the President by executive order exempted heavy oil of 16 degrees gravity or less from price controls and, effective December 21, 1979, this exemption was expanded to include all crude oil of 20 degrees gravity or less.

The President's announcement of his intention to eliminate crude oil price controls was coupled with a legislative proposal for an excise tax on crude oil that would recapture some of the additional revenues going to energy producers. In many ways, this tax replicated portions of the crude oil price control system. However, it eliminated major portions of the economic inefficiency inherent in crude oil price controls.

Most important, decontrol coupled with the windfall profits tax eliminated the subsidy to oil imports. It eliminated the averaging of price-controlled crude oil with expensive imports in the determination of petroleum product prices. As a result, oil consumers faced the full costs of petroleum imports.

Forecasts done during congressional consideration of the Windfall Profit Tax Act indicated that decontrol of crude oil prices would add a cumulative total of $900 billion to oil producers' net revenues between 1980 and 1990, compared to continuation of the exact price ceilings then in effect. Of those net revenues, over $400 billion would have been collected through the normal federal corporate income tax and through state and local taxes. The Windfall Profit Tax Act was designed to collect an additional $227 billion in revenues from oil producers — or about half of the after-tax profits resulting from decontrol.

The windfall profit tax was designed as an excise tax and based on existing categories of price-controlled oil. Crude oil is divided for tax purposes into three tiers, based on its classification under price controls. In each tier the "windfall profit" on selling a barrel of oil is defined as the difference between a tier-specific base price and the actual selling price. This difference is taxed at a rate ranging from 70 percent, for the tier that includes most categories of oil in the lowest tier under oil price controls, to 50 percent for stripper-well oil, to 30 percent for oil exempted from price controls before passage of the tax. Independent producers were taxed at reduced rates on their first 1,000 barrels per day of production, and certain categories of oil were exempted entirely. The windfall profit tax will phase out over 33 months beginning sometime in 1988–1991, depending on when the $227 billion revenue target is reached.

It was recognized throughout the deliberations that the windfall profit tax would lessen the incentive to produce oil in the United States, compared to decontrol without a windfall profit tax. The various tiers and tax rates were designed, albeit roughly, to maximize production incentives within the constraint of raising sufficient revenues to alleviate a major portion of the wealth transfer that decontrol could cause. The tier-three tax on newly discovered oil, heavy oil, and incremental tertiary oil is the source of almost all the lost oil production. Oil in this tier is subject to a 30 percent tax on the difference between the actual selling price and $16.55, adjusted for inflation plus 2 percent for differences in quality and location. For comparison, oil that was exempted from controls in 1979 sold for as much as $29 per barrel in that year.

Because exploration, heavy oil production, and enhanced oil production can involve costs in the $20- to $30-per-barrel range, it is very likely that some projects that would be profitable with $28 oil prices would be made unprofitable by the windfall profit tax. On the other hand, keeping newly discovered and other types of oil in the upper tier of price controls would have held their price under $14 per barrel on average, if 1979 ceilings had been continued.

On the demand side, the windfall profit tax and decontrol completely eliminated the subsidy to oil consumption that existed under price controls, so that for the first time in ten years consumers will face appropriate price signals for efficient use of oil.

Overall, removal of crude oil price controls was achieved through a classic compromise. With the doubling of world crude oil prices in 1979, the economic and other costs of subsidizing the consumption of imported oil and restraining domestic energy production became too great to bear — as did the wealth transfers of decontrol. In an admittedly imperfect compromise, both considerations were given some weight in combining decontrol with a crude oil excise tax. In the process, it became possible to dismantle a major portion of the economic regulation imposed on the oil industry.

CASE 7

OSHA after a Decade: A Time for Reason

Albert Nichols
Richard Zeckhauser
Harvard University

INTRODUCTION

The goal of the Occupational Safety and Health Act (OSHAct) of 1970 was "to assure so far as possible every working man and woman in the nation safe and healthful working conditions." [1] By enacting this legislation, Congress hoped to solve what the House Committee on Education and Labor identified as an "on-the-job health and safety crisis." [2] Indeed, two years after the Act's passage, one of its coauthors expressed the hope that by 1980 injuries would be reduced by "50 percent or something like that." [3] That first decade has passed and the performance of the Occupational Safety and Health Administration (OSHA), the Labor Department agency created to carry out the OSHAct's provisions, has been found wanting. None of a number of studies of the agency's effectiveness has detected an appreciable (harsher critics would say noticeable) reduction in workplace accidents in America.

Copyright © 1981 by Albert Nichols and Richard Zeckhauser. Substantial portions of this paper draw on our earlier studies, "Government Comes to the Workplace: An Assessment of OSHA," *Public Interest*, no. 49 (Fall 1979), and "The Occupational Safety and Health Administration — An Overview," in U.S. Senate, Committee on Governmental Affairs, *Study on Federal Regulation*, appendix to Volume VI, December 1978. We thank the editors of the *Public Interest* for permission to use excerpts from that paper. We thank Richard Claman for valuable research assistance, and Nancy Fairweather, Nancy Jackson, and Michael Klass for valuable comments.

OSHA's problems run deeper than failure to produce appreciable results. The agency has become perhaps the most prominent symbol of misguided regulation intended to achieve social goals. Much of this notoriety derives from a number of ill-advised and readily ridiculed detailed safety standards. Few newspaper readers remain ignorant of OSHA's 140-odd ladder standards, or its meticulous requirements governing the height and coloration of fire extinguishers, or the requirement that life jackets be worn when crossing empty creek beds. To its credit and benefit, OSHA has now eliminated many of its most ridiculous standards and many of its nuisance standards. But those were hardly the most serious difficulties.

OSHA's problems have been much more fundamental than the setting or acceptance of silly standards or the imposition of excessive paperwork. A primary defect in the agency's approach to the occupational safety problem has been its excessive reliance on direct regulation through standards enforced by inspections, as opposed to incentive approaches or voluntary contracting between labor and management. Moreover, until recently OSHA overwhelmingly emphasized occupational safety while virtually ignoring the potentially far more serious problem of occupational health. The agency has now begun to venture into occupational health, but it remains hostile to the idea that the choice between alternative regulations (or regulatory approaches) should be made on the basis of their expected accomplishments and costs — a primary principle for reasoned government action.

A variety of pressures are encouraging OSHA to reform its mode of operation, however reluctantly. The Schweiker Bill currently before Congress would exempt a large number of workplaces from OSHA inspection for such reasons as small size or exemplary safety record.* The Supreme Court recently upheld a circuit court decision overturning OSHA's tightened benzene standard. At the very least, the Court's ruling should force OSHA to make some effort to estimate the health gains associated with future standards. In response to initiatives such as these, OSHA is making more vigorous efforts to target its inspections in productive ways and to consider benefits and costs in setting priorities for standards and enforcement, though not in defining ultimate standards. In looking at the changes that have been made, it is difficult to determine what portion is designed to fend off political pressures and what part is agency identification of superior methods. We should also note that the agency makes continual efforts to rally its supporters, principally the organized labor movement, to its defense.

* Senate bill S.2153, introduced December 19, 1979 by Senator Richard Schweiker, would, among other provisions, exempt firms with low injury rates from routine safety inspections.

We argue here that it is a time for reason. To be constructive, the critics of OSHA should focus on areas in which the fundamental thrust of the agency may be in error, rather than on operational flaws that draw media attention. OSHA itself must awaken to reality. In a time of increasing economic stress, the agency cannot continue to ignore the relationship between the health and safety benefits it tries to promote and the cost of producing them. And Congress must be aware that OSHA is unlikely to have the political freedom or internal desire to reform itself; it may even lack the statutory leeway to do the job.

We first outline the problem that OSHA confronted, in terms of the number of those suffering from health and safety impairment on the job, and the conceptual arguments about why the unfettered labor market might or might not achieve acceptable levels of occupational health. We review the evidence on OSHA's performance to date. We then delve more deeply into the failings of OSHA's approach, paying particular attention to its first major ventures into occupational health. Occupational health will almost certainly be the major area for OSHA activity in the 1980s and is already the focus of fierce debate on appropriate approaches. We conclude by outlining possibilities for beneficial reform of our nation's approach to occupational safety and health.

The Problem at the Outset

The OSHAct was passed during a time of marked enthusiasm for the potential role of the federal government in increasing levels of safety and health in a variety of areas. During a brief period around 1970, Congress passed new legislation regulating coal mine health and safety, air pollution, consumer product safety, and automobile safety.

At the time of the OSHAct's passage, few congressmen appear to have questioned either the need for federal regulation of occupational safety and health or the proposition that the best way to address these problems was through a system of detailed regulations enforced by inspections. Testimony before congressional committees stressed the magnitude of the "problem." In 1970 the National Safety Council estimated that each year more than 14,000 workers died on the job, and another 2.2 million suffered disabling injuries.[4] Supporters of the OSHAct pointed with alarm not only to the annual toll, but to the fact that after many decades of decline, occupational injury rates had risen from the midfifties through 1970. Although good data on occupational illnesses were unavailable then, as now, the limited evidence available indicated that job-related diseases were an even larger problem; one HEW study, extrapolating from very limited data, suggested that 390,000 cases of occupational illness were incurred each year, resulting in as many as 100,000 annual fatalities.[5] Continued rapid growth in the number of chemicals in the workplace was seen as a further cause for alarm.

The data and testimony presented to Congress created an air of crisis, with the implication that swift and decisive action was required and would lead to rapid and significant improvements. Thus, the OSHAct embodies the "enact now, assess later" approach to regulatory development. Leaving aside for the moment the question of how best to approach the problem of occupational safety and health, it is important to consider what levels of attainment should be sought. Subsequently we shall argue that OSHA's failure to address this question appropriately may be the primary source of the agency's major problems in the next decade.

APPROPRIATE LEVELS OF HEALTH AND SAFETY

Some naive critics might be tempted to argue that occupational injuries or illnesses should be completely eliminated. A zero-rate goal, however, is obviously infeasible. Indeed, short of closing our workplaces, we could not prevent some accidents and illnesses even if we devoted 50 percent of our nation's resources to occupational safety and health. A less extreme argument would be that all avoidable accidents and dangerous exposures should be eliminated. But what is meant by avoidable? If these accidents were avoidable at no cost, there would be no debate. The critical question turns out to be one of price. What are we willing to pay in foregone benefits elsewhere to reduce risk in the workplace?

In most areas of our economy, the answer to such questions is provided by the competitive market. The price of a good is the value of the resources it entails put to their best alternative uses. A number of economists from the time of Adam Smith have suggested that this approach is also appropriate to gauge the value of occupational safety and health. They ask: What levels of health and safety would be achieved in perfectly competitive markets with full sharing of information and no externalities? The equilibrium levels that would be produced would bear the features — both attractive and (as the critics of economic approaches will remind us) unattractive — of any competitive equilibrium.

With the hypothetical competitive market outcome as the point of departure, the next question would be in what ways real markets depart from the hypothetical ideal. This method of reasoning, we argue, not only yields a qualitative idea of the magnitude of the problem, but also suggests useful modes of government intervention. We argue further that even someone who rejects the competitive market outcome as an ideal would find that going through this exercise gave him useful information on when and how to intervene.

Wages and Health
in a Competitive Market

Levels of occupational safety and health are determined by the decisions of both workers and employers. Accidents and illnesses impose economic costs on workers, such as lost wages and medical expenses. In many instances, nonpecuniary losses, such as pain, anxiety, and the tragedy of premature death, are substantially more important. To induce workers to accept risky employment, employers have to pay wage premiums over and above normal compensation for otherwise equivalent work. In addition, accidents may impose costs on employers in the form of insurance premiums — both health care coverage and workers' compensation (formerly called workmen's compensation) — and the disruption of production.

In addition to compensating workers for accepting risks, wage premiums play a second role. They provide incentives to firms to improve health and safety levels as a means of reducing their labor costs. Assuming that the market works well, the outcome is efficient; through its actions, the firm minimizes the sum of the costs of preventing accidents and illnesses and the costs of the accidents, such costs being assessed by the workers in terms of wage premiums they demand. Assuming that their increased income would not change their valuations of health and safety risks, this is the same level of prevention that would prevail if the workers themselves owned the firm.

Although the concept of wage premiums for hazardous work is an old one in economics, attempts to estimate the empirical magnitudes of such premiums have appeared only recently. In the first such major study, Thaler and Rosen estimated wage premiums in a high-risk sample of occupations to be of the order of $136,000 to $260,000 per expected life lost in 1967 dollars.[6] Smith, using industry-level data, found much higher premiums, in the range of $1.5 to $2.5 million per expected life lost.[7] Viscusi also found evidence of substantial wage premiums, in the range of $1 to $1.5 million per life lost and $6,000 to $10,000 per nonfatal injury, based on 1969 data.[8] In a complementary line of investigation, Viscusi estimated that workers who perceive their jobs to be "dangerous" or "unhealthy" received about $400 extra per year in 1969.[9] (Over one-half of Viscusi's blue-collar sample rated their jobs as "dangerous or unhealthy.")

Market Imperfections

These and other studies make it clear that workers are at least partially aware of the risks they run and that the wage premiums paid for hazardous work are substantial. They do not tell us, however, whether the market is working at 5, 50, or 100 percent efficiency. Two major problems might occur. First, workers may not be fully informed or fully understand the risks they run. Second, even if workers fully understand risks, other parties besides the firm and worker may have an interest in occupational safety and health decisions; that is, there may be externalities.

Imperfect or Misunderstood Information. The perfectly competitive model assumes that both workers and management know the magnitude of risks and the costs of reducing those risks. This information must be available, transmitted to the affected parties, and understood.

Problems arise at each of these three stages. Not surprisingly, the data relating workplace conditions to health and safety outcomes are poor. Although such information would be valuable across a wide range of workplaces, no individual or firm has sufficient incentive to produce the optimum amount. After all, he would have to bear the full cost while reaping only a small fraction of the benefits. Here is a clear potential role for government — to collect and disseminate information on the causes of occupational injuries and illnesses and on mechanisms for reducing them.

To be useful, information must also be disseminated in a form that is understandable to workers and firms. Experimental and empirical evidence suggests that individuals have a great deal of difficulty processing information about small probabilities, which characterize most occupational safety and health problems.[10] Firms are unlikely to provide accurate information on risk levels to their workers, if indeed they have it themselves. Information problems are likely to be particularly severe with regard to health (as distinct from safety) threats. Even with large-scale, long-term studies using relatively sophisticated statistical techniques, epidemiologists find it difficult to identify occupational carcinogens unless the increased risk is substantial. The chances that an individual worker will notice that working with a particular chemical even doubles his long-term risk of lung cancer is almost nil. By contrast, safety problems are likely to result in much more immediate effects that workers or their representatives can detect.

It seems quite possible that workers are reasonably well informed about the relative riskiness of different occupations and industries but cannot tell, for example, whether one metal-stamping plant is safer than another. If so, wage premiums will still be observed between industries but not between firms within an industry. The impact of such premiums on company behavior will be limited, since, continuing the example above, improvements in health or safety at one metal-stamping plant will not lower wage premiums at that plant, except indirectly through a minor lowering of the overall industry risk level. The critical element for effective market behavior is that each firm receive full recognition, and hence full credit, for improvements in its safety performance.

Externalities. As is well known, competitive markets will not allocate resources efficiently if transactions generate costs or benefits external to the participants. Externalities provide the primary economic justification for government regulation of pollution; in the absence of intervention, economic factors do not bear the costs their pollution imposes on others and hence devote insufficient resources to reducing it. That externality is direct and physical in nature. In the case of occupational safety and health, instances in which nonworkers are physically harmed are unusual. Most commonly, the externality is financial in nature. To a significant extent, the costs of occupational illnesses and injuries are borne by society at large, and not solely by the individual worker and his employer. The family of a worker killed on the job, for example, is likely to qualify for survivor benefits under Social Security. More generally, the whole medical care system is laced with subsidies, so that when a worker seeks medical care, a substantial portion of the cost is borne by taxpayers as a whole. The retired worker who develops cancer as a result of earlier occupational exposures to a carcinogenic chemical, for example, is likely to have his medical bills paid by Medicare. Private insurance plans also generate financial externalities of precisely this sort. If their participants have no mechanism to influence each other to choose appropriately low risk levels, government efforts to reduce privately accepted levels of risk might be justified.

Before rushing to accept government intervention on the basis of financial externalities, we should ask: (1) What is the relative importance of such externalities for job-related injuries and illnesses? (If firms and workers bore the full expected costs of their risk-accepting actions, would they be much more cautious?) (2) Might some other mechanism, such as greater experience rating for workers' compensation, or merit rating for medical insurance based on behavior, be a better way to reduce the externality? (3) How well can we expect government intervention to perform? Note also that the financial-externalities argument for government intervention, to the extent it is relevant, applies to a broad range of human activity. When people choose to smoke, overeat, or engage in any activity that might prove deleterious to their health, those who contribute to their medical care are adversely affected.

Workers' compensation was originally viewed in part as an incentive for employers to provide greater safety. In fact, however, only the largest firms are fully experience-rated (i.e., pay a premium that reflects their past safety record) or, equivalently, self-insured. For small- and medium-sized firms, most of the cost of workers' compensation is unrelated to the firm's own safety record.

The relative importance of externalities seems to be much stronger for occupational health than for safety. Because there is often a long latency period before adverse reactions are identified, it may be hard to trace such conditions back to particular workplaces. Few cases of illness result in any payment of workers' compensation. In many circumstances, the health-program equivalents of workers' compensation are funded at least in part by the government, or on an industrywide basis, without attention to the particular conditions at a workplace. Thus, even though the Black Lung Fund is financed by a per-ton tax on coal, on this basis alone no individual firm has sufficient incentive to reduce exposure to dust in coal mines.

It is important to distinguish the importance of externalities across different types of health problems. The major effect of exposure to noise, for example, is to impair hearing, but not to a degree that is disabling. Thus workers bear most of the costs in the form of reduced function and enjoyment. The asbestos worker, who may develop lung cancer ten or twenty years after exposure, presents quite a different problem. The costs of providing him with medical care and of supporting his family if he dies or is disabled are likely to be widely spread. Note also that the problem of inadequate information provides stronger support for intervention with asbestos than with noise. The presence of noise is obvious, and its link to hearing loss is easy to comprehend. By contrast, substances such as asbestos are carcinogenic at levels too low to detect with the unaided senses, and the ultimate link to health loss may well be too obscure or too delayed for an individual worker to notice.

In summary, problems of externalities and imperfect information are the two primary theoretical justifications for government intervention to promote occupational safety and health. Both provide their strongest justification for long-term disabling health problems, rather than for less serious threats to health, such as hearing loss, or for safety.

Goals of Intervention:
Efficiency and Equity

Efficiency. Our analysis, like most economic analyses of regulatory issues, focuses on efficiency concerns. In the strictest sense, efficiency in
the sphere of occupational health and safety would require that we
seek to minimize the sum of the two classes of costs that are of concern,
namely: (1) the costs of occupational injury and illness, and (2) the
costs of avoiding safety and health risks in the workplace. In general,
there is a direct trade-off between these two classes of costs. Tightening
an exposure standard, for example, is likely to lower health costs while
raising avoidance costs. As Figure 1 illustrates, the sum of the two
costs (the two crosshatched areas) is minimized where the marginal cost
of further tightening the standard is just equal to the marginal reduction in health costs.

Once the efficiency objective is laid out in this way, one runs into
the hornet's nest of valuing lives or, to describe the problem as it
actually arises, of valuing low-probability risks to lives. Without such
valuation, there would be no metric with which to combine the two
classes of costs.

A more conceptual, though no less emotional, argument against
aggregating costs of avoidance and health loss is that they may be borne
by different parties — business, workers, and members of the general
public in their roles as consumers and taxpayers. This argument would
be more compelling if OSHA had substantial ability to redistribute resources among these groups over the long run. We do not believe it
can, certainly not in anything approximating a modestly efficient
manner.

A major justification for our focus on efficiency is our belief that
governmental efforts to impose occupational safety and health (OSH)
standards above those dictated by efficiency will end up hurting, not
helping, workers in general, at least to the extent that labor markets
over the long run are roughly competitive. Let us say, for example, that
an OSH-promoting measure is promulgated that workers value at
$2,000, but that is inefficient because it costs $3,000 to provide. The
demand curve for labor will fall by $3,000 and the supply curve will
shift down by $2,000. The $1,000 inefficiency will be taken up partly
by a fall in effective wages (dollars plus OSH benefits) and partly by
reduced employment. That some OSHA interventions help some particular workers is not in question. But they do so at the expense of
other workers. That is not the type of redistribution that OSHA's supporters claim to seek.

Fortunately, OSHA's performance can be improved substantially
without confronting the life-valuation issue or resolving the question

Figure 1. Choosing the Efficient Level for a Standard

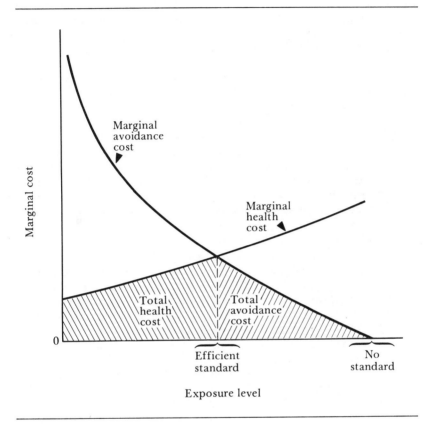

Exposure level

of who gains from what at the expense of whom, if we think of efficiency in the more limited sense of maximizing output (in this case health benefits) for a given amount of input (resources spent on OSH promotion). In the language of policy analysis, OSHA should seek to order its interventions in a cost-effective manner.

OSHA sacrifices cost effectiveness whenever it requires that resources be spent to save lives at high cost when other areas of expenditure would yield more lives saved because those lives can be "purchased" more cheaply. This kind of misordering occurs when a specification standard is used, preventing firms from employing cheaper ways of providing the same benefits. (In evaluating personal protective equipment such as respirators, for example, the cost of using such equipment should include the worker's demand for additional compensation because it is uncomfortable.) When OSHA requires substantial monitoring and medical surveillance of individuals whose exposure to risk is minimal, it creates misordering. When, as with the benzene standard, OSHA concentrates on the politically attractive target of oil and chemical companies, but excludes the local gas station, whose workers may be subject to greater risk, it contributes to cost ineffectiveness. And when OSHA refuses to quantify the benefits of its health-promoting interventions, it deprives itself of even knowing how substantial its misordering might be.

Even if OSHA rejects the view that costs are inherently important, there remains a strong argument why it should pursue cost effectiveness. OSHA, like any governmental organization, has limited political capital, and hence a limited ability to impose resource costs on society. It should therefore direct its limited resources in an efficient manner to achieve maximum production of occupational safety and health.

Equity. We recognize that in discussions of appropriate levels of occupational safety and health, most observers find equity a compelling criterion. Most agree that safety and health threats to workers vary significantly from industry to industry and from occupation to occupation, and that those exposed to the highest risks are disproportionately the poor and the unskilled. Moreover, economic theory predicts that the unhindered market would tend to generate such outcomes. Poor people, on average, will be willing to accept risky work for lower compensation than higher-income individuals would demand.

It is on matters of interpretation and inference for policy that the sharpest disagreements arise. The proponents of social programs for occupational safety and health start, for the most part, with the belief that all American workers have what Representative Phillip Burton called the "inalienable right to earn their living free from the ravages of job-caused death, disease, and injury." [11] The notion is that bodily integrity is not a commodity appropriate for trade on the market, any more than one's vote or freedom is.

Those who believe that occupational safety and health levels should be determined through market processes (modified by regulation only to the extent that the conditions assumed by the competitive market model do not hold) argue in response that individuals assuming risks receive wage premiums for doing so. The worker chooses his level of safety for himself. If the government prohibits certain classes of risky activities, it may well be diminishing the economic prospects of the very people it wishes to help, the most disadvantaged members of society.

Why has this argument failed to convince those who view safe and healthful workplaces as a right? First, there is the special nature of health, which is a nonmarket good provided, at least initially, by nature. Second, an undercurrent of paternalistic obligation runs through their thinking; some people — the poor in particular — supposedly will not know enough to choose safe and healthful employment. Third, the correlation between occupational risk and the distribution of income causes discomfort to some proponents of government intervention; losses of life, limb, and workdays draw attention to inequalities in our society that would otherwise be fuzzier in our consciousness. The legislative history of the OSHAct shows quite clearly that equity arguments, with their emotional overtones, were politically effective in securing federal intervention. The implications of these arguments, however, were never spelled out.

GOVERNMENT INVOLVEMENT IN OCCUPATIONAL SAFETY AND HEALTH

State and federal government involvement in the occupational health and safety area has a long history. Government has regulated work practices and workplaces directly and fostered systems to compensate those disabled by job-related injuries and illnesses. Under common-law rules of liability, injured workers always had the right to sue their employers for negligence. This afforded little protection to workers, however, since the process was slow and costly, and employers had a number of sturdy legal defenses.

Workers' compensation laws, administered by the states, were designed to provide workers with more equitable and reliable compensation than was available under tort law and to give employers strong incentives to provide safer conditions. By the time OSHA was enacted, workers' compensation covered roughly 85 percent of all employees. Its cost to employers that year was $4.9 billion, or roughly 1.1 percent of covered payrolls. Still, many deficiencies were perceived in the system. The OSHAct created a commission to study the problem. The commission recommended extension of coverage to all workers, increases in benefit levels (then usually two-thirds of wage), removal of dollar and time limits, and greater coverage of occupational diseases.[12]

OSHA's Approach:
Direct Regulation

Viewing an unacceptable accident rate and a compensation system it felt to be insufficient, Congress wrote the OSHAct to confront the problem of occupational safety directly. The Secretary of Labor, to whom OSHA reports, was charged with promulgating and enforcing standards for protecting workers. In setting standards for "toxic materials or harmful physical agents," for example, the Secretary is directed to "set the standard which most adequately assures, to the extent feasible, on the basis of the best available evidence, that no employee will suffer material impairment of health or functional capacity even if such employee has regular exposure to the hazard dealt with by such standard for the period of his working life." [13] In numerous court battles, thousands of words have been spilled explicating the congressional intent of this passage.

Under the provisions of the OSHAct, OSHA's primary responsibility is to set and enforce standards covering safety and health conditions in the workplace. Most of OSHA's standards have not been written by the agency itself, but rather were adopted en masse in 1971, without critical review, from preexisting federal regulations and from voluntary "consensus" standards written primarily by the American National Standards Institute and the National Fire Protection Association. Of the 4,400 standards adopted in that manner, a few were rescinded fairly quickly, and almost 1,000 were eliminated in 1978. Most of the safety standards are specification standards, detailing, for example, particular types of machine guards or construction requirements for railings. In contrast, the health standards tend to be more performance-oriented, setting, for example, maximum limits for exposure to hazardous substances, but allowing firms some discretion in determining the means by which the limits are achieved. In most instances, however, these exposure limits are supplemented with detailed requirements for medical surveillance and exposure monitoring. More important, in the view of many critics, OSHA has insisted that the exposure limits be achieved by use of engineering controls, such as ventilation or modification of production processes, and has not allowed firms to substitute far less expensive personal protection devices such as respirators or ear muffs (for noise), except where engineering controls are technically infeasible.

Safety regulation through standards leads inevitably to an emphasis on capital equipment — on machine guards, railings, and the like. Many safety professionals question the efficacy of such an approach, since most studies of accidents suggest that far more occupational injuries are caused by worker behavior or temporary conditions than by the types of permanent, equipment-related hazards addressed by OSHA's standards. An early, classic study still cited by some safety experts indicated that almost 90 percent of industrial accidents were due to human error.[14] More recent research has emphasized the interaction of human and mechanical factors. At hearings before the National Commission on State Workmen's Compensation Laws, for example, an official of the National Safety Council estimated that only 18 percent of occupational accidents are caused solely by environmental factors, while 19 percent result from behavioral factors, and fully 63 percent reflect some combination of the two.[15]

Determining the cause of an industrial accident is obviously a difficult and, to a substantial extent, subjective task. Even where careless worker behavior "causes" an accident, redesigned equipment may reduce or even eliminate the consequences of carelessness. Several studies, however, provide more conclusive evidence of the limited potential effectiveness of standards in reducing accidents. Mendeloff asked a group of California state safety engineers to review accident reports; they concluded that only 18 percent of the accidents could have been prevented by a fully effective government inspection program.[16] A report of the Wisconsin state agency concerned with job safety and health estimated that only 25 percent of industrial accidents were due to identifiable physical hazards susceptible to inspection and concluded that worker training and education programs might be more effective than standards. Follow-up studies of accidents in New York and Wisconsin found code violations in only 22 to 39 percent of the cases.[17]

In practice, since inspections are infrequent and will not eliminate all violations, standards-based approaches are likely to perform far below the potential levels suggested above. Before passage of the OSHAct, state occupational safety or health programs varied widely in their stringency; annual expenditures per worker ranged from less than $0.01 to about $2.70.[18] Despite this huge variation in state regulatory efforts, cross-state studies, based on both econometric and case-study approaches, were unable to show that states with tighter standards or more stringent enforcement enjoyed safer or more healthful working conditions.[19] Although much of this evidence suggesting the limited efficacy of standards in reducing accidents was available at the time of the OSHAct's passage, Congress never considered it.

Unfortunately, no studies were or are available on the efficacy of standards in reducing the incidence of occupational illnesses. It may be argued, particularly in the absence of negative evidence, that standards offer more promise for regulating health than safety hazards; in health, a standard can control the hazard itself, rather than some piece of equipment that may or may not contribute to risk reduction. In the health area, OSHA is able to rely much more extensively on performance standards, such as exposure limits. Performance standards, however, are by no means a panacea. The major problem remains one of setting an appropriate exposure level, usually on the basis of very imprecise data.

OSHA's Record on
Injuries and Illnesses

If OSHA had had the kind of dramatic impact on occupational illness and injury rates that its supporters hoped for, that impact would be relatively easy to detect. Unfortunately, the smaller gains that might more reasonably have been expected are difficult to measure. The problem is particularly acute with regard to occupational illnesses. Although the Bureau of Labor Statistics publishes data on occupational diseases, they are of limited utility because they tend to reflect only those illnesses that are obviously work-related, such as rashes caused by contact with certain substances.

Some of the most serious occupational diseases, particularly cancers, are not identifiable as such; it is usually impossible to tell, for example, whether a particular case of lung cancer in an asbestos worker was "caused" by exposure to asbestos, by smoking, or by some other nonoccupational source, even though we know on the basis of epidemiological data and other evidence that asbestos exposure significantly raises the risk of lung cancer. Even if we could measure occupational illness rates, the long latency periods associated with many diseases would mean that recent reductions in exposure would not show up in lower illness rates for many years.

Given the problems cited above, it may never be possible to assess accurately OSHA's impact on occupational disease. Two factors suggest, however, that OSHA's impact to date has been minimal. First, until recently OSHA has not devoted many resources to health. Second, in the small number of cases in which the health benefits of proposed standards have been estimated, the estimates suggest rather modest gains. In our discussion of OSHA's future, we shall return to the salient issue of OSHA's potential impact on occupational health.

In contrast to the situation in health, any significant OSHA impact on injury rates should be observable after almost a decade. From 1972, the first post-OSHA year for which data are available, to 1978, the most recent year for which data have been released, the overall occupational injury and illness rate in the private sector as a whole fell 13.8 percent, for a compound average annual decline of 2.4 percent. That decline, however, was due entirely to a reduction in less serious injuries, those that did not result in any lost workdays. Moreover, more than 100 percent of the overall decline occurred between 1972 and 1975; from 1975 to 1978, the rate rose a total of 3.3 percent.* The lost-workday rate, by contrast, climbed 24.2 percent over the six-year period, for an annual average increase of 3.7 percent. From 1975 to 1978, the average rate of increase was 7.5 percent.[20] In the manufacturing sector, the lost-workday rate rose still faster, at an annual rate of 4.9 percent from 1972 to 1978. This compares with an average yearly increase of only 2.4 percent in the decade preceding passage of the OSHAct.[21]

The raw data on injury rates must be interpreted cautiously, since injury rates are affected by a broad range of factors other than OSHA. It is conceivable that these other factors have changed over time, thus masking the beneficial impact of OSHA. Several studies have attempted to disentangle these factors through multiple-regression techniques. Although the studies are by no means conclusive, they tend to reinforce the impression gained from the raw data: OSHA has not affected injury rates significantly in either a statistical or a practical sense.

Mendeloff has made the only attempt to measure the overall impact of OSHA on national injury rates. He used annual data from 1948 to 1970 to estimate a model of year-to-year changes in the lost-workday injury rate in manufacturing. He then used the model to predict changes in that rate in 1972–1973, 1973–1974, and 1974–1975, after the OSHAct was implemented. For the two earlier periods, his model predicted slightly larger increases than actually occurred, suggesting that OSHA had a slight positive effect. In the last period, however, his model predicted that injury rates would fall more sharply than they did, suggesting the opposite effect. In no case were the results statistically significant.[22] In the same study, Mendeloff tried to measure OSHA's impact in California by looking more closely at the types of accidents judged by safety engineers to be most susceptible to a standards-inspection approach. He found some evidence that such "preventable" injuries were reduced to a level below what would have been expected, leading him to estimate that the effect of the OSHAct was to decrease the overall injury rate by about 2 percent in 1975.[23] His results, however, are open to several objections, including the fact that California operates its own occupational safety and health program, so that results there cannot easily be generalized to OSHA on a national basis.

Another possible explanation for OSHA's apparent failure to have any measurable impact on overall injury rates is that, because of limited enforcement, few firms complied with OSHA's standards dur-

---

* The large decline in 1975 can be explained in large part by the state of the economy; injury rates fall during recessions.

ing the agency's early years. In any one year, less than 2 percent of all workplaces are actually inspected, and the fines for violations were, until recently, trivial. In 1975, for example, they averaged $144 per cited firm. Such small penalties, coupled with low probabilities of inspection, create little incentive to comply with regulations before inspection; again in 1975, only 21 percent of the firms inspected were found in full compliance.[24] Once a firm has been·inspected and found in violation, however, the incentive to comply is much stronger, since the probability of reinspection is much higher, as are the penalties for failure to correct cited violations.

Over time, as the cumulative number of firms inspected increases, as firms replace old equipment with new equipment that meets OSHA's requirements, and as the penalties levied for noncompliance increase (by fiscal year 1979, for example, the average proposed penalty per citation had risen to $511),[25] one might expect compliance with OSHA's standards to grow. To the extent that this argument is correct and the problem is not simply that OSHA's basic approach is flawed, we should see a differential impact on injury rates in those firms or industries inspected most frequently. Three studies have taken such an approach, focusing on the relationship between inspections and changes in injury rates.

During OSHA's first few years, firms in the five industries included in OSHA's Target Industry Program (TIP) were subject to much higher rates of inspection than firms in other industries. Thus, if inspections are effective in reducing serious safety hazards, the TIP industries should have shown greater reductions (or smaller increases) in injury rates. To test that hypothesis, Smith regressed post-OSHA industry-level injury rates against injury rates from 1968 to 1970, changes in employment, and a dummy variable indicating whether the industry was included in TIP. Using several different data sources and either the 1972 or 1973 injury rate as the dependent variable, he obtained mixed results. In some cases the effect of TIP was positive, in other cases negative. In no case, however, were the effects statistically significant.[26]

DiPietro, a Labor Department economist, also obtained inconclusive results using firm-specific data. Her model was quite similar to Smith's for the TIP, expressing each firm's injury rate in 1973 as a function of its injury rate in the prior year, the proportional change in its level of employment, and a dummy variable indicating whether it was inspected in 1973 by state or federal inspectors. She estimated the model separately for each of eighteen industries and, within each industry, for firms in three size classifications. Her results show that in most of the 54 industry/size groups, neither state nor federal inspections had a significant impact on injury rates. Moreover, a substantial majority of the significant coefficients were positive, suggesting that inspected firms had larger than normal increases in injury rates. DiPietro suggests several explanations for this apparently perverse result, including the possibility that firms with higher-than-average increases in injury rates were targeted for more inspections.[27] That is, the causality may have been reversed.

In a more recent paper, Smith has attempted to resolve the issue of causality by distinguishing between "early" and "late" inspections within a given year. His initial results, in which he distinguished only between inspected and uninspected firms, suggested that OSHA inspections increased injury rates by about 10 percent in 1973. He then looked only at plants that had been inspected in 1973, but differentiated between those that were inspected early in the year, in March or April, and those that were inspected late, in November or December. He found that firms inspected early in the year, having more time for inspection effects to operate, had significantly lower injury rates, and that the impact continued into 1974. His results suggested that after some lag, inspections in early 1973 reduced injuries in *inspected firms* on average by about 16 percent, with larger effects in small firms, and smaller effects in medium-to-large firms. The results for 1974 inspections, however, were much smaller and did not achieve statistical significance.[28]

Neither the studies discussed above nor the raw injury-rate data provide conclusive evidence of OSHA's effectiveness in reducing injuries. They do suggest, however, that to the extent OSHA has had any impact on injury rates, that impact has been minimal, far below what the supporters of the OSHAct expected, or at least hoped. Had OSHA's impact been substantial, even the crude measures available would have detected it, and the focus of the debate would be over the magnitude of the effect, not its existence.

Costs of OSHA

In contrast to its minimal impact on injuries and illnesses. OSHA has managed to impose significant costs on the economy as a whole. OSHA's own expenditures of $187 million in 1980 represent only a portion of such costs, most of which are incurred by firms forced to comply with the agency's standards.

Compliance with OSHA's standards can impose a variety of costs, including staff time needed to interpret standards and maintain required records, decreased productivity due to OSHA-mandated work practices, purchase of expensive new equipment, and extensive modification of existing facilities. Firms bear these costs initially, but in most cases pass them on to consumers in the form of higher prices. Workers may bear some of the costs if reduced productivity drives down wages or reduces the ability of U.S. firms to compete with foreign producers. Even to the extent that OSHA-imposed costs reduce corporate profits, workers will be affected indirectly, both as taxpayers (since lost revenues from the corporate income tax will have to be replaced by other taxes) and as shareholders (individually, workers own little equity, but employee pension funds are major shareholders).

Data on the costs of OSHA are scattered, incomplete, and of uncertain accuracy. OSHA itself has made no attempt to develop comprehensive estimates, though it has made prospective estimates of the compliance costs associated with some individual standards. From the results of an annual survey, McGraw-Hill estimates that U.S. firms spent almost $5 billion in 1979 on investment related to employee health and safety.[29] That estimate, however, overstates the cost of OSHA because it includes investments that would have been made even in the absence of the agency. Conversely, it understates OSHA-related costs by not including operating and administrative expenses.

In 1979, the Business Roundtable released its *Cost of Government Regulation Study*.[30] The study, conducted by the accounting firm of Arthur Andersen & Co., estimated the "incremental costs" incurred by 48 companies in 1977 in complying with the requirements of six regulatory agencies, including OSHA. The one-year cost of OSHA for those firms was estimated to be $184 million, excluding such indirect costs as productivity declines and delayed construction. Though the accuracy of this estimate is open to question and the possibility (given the study's sponsor) of anti-OSHA bias cannot be excluded, it suggests that OSHA is costly, especially since the firms studied employ only 5 percent of the civilian work force.

OSHA's own estimates of the costs of its standards provide further evidence on this issue. A 1976 study conducted for OSHA estimated that OSHA's 90 decibels (dBA) noise standard would impose capital costs of $10.5 billion over five years, while the 85 dBA standard that was then under consideration would require capital expenditures of $18.5 billion.[31] Estimates for other standards have been much lower, though still substantial. For example, OSHA has estimated the capital cost of its coke-oven standards to be in the range of $451 to $860 million, with annual costs between $173 and $1,150 million.[32] The benzene standard carries an estimated price tag of $267 million in capital costs, with operating costs of $124 million in the first year and $74 million thereafter.[33] The recently issued generic-carcinogens policy could result in the promulgation of several similarly costly standards each year.

PRUDENT PROTECTION
OF HEALTH: CHALLENGE
FOR THE FUTURE

During most of its first decade, OSHA concentrated the bulk of its efforts on worker safety, with little apparent effect other than to antagonize industry and force the expenditure of several billion dollars. More recently, under the leadership first of Morton Corn and since 1977 of Eula Bingham, both academic experts on occupational health, OSHA has been shifting its priorities toward combating long-term health hazards in the workplace. The staff of industrial hygienists, qualified to conduct health-related inspections, has been expanded, though safety specialists still make up the majority of the inspection force. Concerns about health rather than safety have dominated the development of new standards.

OSHA's increasing attention to health is a mixed blessing. Many observers of OSHA, including ourselves, have argued that the agency should devote more of its limited resources to health hazards, where the rationale for government intervention is stronger and the potential benefits are greater than in the safety area. Health, however, is also an area in which imprudent regulation can prove exceedingly costly, possibly swamping the benefits achieved. Unfortunately, the evidence to date suggests that OSHA is not following the careful and selective approach to health hazards needed to secure major gains in worker health without imposing unreasonable costs.

Throughout its existence, OSHA has argued that its legislative mandate prohibits it from considering the costs of its regulation except where they are so high as to make compliance infeasible without driving a major portion of an affected industry out of business. The agency has refused steadfastly to perform benefit-cost or cost-effectiveness studies. Even when forced by court rulings or presidential orders to conduct economic analyses of standards, it has focused on the ability of the affected industry to bear the costs, rather than on whether the benefits to be derived bear any kind of reasonable relationship to the costs imposed. Two recently promulgated regulations, one covering benzene and the other a "generic" policy for regulating carcinogens in the workplace, illustrate OSHA's approach in the critical health area.

Benzene

In May 1977, OSHA issued an emergency temporary standard (later stayed by court order) lowering the exposure limit for benzene from

10 parts per million (ppm) to 1 ppm averaged over an eight-hour working day. Shortly thereafter, the agency proposed a new permanent standard, which supplemented the 1 ppm exposure limit with a variety of requirements for medical surveillance and exposure measurements of workers in plants using benzene.[34]

Benzene has long been recognized as a hazardous substance. Very high levels of exposure result in severe acute effects, sometimes in death. There is also little doubt that long-term, high-level exposures, in excess of 100 ppm, raise the risk of leukemia. There is much dispute, however, about whether exposures at levels below the preexisting standard pose any significant threat to worker health.[35] OSHA's sense of urgency in issuing the emergency temporary standard was based almost entirely on a single study by the National Institute for Occupational Safety and Health of workers exposed to benzene in the process of manufacturing clear plastic film at two plants in Ohio.[36] That study showed an increased incidence of leukemia among workers who began their employment before 1950. Critics of the study point out that little is known about the workers' exposure levels, with some evidence indicating that exposures were routinely in excess of 100 ppm, sometimes as high as 1,000 ppm. Moreover, although the follow-up period extended to 1975, there were no leukemia deaths after 1961, suggesting that lower exposure levels in later years did not cause leukemia.[37]

OSHA's position on benzene, as on other carcinogens, is that no safe exposure level can be established, so the standard should be set as tightly as technical feasibility will allow. Costs come into play only if significant numbers of firms will be driven out of business. As noted earlier, OSHA's contractor estimated that the benzene standard would require $267 million in capital expenditures with operating costs of $124 million in the first year and $74 million in subsequent years. Fully two-thirds of the estimated first-year operating costs are associated with detailed requirements for medical testing and exposure monitoring; only one-third are for activities designed to lower exposures.[38] Nowhere does OSHA indicate whether it believes these hundreds of millions of dollars will save one life, a dozen lives, or a hundred lives per year. Using a linear dose-response model that tends to overestimate risk, Harvard physicist Richard Wilson estimates that the new standard will not save even one life per year.[39] Quite simply, OSHA made no attempt to estimate the health benefits, arguing that it was not required to do so.

OSHA promulgated its permanent benzene standard in February 1978. In October of that year the Fifth Circuit Court of Appeals struck down the regulation, interpreting the OSHAct to require at least some minimal comparison of costs and benefits: "OSHA's failure to provide an estimate of expected benefits for reducing the permissible exposure limit, supported by substantial evidence, makes it impossible to assess the reasonableness of the relationship between costs and benefits." [40] The decision was a major blow to OSHA's know-nothing policy.

In July 1980, the Supreme Court upheld the Fifth Circuit's decision by a 5 to 4 vote. Unfortunately, the implications of the decision for OSHA's policies are not clear, since the Court's majority could not agree on a single opinion. Four of the justices interpreted the OSHAct to require that before imposing such regulations as the benzene standard, OSHA must show that "the toxic substance in question poses a significant health risk in the workplace." [41] Three of these four justices concluded that since OSHA had not passed even that threshold, the Fifth Circuit's requirement for a "reasonable correlation between costs and benefits" need not be addressed. Only Justice Powell went on to argue "that the statute also requires the agency to determine that the economic effects of its standard bear a reasonable relationship to the expected benefits." [42] The fifth justice in the majority based his decision on the grounds that the relevant portion of the OSHAct invalidly delegates legislative authority to the secretary of labor. [43]

What impact will this split decision have on OSHA's policy toward benzene and other potentially toxic chemicals? The plurality opinion may imply that OSHA could quickly reissue the benzene standard in substantially the same form merely by gathering some expert scientific testimony in support of its position that exposure to benzene and other carcinogens is hazardous no matter how small the dose. We suspect, however, that OSHA will go somewhat further and attempt to make quantitative risk estimates, though it will not perform benefit-cost analyses.

Generic Regulation of Carcinogens

Many of the features of the benzene standard have been incorporated into OSHA's generic carcinogen policy, first proposed in October 1977 and finally promulgated in January 1980. [45] The purpose of the policy is to substantially accelerate the pace at which standards covering carcinogenic substances can be issued. It establishes criteria for categorizing suspect carcinogens and includes model standards for each category. A variety of important issues raised in past hearings are declared closed, not to be considered in setting standards for individual substances. As OSHA itself has noted, "The rulemaking, as described below, may well be the most important single proceeding OSHA has ever had or will ever conduct in the future in this area." [46]

The basic concept of a generic approach to regulating carcinogens is appealing. NIOSH estimates that there are as many as 2,000 possible carcinogens in U.S. workplaces. Under a substance-by-substance approach, only a handful of those substances could be regulated in the foreseeable future. Looking at a number of substances simultaneously, on the other hand, would permit trade-offs to be identified and made more consistent and allow scientific evidence and cost data developed for one substance to be brought to bear on others. Both the quality of standards and the speed with which they are issued could be increased. Unfortunately, OSHA's generic policy reveals little concern with improved decision-making, though the final rule is an improvement over the initial proposal. Rather, the overwhelmingly dominant goal appears to be to speed up a deeply flawed process.

Two aspects of OSHA's policy reveal the sacrifice of quality to speed: (1) the sole criterion for categorizing substances is the number and type of tests showing carcinogenicity, and (2) only two categories are established to encompass as many as 2,000 substances. In its rush to regulate, OSHA has ignored a host of vital distinctions.

The classification system ignores evidence of the potency of potential carcinogens, except indirectly as a factor in setting priorities for initiating regulatory action. Deriving dose-response curves is difficult and fraught with uncertainty, particularly when the data must be extrapolated from very high to very low doses or from laboratory animals to humans. Scientists, however, recognize that carcinogens differ widely in their potency, posing risks that may differ by several orders of magnitude at the same concentration. Thus any sensible regulatory system should attempt to make at least crude distinctions based on potential risk.

Substances classified in category I will be subject to an exposure limit set at the "lowest feasible level," unless a "suitable substitute" is available, in which case no exposure will be permitted. As in the past, OSHA defines feasibility primarily in technical terms, with economic considerations confined to narrow issues of financial viability: "The cost of achieving this level are (sic) compared with the economic capabilities of the affected industries. The regulation issued is designed to be achievable from an economic perspective." [47] OSHA does list the cost of regulation as a factor to be considered in setting priorities, though it is sixth in a list of seven, ahead of coordination with other agencies but behind similarities in molecular structure to other substances.

Substances for which the evidence (though not necessarily the potency) of carcinogenicity is weaker will be classified in category II. The exposure limits for such substances need not be as "low as feasible," but many of the other requirements imposed on category I substances, such as medical surveillance and exposure monitoring, will apply. Since the cost estimates for the benzene standard suggest that these requirements may be extremely expensive, it is not clear that the distinction between the two categories will be as important as it might first appear. The generic policy also codifies OSHA's past insistence that exposure limits be met by engineering controls or work practices, rather than by personal protection (primarily respirators), even though the latter is often far less expensive.

The cost effectiveness of OSHA's new generic-carcinogens policy cannot be analyzed because we do not have reliable estimates of its costs or benefits. An industry group, the American Industrial Health Council, sponsored a study of the costs. It found that initial costs were likely to range between $9 and $88 billion, with annual costs between $6 and $36 billion.[48] Although we doubt the accuracy of any such estimates, given the uncertainties involved, it is clear that the policy will impose enormous compliance costs if it accelerates the process of issuing standards. Given our experience with the benzene case and other standards, we doubt whether under any reasonable set of assumptions the benefits in most cases will be commensurate.

DIAGNOSIS OF OSHA'S FAILINGS

Why has OSHA disappointed to date? How might an understanding of its shortcomings lead to sensible policy for the future? The major problems, we argue, stem from OSHA's failings in three areas:

1. It has moved from preconception to policy, rather than relying on available and accumulating evidence.
2. It decided at the outset to employ a standards approach, although in many circumstances contractual approaches between management and labor or incentive approaches might be superior.
3. It settled on the single objective of maximum protection achievable through the use of controls on capital equipment. This approach excluded consideration of cost except in extreme circumstances.

The Missing Link — Detailing and Weighing Costs and Benefits

The OSHAct makes no explicit provision for weighing costs against benefits. This need not imply maximum possible protection, though the language of the Act is not reassuring in this regard. The concept that absolute protection should be afforded to workers is qualified only in such ambiguous phrases as "so far as possible" and "to the extent feasible." OSHA has taken advantage of this ambiguity and has interpreted "feasibility" primarily in technical terms: Is the technology available to meet a standard? Economic feasibility enters only in extreme cases, when a standard threatens the viability of a substantial number of firms in an industry. The economic feasibility of the benzene standard, for example, was established by reference to the robust financial status of the petroleum industry. It is as though spending dollars does not count unless someone may be forced out of business. OSHA claims that it does consider economic factors in setting the time allowed for abating violations, but again the key consideration is the financial capability of the affected firm or industry, not whether the gains in health or safety justify the expenditure.

As noted earlier, OSHA has consistently refused to subject its standards to any kind of benefit-cost analysis, repeatedly observing that there is no widely accepted method for assigning dollar values to improvements in health or longevity. Although the observation is correct, it does not justify OSHA's failure to integrate cost and benefit considerations into its policy decisions. The rationale for government intervention in workplace safety and health is not that costs should be divorced from benefits, but rather that some costs and benefits may be misperceived by, or are not borne by, private decision-makers.

Since OSHA's procedures have been formulated with minimal concern for economic resources, it should not be surprising that the outcomes are frequently inconsistent and wasteful. For a particular firm, compliance with either standard A or standard B may reduce the number of expected accidents by 10 percent per year. Yet compliance with A may cost only a tenth as much as compliance with B. All parties would be better off if regulatory efforts were adjusted so that low-cost means of increasing workplace safety and health were pursued more vigorously and high-cost measures relaxed.

This argument is only slightly less compelling when we look across industries or classes of workers. Most would agree that we should not, for example, spend $50 million to save one life through medical exams for workers exposed to substance A, while sacrificing another through exposure to substance B to save $500,000. Significant gains could be achieved if resources were directed where they were most productive. In the hypothetical example above, for instance, 99 additional lives could be saved if $50 million were redirected from medical exams to efforts to reduce exposure to substance B. If this process of resource-shifting continued, always seeking the area where the greatest gain could be achieved for a given level of expense, a cost-effective outcome would be reached. Significantly, the cost of securing additional safety and health would be the same in all areas of expenditure.

We conjecture that greater gains can be achieved by making current expenditures cost effective than by increasing overall expenditures by, say, 20 percent. The pursuit of a cost-effective strategy would yield an additional benefit: it would automatically generate information on the cost of further increases in the level of occupational safety and health. This information, now unavailable, should be invaluable to Congress and the executive branch in their decision-making. It is to be hoped that it would also have a significant influence on OSHA itself. In our discussion of the benzene and generic-carcinogen standards, we have outlined the misappropriation of resources that comes from failing to consider both benefits and costs.

Most OSHA standards receive much less economic scrutiny than any of the standards we have discussed. None of the more than 4,000 consensus standards received any cost analysis whatever before adoption. Even under an executive order requiring inflationary-impact studies, most of the analyses have been designed to show that the economic thresholds requiring preparation of complete analysis have not been exceeded. The danger, of course, is that although the economic impact may be "small" relative to the economy as a whole, the gains in worker safety and health, when expressed in comparable units, may be much smaller. No meaningful discussion of costs is possible without some idea of the benefits to be derived, whether measured in dollars or in some other unit, such as lives saved or disabling accidents avoided.

Alternatives to Standards

If direct regulation through a standards and inspection system is to succeed, it must gain widespread acceptance and legitimacy. Otherwise, as OSHA's experience makes clear, it is likely to be frustrated, at least for a significant period, by noncompliance and opposing actions that bring about delays in the courts and other rule-making bodies. Any effort at regulation will also be hurt by administrative shortcomings; OSHA is frequently chided for its management failings. But even startling gains in management will accomplish little if the basic regulatory approach is flawed. At least two additional approaches should be considered, either as alternatives or as complements to standards: expanded provision of information and financial incentives. Both of these approaches seek to harness market forces rather than supersede them.

Provision of Information. Inadequate information may prevent the market from achieving appropriate conditions. The government might provide information in a variety of ways. In some cases it may need only to assemble and analyze existing studies and data. In others, new research — including laboratory experimentation, epidemiological studies, and technical and economic analyses — will be required. The government should also play a role in interpreting and disseminating the information thus obtained. This information could be provided through pamphlets and other written materials or through training for workers and employers. In some cases the government might require that firms provide particular information or training to their workers. Government provision of information could be particularly useful where health and safety issues are made part of labor-management negotiations, a possibility to which OSHA should give more attention.

Current government efforts do include a variety of attempts to provide information. NIOSH conducts and sponsors research. OSHA itself distributes various training materials and booklets and offers a limited number of courses for workers and management. These efforts, however, are tiny in comparison to the resources devoted to enforcement. In part, this represents congressional sentiments rather than agency choices; over the past several years Congress has made its deepest cuts in those portions of OSHA's budget that relate to the provision of information and analysis.

Provision of information will be complementary to whatever other activities the government undertakes. Better information should increase the efficiency of private markets. It will also increase equity to the extent that it increases workers' awareness of the risks they face and enables them to demand compensation or protection.

Incentive Mechanisms. Economists frequently argue that where markets fail to achieve desired outcomes, the appropriate solution is not direct control, but rather modification of the incentives available to market participants. Incentive schemes secure their efficiency advantage by allowing those who are regulated to select their optimal response. In this way individual differences are respected, freedom of action is enhanced, and the costs of inadequate information on the part of the regulator are substantially diminished.

The principle of levying taxes on offending parties when externalities are involved is well established in economics, particularly in relation to pollution issues, where the taxes are referred to as effluent charges. The primary advantage of taxes over a system of uniform standards is that they allow firms to find the most efficient means of reducing the externality and lead to an efficient outcome, in the sense that for any given level of control, expenditures are minimized. Taxes also provide firms with an incentive to develop new procedures for reducing hazards still further — unlike standards, which may block the adoption of innovative technologies. Furthermore, a tax system has the advantage that firms that do not or cannot respond to the incentive pay a penalty.

Even if the injury rate in a hazardous industry is not reduced, the prices of the goods produced will rise, thus shifting demand toward goods produced by less hazardous techniques. (David Lloyd George reportedly noted that workers' compensation puts this principle to work: "The cost of the product should bear the blood of the working man.")

Incentive mechanisms hold particular promise for occupational safety. In place of virtually all of its several thousand detailed safety standards, OSHA could levy a tax on employers for each injury sustained by their workers.[49] An injury tax would give firms generalized incentives to improve safety programs. It would stimulate them to control the whole range of factors that contribute to accidents, not just the limited number of physical conditions susceptible to direct regulation. The mix of activities would vary from firm to firm. Some would probably continue to rely solely on the mechanical safeguards required by standards, but others undoubtedly would try innovative approaches, such as safer work practices and new training programs. Moreover, as the cost of accidents rose, safety records would probably become more important in promotion decisions, thus transmitting incentives down to the lowest levels of management. Firms with unusually good safety records, such as Du Pont (whose injury rate is only a small fraction of the chemical industry's average), are generally suffused with safety-consciousness at all levels.

An injury tax would be relatively easy to administer. It no longer would be necessary to inspect individual workplaces on a regular basis. Firms could either report themselves, as they do for income taxes, or the tax system could be tied to workers' compensation claims, for which the administrative mechanism is already in place. Tying the fines to workers' compensation would give workers an incentive to police compliance by their employers.

Even if it is not coupled with a tax to reflect externalities, workers' compensation should be modified to enhance the incentives for firms to provide safer working conditions — to "make safety pay." But to promote an appropriate level of safety, a firm's compensation costs must reflect its own accident rate, and not simply the average experience of similarly sized firms in the same industry. One way of moving toward this goal would be to require that insurance policies for workers' compensation include significant deductibles and co-insurance rates, both keyed to the firm's size.

What benefits would come from a well-conceived incentive approach to occupational safety? On the resource side, we could avoid the costs of OSHA's irrelevant impositions. Equity would be increased by having workers' compensation pegged at levels that reflect full economic losses. Occupational safety might improve noticeably — but with any reasonable level of incentive, it is unlikely that the accident rate would be cut dramatically. As distasteful as it may be, given the competing claims for resources, we may have to accept a significant level of occupational accidents as an inevitable cost of producing goods and services.

A TIME FOR REASON

OSHA must look to the future, not try to undo its past. Physical standards cannot solve the problem of safety; there are simply too many causal factors. To be effective in this area, OSHA will have to rely heavily on incentive approaches, voluntary contracting between management and labor, and exemptions for firms with strong safety programs or exemplary safety records.

In occupational health, we must expect realistically that OSHA will continue to rely primarily on the direct regulatory approach, employing standards and inspections. This seems inevitable, given the continuing political appeal of direct regulation, OSHA's proclivity for a standards-and-inspection system, the loss of agency power inherent in any other approach, and the practical problems of implementing an incentive-based scheme.

Still, we might hope that where both risks and costs are significant and where workers can be well informed or have well-informed representatives, OSHA decisions could be made in the collective bargaining arena. Organized labor, however, shows no propensities in this direction. It appears that collective bargaining as a solution to setting reasonable occupational health standards is likely to have a career not unlike that of effluent charges for the environment: praised by economists, neglected for the most part by others (including policy makers), successful where employed.[50]

The primary danger as OSHA expands its role in occupational health is not that it will employ the wrong tool or approach, but rather that it will continue to set standards in an unreasonable fashion. In its past actions, as exemplified by its standards for coke ovens, benzene, and carcinogens, OSHA has taken refuge in an extreme and narrow definition of its mandate. It seeks to provide maximum protection to workers independent of economic considerations, except in the rare circumstances where the viability of an industry is at stake.

The purpose of our regulatory system, in situations where the market is performing poorly, is to seek to achieve the outcomes that our citizens would desire for themselves. If OSHA accepted this objective, it would seek reasonable trade-offs between health risks and the costs of avoiding these risks, for that is precisely what our citizens do in a wide range of their activities. As we have pointed out, OSHA refuses even to provide the information that would enable outside observers to determine what trade-offs are being made implicitly.

To persuade OSHA to provide information on the expected costs and benefits of its health interventions would be a gain. To induce the agency to establish its priorities and guide its interventions on this basis would represent an improvement of the utmost importance. But let us not suppose that progress will be easy.

Can OSHA Perform Effectively?

The failures of OSHA and the proximate reasons for those failures are easier to document than the ultimate causes and underlying motivations. Some argue that the seeds of failure were sown with the creation of the agency. Placing it within the Labor Department assured that it would be subject to intense and continuing pressures from organized labor. Its relation to other important interest groups in society would inevitably be one of confrontation.

Others blame the statutory language establishing the agency's mission. The failure to modify "feasibility" with "economic" set the course for neglecting economic costs. The problem cut deeper than mere neglect of economics, however. No language in the original statute explicitly required the agency to demonstrate even a moderate health benefit when establishing a standard. The recent Supreme Court ruling on the benzene standard appears to impose such a requirement, though it leaves open the question whether the agency must give any consideration to the relationship between health benefit and costs imposed. We hope that the ruling on the coke oven standard will require that OSHA attempt to strike at least some balance between protection and cost, but given the narrow and divided decision in the benzene case and the imprecision of the legislative language that created the agency, we are not optimistic.

Other critics assert that OSHA's problems to date relate to an inadequate opportunity to mature — for example, to bring economic analysis into the agency, or to develop means for setting priorities on standards as well as on inspections. They might point with hope to some beneficial steps that OSHA has taken with its generic-carcinogen policy. OSHA has also been making overtures toward allowing labor-management agreements on safety and health measures to supersede some portion of the agency's regulatory interventions. If such steps spring from deep-seated feelings within the agency and if bolder strides can be expected in the future, then internal reform may hold promise.

Our view is more pessimistic. The two major failings we identify are that OSHA refuses to (1) give alternative modes of intervention and protection fair consideration and trial, and (2) make estimates of economic costs and contributions to health and safety the primary considerations in setting standards. We do not believe that these failings can be remedied internally.

If reform is desired, Congress will have to play a major role. Dissatisfied with OSHA's performance, Congress has amended the agency's mandate in marginal ways, such as exempting certain classes of firms from fines or reducing record-keeping requirements. It is now time for more fundamental change. Congress should rewrite its legislation of a decade ago, requiring OSHA to pay attention to both performance and cost in choosing where and how it intervenes.

NOTES

[1] Occupational Safety and Health Act (OSHAct) of 1970, Section 2(b).

[2] House Education and Labor Committee report on the OSHAct reprinted in Bureau of National Affairs (BNA), *The Job Safety and Health Act of 1970* (Washington, D.C.: Bureau of National Affairs, 1971), p. 152.

[3] Representative William Steiger, U.S. Congress, House Committee on Education and Labor, Select Committee on Labor, *Occupational Safety and Health Act of 1970 (Oversight and Proposed Amendments)*, 1972, pp. 274–278.

[4] BNA, *Job Safety*, p. 13.

[5] N. A. Ashford, *Crisis in the Workplace* (Cambridge, Mass.: MIT Press, 1976), p. 47.

[6] R. Thaler and S. Rosen, "The Value of Saving a Life: Evidence from the Labor Market," in N. E. Terleckyz (ed.), *Studies in Income and Wealth*, Vol. 40 (National Bureau of Economic Research, 1975).

[7] R. S. Smith, *The Occupational Safety and Health Act* (Washington, D.C.: American Enterprise Institute, 1976), Appendix B.

[8] W. K. Viscusi, "Labor Market Valuations of Life and Limb: Empirical Evidence and Policy Implications," *Public Policy*, 26 (1978), 359–386.

[9] W. K. Viscusi, *Employment Hazards: An Investigation of Market Performance*, Ph.D. thesis, Harvard University, 1976.

[10] See, for example, A. Tversky and D. Kahneman, "Judgment under Uncertainty: Heuristics and Biases," *Science*, 185 (1974), 1124–1131.

[11] BNA, *Job Safety*, p. 199.

[12] National Commission on State Workmen's Compensation Laws (NCSWCL), *Compendium on Workmen's Compensation* (Washington, D.C., 1972), p. 6.

[13] OSHAct, Sec. 6(b).

[14] H. W. Heinrich, cited in NCSWCL, *Compendium*, p. 287.

[15] *Ibid.*, p. 288.

[16] J. Mendeloff, "An Evaluation of OSHA Programs' Effect on Workplace Injury Rates: Evidence from California through 1974," report submitted to U.S. Department of Labor, July 1976.

[17] The New York Study is cited by W. Y. Oi, "On Evaluating the Effectiveness of the OSHA Inspection Program," report submitted to U.S. Department of Labor, May 1975, p. 42. The two Wisconsin studies are cited by Ashford, *Crisis,* pp. 113–114.

[18] BNA, *Job Safety,* p. 14.

[19] For the econometric evidence, see J. Chelius, "The Control of Industrial Accidents: Economic Theory and Empirical Evidence," *Law and Contemporary Problems,* 38 (1974), 700–729. For a case study, see P. E. Sands, "How Effective Is Safety Legislation?" *Journal of Law and Economics,* 11 (1968), 165–174.

[20] All post-OSHA injury-rate data have been obtained from annual press releases from the Department of Labor, Bureau of Labor Statistics.

[21] *President's Report on Occupational Safety and Health* (Washington, D.C., May 1972), p. 71.

[22] J. Mendeloff, *Regulating Safety* (Cambridge, Mass.: MIT Press, 1979), pp. 102–105.

[23] *Ibid.*, pp. 105–115.

[24] *Job Safety and Health,* 4 (May 1976), 3.

[25] Information obtained from computer printouts generated by OSHA's Office of Management Data Systems.

[26] Smith, *OSHAct,* Appendix C.

[27] A. DiPietro, "An Analysis of OSHA Inspection Program in Manufacturing Industries, 1972–73," unpublished paper, U.S. Department of Labor, August 1976.

[28] R. S. Smith, "The Impact of OSHA Inspections on Manufacturing Injury Rates," *Journal of Human Resources,* 14 (1979), 145–170.

[29] Information obtained from McGraw-Hill, based on "McGraw-Hill Survey of Investment in Employee Safety and Health."

[30] Arthur Andersen & Co., *Cost of Government Regulation Study* (New York: Business Roundtable, 1979).

[31] Bolt, Beranek & Newman, Inc., "Economic Impact Analysis of Proposed Noise Control Regulation," report prepared for OSHA, April 21, 1976.

[32] U.S. Department of Labor, OSHA, *Inflationary Impact Statement: Coke Oven Emissions* (Washington, D.C., February 27, 1976).

[33] Arthur D. Little, Inc. (ADL), "Technology Assessment and Economic Impact Study of an OSHA Regulation for Benzene," draft report to OSHA, undated.

[34] *Federal Register,* 42:103 (May 27, 1977), 27452–27478.

[35] For a survey of the health effects of benzene, see U.S. Environmental Protection Agency, *Assessment of Health Effects of Benzene Germane to Low-Level Exposure* (Washington, D.C., 1978).

[36] P. F. Infante et al., "Leukemia Among Workers Exposed to Benzene," National Institute of Occupational Safety and Health, Cincinnati, April 28, 1977.

[37] These criticisms, made at the OSHA hearings on benzene in July and August 1977, are summarized by E. W. Warren et al., "Post-Hearing Brief of API, NPRA, and Individual Companies," Kirkland, Ellis & Rowe, Washington, D.C., September 22, 1977.

[38] ADL, "Technology Assessment," pp. 1–9.

[39] A dose-response function shows the relationship between the level of exposure and the risk of contracting cancer. Under the linear dose-response model, risk is assumed proportional to exposure, so that even very low levels of exposure to a carcinogen pose some risk. For the specific estimate cited for benzene, see R. Wilson, "Testimony for American Industrial Health Council, OSHA Hearings on Identification, Classification and Regulation of Toxic Substances Posing a Potential Occupational Carcinogenic Risk," unpublished paper, Harvard University, undated.

[40] *American Petroleum Institute* v. *OSHA*, 581 F.2d 493 (1978).

[41] *Industrial Union Department* v. *American Petroleum Institute*, 100 S. Ct. 2844 (1980), opinion of Justice Stevens.

[42] *Ibid.*, opinion of Justice Powell.

[43] *Ibid.*, opinion of Justice Rehnquist.

[44] U. C. Lehner, "Regulations Limiting Worker Exposure to Benzene are Voided by High Court," *Wall Street Journal* (July 3, 1980).

[45] For the final rule, see OSHA, "Identification, Classification and Regulation of Potential Occupational Carcinogens," *Federal Register,* 45 (January 22, 1980), 5001–5296.

[46] *Ibid.*, p. 5007.

[47] *Ibid.*, p. 5245.

[48] Cited in *ibid.*, p. 5238.

[49] For an extended discussion of the merits of an injury tax, see R. S. Smith, "The Feasibility of an Injury Tax," *Law and Contemporary Problems,* 38 (1974), 730–744.

[50] For an extensive analysis of the current and potential roles of labor-management negotiations in improving OSH, see L. S. Bacow, *Bargaining for Job Safety and Health* (Cambridge, Mass.: MIT Press, 1980).

CASE 8

Federal Environmental Regulation

Larry E. Ruff
Brookhaven National Laboratory

The policy response to the emergence of environmental problems in the United States has been straightforward; the traditional processes and theories of economic regulation have been applied with a minimum of modification. But the differences between environmental problems and the economic difficulties that have led to economic regulation in the past are significant. These differences and their policy implications are crucial to understanding the nature of the environmental regulation problem and will be discussed in the first part of this chapter. Then the recent history of environmental regulation in the United States will be outlined to demonstrate the difficulties caused by failure to recognize the difference between environmental and economic regulation.

THE ENVIRONMENT, THE REGULATORY PROCESS, AND THE MARKET

For the purposes of this analysis, the critical feature of most situations involving economic regulation is that a functioning market already exists and plays a central role, so that the regulator need worry only about matters at the margin. For example, the CAB may have a legal mandate to promote and regulate commercial aviation, but it is the power of economic forces, more than the managerial genius and regulatory power of the CAB, that gets aircraft built, keeps supply in line with demand, decides what service should be offered, and so on. The same applies to the FDA, the ICC, the FCC, and other regulatory agencies: the positive and dynamic features of the industry and the generally satisfactory nature of transactions in it are the result of market forces. Successful economic regulation tries to provide some stability, prevent some mistakes, and take care of some marginal inefficiencies and inequities, without interfering too much with the normal workings of the market.

Environmental problems, however, are quite different in form because there is no market to be regulated. The "market failure" that causes an environmental problem is not between buyers and sellers in the market for pollution control equipment, or between buyers and sellers of the steel or paper from the polluting mills; rather, it is between the "buyers" and "sellers" of the environmental resources themselves. Clean air, clean water, wilderness areas, and the earth's ozone layer are resources that provide nature and human society with a whole array of indispensable services, supporting recreation, industry, agriculture, health, and the very life-sustaining processes of the earth. When human society makes few demands on these resources, the supply is adequate for all. But as human numbers, concentrations, and activities grow, these demands begin to compete and interfere with one another, subjecting the environmental resources to more demands than they can meet. For most valuable resources, such conflicts are mediated by supply and demand in a market. But for most of the resources affected by pollution, no natural markets exist and the market failure is total.

Public policy could and should seek to create some market-type institutions for managing environmental resources, but (at least in the United States) it has not yet done so. Thus, environmental regulation must cope with a situation fundamentally different from that in which most economic regulation takes place — the environmental regulator is trying, not to correct existing market forces that are basically supportive of his goals, but to solve a complex economic problem *without* the help of market forces. Thus, one cannot logically argue that environmental problems could be "left to the market" in the same way that, say, transportation or consumer-product safety or cable television could. Nor can one assume that the best solution to this fundamentally different kind of problem is to beef up the traditional tools of economic regulation and apply them without modification. Instead, policy should seek to develop the kinds of social institutions that handle difficult economic problems elsewhere in society, most of which are based on market forces.

If policy does not provide some supportive market forces, the job of the environmental regulator is much more difficult than the job of most economic regulators. The environmental regulators do not get much help from the market in developing technology, sorting out priorities, providing information about alternatives, stimulating competition, or reducing frivolous demands on them or the environment. They are quickly drawn into detailed technical and economic issues across a broad spectrum of the society. Because so much money hangs on each detail and because delay is worth so much, litigation is extensive and political pressure intense. Some of this is inherent in the complexity of environmental issues, some of it could be handled by providing more staff, budget, and independence to the regulators, but a large part of it is due to the difficulty of solving by purely administrative means the kind of economic problems that are generally, and with good reason, left to market forces.

If environmental markets did exist, they would require those who "use up" environmental resources — that is, who degrade them so that less are available for other uses — to pay for the privilege. The resulting economic incentive would encourage conservation of the environmental resource, immediately and over time, via all the ingenious means that economic forces are capable of stimulating. These markets do not exist because of the difficulty of defining "property rights" in environmental resources and defending them against those who would encroach on them. Unlike land or animals, which have undergone the historic transformation from free goods to economic commodities, environmental resources cannot usually be appropriated and defended — and hence "owned" — by individuals. But if public policy were to define and defend such property rights and provide the institutional and legal framework within which these rights could be traded, then some of the advantages of markets could be realized in managing valuable environmental resources.

Environmental markets established by public policy could take either of two basic forms, with any number of variations and combinations possible to accommodate the details of a specific situation. A system of discharge prices could be used, in which the processes of government would decide the prices that must be paid by any source that discharges pollutants of certain types at various times and places, allowing the resulting economic disincentive to determine how fast and how far the discharges will be reduced. Or a system of marketable discharge rights (MDRs) could be used, in which the regulatory authorities would decide how much of which discharges would be allowed in an area, define a set of certificates, rights, or permits limiting total discharges to the chosen level, and then allow these rights to be traded in a (regulated) market. Often, the best system would be some combination, in which a set of marketable discharge rights would be issued, reflecting the desired total level, and then a high price imposed on all discharges not covered by the rights, to accommodate uncertainty and variability.

Whatever the details, the basic advantage of market forces in pollution control is that they can be effective and efficient in reducing pollution discharges without requiring the authorities to inquire deeply into the internal characteristics — the technology, economics, or motivations — of individual sources or requiring the crude tools of legal processes to force costly measures on reluctant actors. Each unit of the same pollutant should, in a pure market system, be charged the same discharge price (or have the same kind of MDR) unless the *external* impacts of different emissions are different. The dischargers' arguments that technology is unavailable, or that "good-faith efforts" are being made, or that the cost of control is too high, may be listened to sympathetically, but no official decides that, for these reasons, some units of pollution are good and some bad. If the external impacts are similar, the discharge price is similar, independent of factors internal to the source. Ultimately, each source must evaluate its own options and decide what combination of pollution control costs and pollution charges it will pay.* Instead of arguing about internal technical details with each source and then defending decisions in court, where their adversaries have better information and all the protections of law, the public authorities can concentrate on the external aspects of the problem — where the pollution comes from, where it goes, what it does when it gets there, and how much it is worth to reduce it further — and adjust the market parameters accordingly.

In choosing among policies, suggestions that market devices be used to help manage environmental resources are too often put to the wrong test. Perhaps because economists have gone to such great lengths to demonstrate the logical beauty of market concepts applied to environmental resources, the policy suggestions are usually dismissed by pointing out the impossibility of implementing them the way economic theory prescribes. But the important question is whether, in practice, they would yield net advantages if used to replace or complement the real alternatives based on regulatory processes. Thus, this chapter reviews the history of air and water pollution control regulation in the United States, culminating in the massive regulatory programs of the 1970s, in order to illustrate how far regulatory reality is from regulatory theory (to the extent that logical theory actually backs regulatory processes). It is this real-world regulatory alternative, and not just eco-

---

* In fact, if it turned out to be more costly or time-consuming to reduce discharges than originally thought, the appropriate policy response might be to raise the discharge price. This possibility might provide an incentive to look for solutions to technical problems of pollution control.

nomic theory, that should be used to judge proposals for using market forces in pollution-control policy.

EVOLUTION OF ENVIRONMENTAL REGULATION IN THE UNITED STATES

Attitudes and policies toward pollution have undergone a steady evolution in the United States. Initially, pollution was regarded as simply one way an individual might harm or inconvenience others, who could then go to court and seek redress under civil law. Gradually, it became clear that rules and guidelines were necessary to assist the courts, and antipollution statutes began to appear; these laws attempted to define certain behavior as unacceptable but still relied on the courts to apply these vague definitions. Eventually, pollution control became accepted as a problem in the management of social resources, and progressively more elaborate regulatory schemes were developed, culminating in the 1970 Clean Air Act and 1972 Federal Water Pollution Control Act. Throughout this evolution, however, United States policy has continued to treat environmental problems as purely regulatory ones, without recognizing the possibility that market forces might be useful in managing valuable social resources.

Pre-1970 Federal Legislation

As long as pollution was regarded as a problem between identifiable polluters and victims, there was little reason for federal action, except where polluters and victims were located in different states. Thus, except for a 1924 law regulating oil pollution in tidal waters, the federal government was quite slow in enacting pollution control legislation. After a series of efforts in 1936, 1938, and 1940, the first federal pollution control law went into effect in 1948.

The Water Pollution Control Act of 1948 left control of intrastate waters to the states and established an extremely cumbersome procedure for abating interstate pollution. Under this procedure, the federal authorities could act only upon the request of state officials or when interstate damage could be proven, and then could not act very strongly. Over the years, a series of amendments attempted to expand and streamline this process by extending federal authority to all navigable waters and allowing federal enforcement in certain situations without state approval. In 1956, federal funds were made available on a matching basis for municipal sewage treatment plants. But progress was slow.

With respect to air pollution, the federal government was even slower to act. Despite the death of some twenty persons during an acute air pollution episode in Donora, Pennsylvania, in 1948, and the demonstration by scientists in the early 1950s that Los Angeles smog was caused by auto emissions, it was not until 1955 that a federal air pollution control act was enacted and a small program of research, training, and demonstrations established.

The Clean Air Act of February 1963 (P.L. 84-159) was the first air quality legislation giving the federal government enforcement powers. This Act was modeled after the earlier water pollution control law and was no more effective. In 1965 a second title (P.L. 89-272) was added to the Act, authorizing the Secretary of HEW to set emission standards for automobiles as soon as practicable, giving "appropriate consideration to technological feasibility and economic costs."

By the mid-1960s, these early federal ventures into pollution control were widely felt to be seriously defective. Thus, the 1965 Water Quality Act and the 1967 Air Quality Act* adopted a rather different approach. Under these Acts, the Secretary of HEW was to produce "criteria" documents describing what was known about the effects of air and water pollution on people, other organisms, materials, and so on. Each state was then to establish ambient (i.e., "surrounding") air and water quality standards for the several air quality control regions and water bodies within the state, based on the intended uses of the region and HEW's description of the characteristics of air and water that were consistent with these intended uses. These ambient standards would be stated in terms of measurable quantities (e.g., micrograms per cubic meter of sulfur dioxide in the air, temperature and oxygen content of the water, number of bacteria per milliliter) and, once approved by HEW, would not have to be reconsidered every time an action was taken against a polluter.

The next part of the new strategy was the translation of these ambient standards into specific effluent and emission levels for individual sources. Each state was required to develop implementation plans describing the effluent and emission limitations it would enforce and other steps it would take to accomplish the ambient standards in each region and basin. If any state failed to produce ambient standards

* Public Law 89-234 and Public Law 90-148, respectively. Although the Acts were administered by different agencies and were different in details and terminology, they were quite similar in basic structure and logic and are described here in a single, somewhat stylized form.

or implementation plans acceptable to the Secretary of HEW, he could promulgate his own. Once a plan had been promulgated, the Secretary could take enforcement actions against individual polluters if any state failed to do so. Funds were also provided for research and for municipal facilities.

From the perspective of legal and regulatory theory, the strategy adopted in the mid-1960s was quite reasonable; unfortunately, it did not work very well in practice. By 1970, the National Air Pollution Control Administration (NAPCA) had not defined the air quality control regions and had published the criteria documents for only two pollutants. Not a single state had a complete set of ambient standards and implementation plans, and the plans that did exist had not been reviewed for adequacy by NAPCA. No enforcement actions were ever taken under the procedures of the 1967 Act. And for mobile-source emissions, the standard-setting process seemed unlikely to accomplish the needed emission reductions. With respect to water pollution, the only part of the process that worked reasonably well was the establishment of water quality standards — that is, the goals in terms of physical and chemical characteristics of water bodies. But the process began to break down at the level of translating these goals into enforceable regulations; deciding what total discharge levels were consistent with the desired water quality and which discharges should be allowed how much of this total proved too much for the states. The enforcement process remained unworkable. Even though it was not necessary to prove that a specific discharge endangered the public health and welfare, one still had to prove that a specific discharge was the cause of a violation of the water quality limitation. Progress under the 1964 Water Quality Act was disappointing.

As frustration with progress was growing in the late 1960s, the possibilities offered by the Refuse Act of 1899 were discovered. This old law, which had never been used to control pollution, allowed the Secretary of War (Defense), acting through the Army Corps of Engineers, to prohibit any industrial * discharge that had not been granted a permit and put whatever conditions he chose on any permit he chose to issue. Soon after this Act was applied to pollution, however, the courts ruled that the administrator could not simply grant or withhold a permit as he saw fit and must, in fact, prepare an environmental impact statement † on every major action — the Refuse Act permit program died aborning. Even in its brief lifetime, however, the advantages inherent in a permit system, in which operating without a permit is

* The courts had held that municipal discharges were not covered.
† The EIS is a procedural requirement of the National Environmental Policy Act, discussed below.

unlawful and the permit can be used to impose specific conditions, had been demonstrated.

Environmental Legislation of the 1970s

In 1969 and 1970 "the ecology" became an important issue on the American political scene. There was widespread dissatisfaction with the way environmental matters were being disregarded in important decisions and with the ineffectiveness of those programs of regulation that had been established. In 1969 the National Environmental Policy Act was enacted, establishing the Council on Environmental Quality as an advisory body to the President and declaring it to be national policy that the government shall endeavor "to create and maintain conditions under which man and nature can exist in productive harmony." [1] NEPA's most important substantive requirement was that federal agencies must prepare a detailed statement describing the environmental impact of any proposed action that might significantly affect environmental quality and must study reasonable alternatives to the proposed action.[2] The Clean Air Amendments (CAA) of 1970 and the Federal Water Pollution Control Amendments (FWPCA) of 1972 were enacted to expand the federal role in environmental regulatory policy; these laws, in slightly amended form, provide the basis of the programs in place in 1980.

The 1970 CAA kept the overall structure of the 1967 legislation, which set emission standards for new automobiles and required the states to develop implementation plans describing how ambient air quality standards would be accomplished. The changes introduced into this process by the 1970 Act were, however, profound: the Congress itself set the levels and deadlines for the automobile standards; EPA was directed to establish, on the basis of narrow considerations, national ambient standards within months; the states were required to develop and enforce plans to meet these ambient standards on strict timetables, or have EPA do so for them; and citizen groups were given standing in court to sue the Administrator if EPA failed to act as directed. The 1970 Act also introduced, for the first time, national emission standards for certain stationary sources and contained language that the courts interpreted to require a policy of "nondeterioration" of clean air areas.

The 1972 FWPCA maintained most of the provisions of the earlier water legislation, but only in an effort not to disrupt those state programs that were accomplishing something. On the whole, the 1972 Act took an entirely different philosophical tack, based on the uniform application of the best technology everywhere. The Act required that all point-source discharges use the "best practicable control technology currently available" (BPT) by July 1977, and the "best available technology economically achievable" (BAT) by July 1983. Other sections of the Act required national effluent standards for new sources, for sources that discharge to publicly owned treatment plants ("pretreatment" standards), and for sources of toxic pollutants. To accomplish this the Act set ambitious goals and rigid deadlines, established complex bureaucratic processes, promised billions of dollars to pay for the bulk of the municipal cost of accomplishing the goal, and provided for "citizen suits" to force action.

The all-new, post-1970 federal pollution control policies were widely hailed as dramatically different approaches to the management of environmental resources. And, indeed, in their extension of federal authority, "economics-be-damned" attitude, use of rigid goals and deadlines backed up by citizen standing in court to force action, and level of financial commitment they were quantitatively different. In the more qualitative dimensions, however, the new policies were nothing but logical extensions of the old; they continued to assume that environmental problems could be solved by traditional administrative mechanisms without help from market forces.

IMPLEMENTATION OF THE 1970 CLEAN AIR ACT

The principal regulatory innovations of the 1970 Clean Air Act Amendments were the use of legislatively set, uncompromisable, health-protection goals and rigid deadlines to force action. And the principal fact of life since then has been the periodic postponement of deadlines and revisions of timetables by Congress, the courts, and EPA. This observation by itself does not necessarily demonstrate that the CAA was unwise either in setting these rigid deadlines or in relaxing them as it became clear they would or should not be met. However, it does suggest that setting rigid deadlines and constraining the regulatory authorities do little to overcome the basic problems with regulation in this area. This is illustrated below for the most important features of the CAA.

Mobile-Source Emission Standards

The 1970 Amendments required that emissions of pollutants from new automobiles (on a grams-per-mile basis) be reduced by 90 percent within five years. The Administrator was allowed to grant only a single, one-year extension, and then only if he found the manufacturers were making serious efforts but could not comply for technical reasons. The burden of finding a solution and bearing the costs was to be on the manufacturers.

The manufacturers did the rational thing under the circumstances — they set out to prove it was impossible to meet the standards and applied for an extension of the 1975 hydrocarbon (HC) and carbon monoxide (CO) standards. When EPA Administrator Ruckelshaus rejected their application, the automobile manufacturers took the issue to court. In *International Harvester* v. *Ruckelshaus,* the court remanded the issue back to EPA, on the grounds that EPA had not adequately refuted the manufacturers' claim of technical infeasibility, and that the economic consequences would be disastrous if events proved EPA to be wrong. EPA granted the extension for HC and CO, setting an interim standard for 1975 automobiles, and three months later granted a one-year extension for the 1976 nitrogen oxides (NOX) standard.

EPA and the courts had now done all they legally could to relax the deadlines, and the battleground shifted to the political arena. The Arab oil embargo and the "energy crisis" provided a convenient opportunity for statesmanlike reconsideration of those earlier decisions made at the height of the "environmental crisis," and the Energy Supply and Environmental Coordination Act of 1974 (ESECA) was the result. Among other things, ESECA moved back by two years the original deadlines for accomplishing the 90 percent emission reductions and allowed the Administrator of EPA to grant a further one-year delay for HC and CO; this he proceeded to do in March 1975. In 1977, Congress amended the CAA again, postponing the emission reductions two more years.

As a result of the federal regulatory program under the 1970 CAA, the emission levels from new automobiles declined, but much more slowly than originally contemplated by the 1970 Act, as illustrated in Table 1.

National Ambient Air Quality Standards

The national ambient air quality standards (NAAQS) for the six pollutants explicitly mentioned in the 1970 amendments were promulgated as required; a seventh "criteria" pollutant, lead, has since been added. Only one legal challenge has been made to the NAAQS, even though that one resulted in EPA's relaxing a standard.[3] Independent scientific

Table 1. New Automobile Emission Characteristics[a]

	HC	CO	NOX
Actual 1970 emission levels	4.1	34.0	4.0
1970 CAA standard for 1975–1976 [b]	0.41	3.4	0.4
Actual 1975 standards	1.5	15.0	3.1
Actual 1978–1979 standards	1.5	15.0	2.0
1977 amendments standards for 1980–1981 [c]	0.41	7.0–3.4	1.0

a All numbers are in grams per mile.

b To be met in 1975 for HC and CO, in 1976 for NOX.

c To be met in 1980 for HC, in 1981 for NOX; for CO, standard is 7.0 in 1980, 3.4 in 1981.

reviews of the NAAQS by the National Academy of Science and others have "found no substantial basis for changing the standards." [4] Since the CAA gives great discretion to the Administrator in choosing (primary) standards that protect public health with an adequate margin of safety, since the scientific evidence is poor, and since Administrator Ruckelshaus was careful to err on the side of protection in initially setting the NAAQS, it is not surprising the courts and the scientific establishment are reluctant to question his judgment.

Perhaps a more important reason for the lack of legal challenge to the NAAQS is that most participants in the struggles over air pollution control quickly realized that, despite the intent of the 1970 Amendments that health protection should drive the program, the real issues would continue to be technology and economics. The "threshold theory" * on which the concept of NAAQS was based has never had firm scientific support but was thought to be necessary for an effective regulatory program. As it has become clear that in some cases the costs of meeting the chosen NAAQS would be prohibitive, and that doing so would not, in fact, eliminate all adverse effects of even the criteria pollutants, the NAAQS have become less important. The debate has shifted to such questions as technical and economic feasibility and the extent of pollution damage compared to the social costs of preventing

* This theory states that there is a level of pollution at which effects become significant more or less abruptly. Below the threshold level, effects are insignificant; above the threshold they are serious. Thus, the threshold — if there is one — is a natural policy goal whatever the costs of achieving it.

it. Nonetheless the NAAQS remain on the books and play an important administrative role in the air pollution control program.

Controls on Existing Stationary Sources

Under the CAA, existing stationary sources are to be controlled to levels specified in the State Implementation Plan (SIP), with the SIP levels chosen to accomplish NAAQS. However, the stationary-source regulations in the SIPs are, in general, vague and imprecise, not at all the kind of clear, enforceable rules that regulatory theory says they should be. The early plans were often unclear about which sources were subject to what regulations, whether or not they were in violation, or what they would have to do about it and when.

Since the CAA and EPA's regulations clearly require "schedules, and timetables for compliance," [5] EPA could not approve SIPs that did not include compliance schedules. Eventually some of the states produced compliance schedules acceptable to EPA, generally by publishing a list of all major sources and saying they would all have to be in compliance with all the general rules by mid-1975, the date when NAAQS had to be met. Where a state failed to produce acceptable compliance schedules, EPA produced its own. After several years most states had adopted statutes and regulations making certain polluting activities unlawful and specifying in more or less detail the schedule on which particular sources or classes of sources were supposed to stop violating these laws by July 1975.

Unfortunately, the "enforceable" regulations were (and still are) typically little more than starting points for negotiations between the control agency and the individual sources, each of which will argue that: (1) he is in compliance with the regulations; (2) if not, it is because the regulation is unreasonable as a general rule; (3) if not, then the regulation is unreasonable in this specific case; (4) if not, then it is up to the regulatory agency to tell him how he can comply; (5) if forced to take the steps recommended by the regulatory agency, he cannot be held responsible for the results; and (6) he needs more time. The regulatory agency, unable to fight every battle, will define the regulations so that most sources are in compliance or can easily become so and will work out agreements promising future action by the worst violators. These agreements then become the "enforceable regulations" and, if they are not complied with, another round of negotiating begins.

EPA estimates there are more than 200,000 existing stationary sources subject to emission limitations in SIPs.[6] Approximately 23,000 of these are "major" sources, each capable of emitting more than 100 tons of a pollutant per year, and collectively accounting for about 85 percent of all air pollution from stationary sources. Over 20,000 of these major sources were in final compliance with the applicable emission limitations as of October 1977 — not necessarily because they had *done* anything in response to the regulations, but typically because they had long used the required "best engineering practices." Another 1,276 major sources were meeting interim requirements specified in compliance schedules — that is, were taking promised actions that might eventually bring them into compliance.

Although EPA points to this 94 percent compliance rate with pride, as of October 1977 there were still 1,225 major sources known to be out of compliance, and 179 for which the compliance status was unknown. And these noncompliers — which include power plants, steel mills, smelters, and so on, where control costs are high and resistance is strong — are the serious sources of air pollution. Thus by 1977, despite the regulatory innovations and toughness of the 1970 CAA that was supposed to eliminate air pollution by 1975, the same old regulatory story had reappeared; virtually all serious emitters were, or could be defined to be, in violation of the law, and EPA was pushing, prodding, and negotiating as best it could.

Transportation and Land-Use Controls

The SIP process has been, if anything, even less successful in dealing with transportation and land-use controls. The states have taken the position that the federal emission standards for new automobiles would do all that could be done to control mobile-source pollution. Recognizing the magnitude of the problem, EPA Administrator Ruckelshaus tried to be reasonable and give the states an additional two years to develop enforceable transportation control plans. But court suits brought under the citizen-suit provisions of the CAA forced EPA to rescind this extension. This led to the absurd situation in which EPA was forced to promulgate a SIP for California that required reduction of gasoline usage in the Los Angeles basin by 87 percent during the summer smog season.

EPA tried to get the states to propose and implement measures to control transportation and "indirect" sources (e.g., traffic-drawing facilities, such as shopping centers) as part of an effort to accomplish NAAQS, and failed. When EPA tried to impose its own plans, which required surcharges on parking, the management of parking supply, and preferential bus and carpool lanes on highways, Congress and the courts intervened. The 1977 Amendments to the CAA have recognized that the NAAQS are not going to be met everywhere, and they allow the Administrator to extend the compliance date for NAAQS by five years anywhere, and by as much as ten years in regions where transportation control measures are necessary for attainment.

New-Source Performance Standards

New-source performance standards (NSPS), applicable to any new or "modified" source, are to be set and enforced by EPA, on the basis of the best system of control available, for any category of emitters that the Administrator determines to be a significant contributor to air pollution.

The original theory behind this provision seemed simple enough; EPA, using only technological and economic criteria, would pick a standard for a category or subcategory, establish its enforceability, and require every new source to meet it or not operate. Unfortunately, given the complexity of industrial operations and the diversity among sources, even new sources are not so simply controlled, as illustrated by the fact that the five NSPS promulgated by EPA in 1971 were still being litigated in 1976.

The issues involved in some of the early legal challenges to the NSPS are instructive. For fossil-fuel-fired steam generators (i.e., power plants) the NSPS for sulfur dioxide was set at 0.8 lb/MMBtu for liquid fuel and 1.2 lb/MMBtu for solid fuel, in an attempt to force the use of low-sulfur coal or the adoption of stack-gas scrubbers on new coal-fired boilers;[7] the NSPS were remanded to EPA for reconsideration, where they were debated for several years. In the case of the Portland cement NSPS, the court ruled that EPA could properly impose a stricter standard on one industry than on another where technology was unavailable, thereby penalizing the more progressive industry; the court also noted that EPA would have to take into account the competitive nature of certain industries.[8] The same case also challenged the application of the NSPS during periods of startup, shutdown, and malfunction; on the remand, EPA changed its NSPS certification procedures so that tests will be run only during "normal" operation — that is, when the plant operator has everything finely tuned.

Thus, even in the apparently simple case of setting technology-based standards for new sources, the familiar regulatory pattern has developed. EPA must consider a broad range of technical and economic issues, make many distinctions, and make and defend many difficult judgments. However, because an EPA permit is required before construction can begin, delay and indecision in the regulatory process prevent, rather than permit, pollution from a specific source. Judged by its ability to prevent pollution from new sources, the NSPS provision may be successful. But judged by its ability to manage the expansion of industry and the replacement of old sources by new with a minimum unnecessary delay, uncertainty, conflict, and bureaucratic intervention, the NSPS provision leaves something to be desired.

The 1977 Amendments to the CAA introduced a new NSPS concept by requiring the use of technological controls on all new sources burning solid fossil fuels, independent of ambient air quality or the uncontrolled emissions levels. EPA is to specify the fixed percentages by which sulfur, nitrogen oxide, and particulate emissions must be reduced below their uncontrolled levels. Thus, using inherently clean fuels will no longer be an acceptable method of emission control for solid-fossil-fuel combustion, and the relevance of the ambient air quality standards has been further reduced.

For sulfur, which is inherent in coal, the concept of a uniform percentage is definable but extremely difficult to implement. If the sulfur-removal percentage is set too strictly, some promising coal-using technologies, such as fluidized-bed combustion and solvent refining, may never be developed because of the risk that they will control only (say) 90 percent. If this happens, large costs will be imposed for little or no environmental gain.

This provision is yet another example of regulatory dynamics at work. Unhappy with events, Congress tried to cut through the complex processes of the CAA (which were themselves initially regarded as a major simplification) by ruling it unnecessary to make distinctions. However, it probably will soon be clear that the costs of ignoring economic and technical complexities are too great, and the regulatory/legal process will bog down, forcing Congress to reconsider. The result will be several years of delay and uncertainty, followed by adoption of a more complex regulatory procedure.

Nondeterioration of Air Quality

When the Supreme Court ruled in 1973 that EPA must prevent "significant deterioration" of air quality, EPA proposed a zoning plan that would divide the clean air regions of the country into three classes, depending on the extent to which air pollution in each area would be allowed to increase. Initially, all clean air regions would be put in Class II, in which emission increases would be allowed if new sources used best available control technology. State governors could then classify regions as either Class III, in which deterioration in air quality to the secondary NAAQS would be allowed, or Class I, in which only very limited increases in ambient concentrations would be allowed; the federal government would also put some federal lands, such as national parks, into Class I.

Regulations to this effect were promulgated in November 1974 and immediately came under attack from all sides. However, in the 1977 Amendments, Congress in large measure adopted the EPA approach, using the three-way classification concept and requiring "best available technology" to be used by any new source in an area where NAAQS were met as of 1977. The regulatory mechanisms involved in implementing this provision are administratively cumbersome, requiring both a full year of site study and the demonstration that a new source will not increase ambient concentrations of pollutants more than specified amounts in specified locations. If they were to become effective, these prevention-of-significant-deterioration (PSD) provisions, like the new NSPS policy, would probably significantly constrain industrial development; it is likely, however, that they will be changed when their costs become apparent.

Trends and Prognosis in Air Pollution

State air pollution control programs were in place before the 1970 CAA superimposed its elaborate mechanisms and ambitious goals on them, and the environmental awakening of 1969–1970 by itself would surely have stimulated them into greater effectiveness. At the same time, economic trends, notably the historical shift from coal to oil as the preferred energy source, were having an independent effect on air pollution. These influences, combined with the fact that systematic monitoring of pollution is a recent activity, make it extremely difficult to be very precise about the impact of the CAA on air pollution. Nonetheless, it is instructive to look at the evidence that can be found on trends.

In terms of national emission trends for the criteria air pollutants, only total suspended particulates (TSP) showed any significant decrease from 1970 to 1977 (the last year for which data are available), and this is largely the result of applying simple dust-control measures on smelters, steel mills, power plants, and open burning. Emission of sulfur oxides (SOX) and volatile organic compounds (VOC) decreased less then 10 percent over that period, while emissions of nitrogen oxides (NOX) increased 15 percent and emissions of carbon monoxide remained essentially unchanged. Table 2 presents the EPA estimates of national emission trends.

Table 2. Summary of National Emission Estimates, 1970–1977
(10^6 Metric Tons/Year)

Year	TSP	SO_x	NO_x	VOC	CO
1970	22.2	29.8	19.6	29.5	102.2
1971	20.9	28.3	20.2	29.1	102.5
1972	19.6	29.6	21.6	29.6	103.8
1973	19.2	30.2	22.3	29.7	103.5
1974	17.0	28.4	21.7	28.6	99.7
1975	13.7	26.1	21.0	26.9	96.9
1976	13.2	27.2	22.8	28.7	102.9
1977	12.4	27.4	23.1	28.3	102.7

Source: "National Air Quality, Monitoring, and Emissions Trends Report, 1977," U.S. EPA, December 1978.

Trends in ambient air quality are harder to define and measure because, typically, some regions improve and others deteriorate. In some cases these changes can be weighted by population exposed, but data are limited. One indicator of overall progress is EPA's Pollutant Standards Index (PSI), which "is an indicator of daily maximum pollution levels; the figure is above 100 when any of the five criteria pollutants reaches a level considered to affect human health adversely." [9] CEQ reports that, in the sixteen cities for which trend data are available, "between 1973 and 1976, the number of days when PSI values exceeded 100 declined from 2,545 to 2,344, an 8 percent improvement. The severity of pollution also declined; the number of days when the PSI rose above 200 dropped from 447 to 318, a 29 percent improvement." [10]

Measures such as the number of days the PSI exceeds 100, or such as the population exposed to pollutant concentrations exceeding the NAAQS, can be misleading because they assign too much significance to the NAAQS; for example, a small improvement in air quality that causes a NAAQS to be barely met is treated as significant, while a large improvement that does not change the compliance status of a region is ignored. Thus, simple average concentration levels (weighted by population exposed where the data allowed it) may provide better measures of health-relevant trends. Trends in averages, however, can be misleading because a fixed set of monitoring sites must be used, making it difficult to take account of changes in the geographic spread of pollution; since most monitoring sites have traditionally been in central cities, trends in averages tend to miss the "spreading out" of air pollution that is taking place.

In terms of simple averages of a more or less fixed set of monitoring sites, EPA reports[11] that nationwide average TSP levels decreased by 8 percent from 1972 to 1977; essentially all of this improvement had occurred by 1975, with no change or a slight deterioration from 1975 to 1977. A similar pattern holds for SOX levels, with average concentrations declining perhaps 10 percent from 1972 to 1975, and changing little since.

For carbon monoxide, which is more localized and not as extensively measured as some of the other pollutants, average (and especially peak) concentrations have decreased in central cities as a result of improved vehicle emission characteristics but have probably increased in areas with increasing automobile traffic. Average photochemical oxidant ("ozone," the principle component of Los Angeles-type "smog") concentrations have, in California, decreased about 10 percent from their 1974–1975 peak; in the rest of the country they have increased, with the net result that national average concentrations have increased about 10 percent from 1972 to 1977. Concentrations of volatile organic compounds have been essentially unchanged nationally over that period. Nitrogen dioxide concentrations show erratic year-to-year behavior, but with more increases than decreases.

These various indicators of trends clearly do not show the kind of dramatic improvement promised by the CAA in 1970. And the future is not likely to be one of more dramatic progress. Further control of existing stationary sources and of motor vehicles will come slowly, as energy-related variances are granted and the general trend toward relaxing pressure continues for economic reasons. The NSPS and PSD provisions may make new sources cleaner than they would be under some less restrictive policy, but their net effect is likely to be to *add* to air pollution by discouraging the substitution of new, cleaner plants for old, dirtier ones. And the inevitable national shift to coal will not help. Thus national emission trends are not likely to look any better in the next five years than they have in the last five.

Furthermore, even if emission levels do decline, ambient levels and the associated health effects will decline even more slowly. In many areas background levels of natural particulates or oxidants are near primary NAAQS, so that even total elimination of man-made emissions would leave ambient levels high. Sulfates, which may be the real culprit in air pollution, are formed in the atmosphere in amounts that are not directly related to sulfur dioxide level. And even complete accomplishment of the NAAQS, which supposedly would eliminate all adverse health effects associated with the criteria pollutants, would, in fact, do no such thing. Thus it is quite possible that most significant air pollution problems would not be much reduced even if emissions were controlled more effectively than they are likely to be.

IMPLEMENTATION OF THE 1972 FEDERAL WATER POLLUTION CONTROL ACT

The principal regulatory feature of the 1972 FWPCA is the National Pollutant Discharge Elimination System (NPDES), which consists of two parts: the promulgation of federal effluent guidelines and standards, and the incorporation of these into permits for individual dischargers. The principal nonregulatory feature is a massive federal public works program to build municipal sewage collection and treatment systems throughout the country.

Effluent Guidelines and Standards

Under the 1972 FWPCA, EPA was to publish "effluent guidelines" specifying, for categories and subcategories of existing sources, the levels of control attainable with the "best practicable technology" (BPT) by 1977 and with the "best available technology" (BAT) by 1983. In addition, EPA was to promulgate (1) effluent standards for new sources reflecting the "best available demonstrated control technology," (2) pretreatment standards for existing and new sources to control discharges into publicly owned treatment works, and (3) effluent standards for toxic pollutants.

The apparent intention of the drafters of the 1972 FWPCA was to take differences among dischargers in such factors as age, size, location, and process into account in the definition of a few subcategories so that, once the effluent guidelines and standards had been issued and legally established, individual plants within a subcategory would all have to meet the same requirements. This would minimize both the competitive economic effects of the standards and the success of challenges to the application of an effluent limitation to a particular discharger. However, as soon as the 1972 FWPCA was enacted, EPA Administrator Ruckelshaus recognized and warned against the quagmire into which Congress was pushing him. In a speech he said:

> There is no way that anyone sitting in Washington can properly prepare a document which specifies the effluent limitations for all of the tens of thousands of plants around the country. Every plant involves individual factors which differentiate it from others and directly affect what would be the best practicable control technology for that plant.... To do the job on specific plants will take the full-time efforts of hundreds of federal and state pollution control people, working as a team, and it's going to take years to accomplish.

More recently, the staff of the National Commission on Water Quality noted that

the EPA effluent limitation strategy ... in effect sometimes causes a "force fit" of a simplistic set of numbers to wastes from industrial production processes. The more complex the industry and the more variable its production processes, the more difficulty EPA has encountered in applying this regulatory strategy. As the trend in most industries is toward more sophistication, variation, change and complexity in production, problems for the regulator are not likely to decrease, but rather increase. As new source performance standards and Phase II (1983) requirements for application of BAT become effective ..., the process will require even more knowledge.

If anything, these observations understate the problem, since they are concerned primarily with the technical aspects of setting effluent guidelines; economic considerations add yet another dimension of variability.

These realities have had just the result one should expect. The EPA effluent guidelines and standards have taken prodigious amounts of EPA resources to produce and have led to a staggering array of technical distinction and subcategorization, which has still been inadequate to make the guidelines the kind of equitable, unchallengeable regulations the framers of the law anticipated. For example, the effluent guidelines promulgated for the Canned and Preserved Seafood Processing Point Source Category contain 33 subcategories — Conventional Blue Crab, Mechanized Blue Crab, Nonremote Alaskan Crab Meat, Remote Alaskan Crab Meat, Nonremote Alaskan White Crab and Crab Section, Remote Alaskan White Crab and Crab Section, Dungenas and Tanner Crab in the contiguous states, plus similar categories for shrimp, oysters, clams, scallops, herring, salmon, catfish, tuna, abalone and fish meal — and still EPA has to add to the guidelines for each subcategory the admonition that "these limitations should be adjusted for certain plants in the industry." And seafood processing is certainly one of the simpler industrial processes; EPA has defined 63 subcategories of inorganic chemicals, 35 subcategories of iron and steel manufacturing, 66 subcategories of canned and preserved fruits and vegetables, and so on, for a total of 642 subcategories.

To make matters worse, in 1976 EPA entered into a settlement agreement with several environmental law groups, agreeing that it would (among other things) issue effluent guidelines covering old sources, new sources, and pretreatment standards for 65 toxic pollutants (some of which are groups of chemicals) from 21 major industrial categories and to do so on a definite schedule over the next fifteen months. These requirements were incorporated into the 1977 FWPCA Amendments; the 1978 CEQ Report says that EPA has a "formidable task" in implementing this requirement.

The Industrial Permit System

The difficulties described above refer only to the process of getting effluent guidelines and standards promulgated; the next step is translating them into NPDES permits. Although the drafters of the Act apparently thought this would be easy once the guidelines were drawn up, it has not (and could not have) worked out that way. In fact, the staff of the NCWQ said that "it is within the permit system that the controversy over effluent limitations is most significant."

Even when there is general agreement that an existing effluent guideline is applicable, a particular discharger can request an adjudicatory hearing to challenge the specific requirements in a permit. As of September 12, 1975, EPA had issued about 2,000 permits to major industrial dischargers, and 665 of these had requested adjudicatory hearings. After denying 106 and "settling" 109 of the requests, EPA still had 450 major industrial permittees awaiting the protracted and complex hearing process. The challenges to the permits have been based on the predictable arguments — the general effluent limitation is not applicable to a specific plant or the permit conditions are unreasonable. Until a permit has been adjudicated, no enforcement action can be taken. If EPA denies the request for an adjudicatory hearing or finds against the discharger, there remains the option of going to court.

All these difficulties made it clear in 1976 that the BPT discharge levels would not be met everywhere by mid-1977, as required by the FWPCA. Since EPA had no legal authority to issue or approve permits that allow time extensions beyond this statutory deadline, EPA adopted a substitute policy — the "enforceable regulations" in the permits would not be enforced! EPA issued a remarkable set of memoranda stating that, since "some dischargers cannot be expected to accept permits requiring achievement of BPT by July 1, 1977," EPA must be reasonable. If enforcement activity were tried, most permittees would contest the schedules in the permits through adjudicatory hearings and judicial appeals, thus "deferring . . . achievement of BPT for substantial periods of time." So, instead of trying to enforce the regulations, a "discharger which has proceeded in good faith . . . should be dealt with by (1) issuing a permit requiring the achievement of BPT by July 1, 1977 and (2) simultaneously issuing an Enforcement Compliance Schedule Letter . . . stating the permit issuing authority's intention to refrain from enforcing the July 1, 1977 requirement." [12]

This EPA policy was remarkable only in its candor. Seldom does a regulatory agency state so openly the basic ineffectiveness and unenforceability of its regulations. In amendments to the FWPCA adopted in 1977, EPA was granted authority to allow extra time to dischargers making "good faith efforts" to comply, making noncompliance legal. By July 1, 1977, the original deadline for BPT to be installed, 724 of the 3,798 major industrial dischargers were not in compliance with the existing limitations, and the EPA was still defining the BACT, toxic pollutant, and other effluent limitations.[13]

The industrial water pollution control program is, then, in about the same situation as the air pollution control program: "pollution" is now illegal; most significant dischargers are or soon will be in violation, unless EPA shows real imagination in defining "compliance"; any attempt to force compliance will succeed only in embarrassing the agency and disrupting what is left of the program; so EPA will leave the "enforceable regulations" on the books and work out quiet arrangements with the polluters on a case-by-case basis.

Municipal Water Pollution Control

The FWPCA has never expected the federal government to force control on impecunious local governments and relies on massive federal funds and state planning processes to get municipal and regional waste treatment facilities built in a timely and cost-effective fashion. Since the municipal construction grants and the planning processes are not regulatory programs, they will not be discussed in detail here; they must, however, be dealt with briefly because municipal pollution is so important to the FWPCA strategy and to any alternative that might be suggested.

Because of the 1977 deadline for meeting secondary treatment standards, the initial emphasis in the construction grants program was on getting money obligated and spent, even though there are serious questions concerning the cost effectiveness of expenditures. While this effort was underway, the estimate of municipal needs escalated dramatically above the $18 billion estimated in EPA's 1971 "Needs Survey." The Needs Surveys of 1973 and 1974 took into account the more stringent treatment requirements of the FWPCA, added some communities, included the cost of extending and rehabilitating sewers, and, most notably for 1974, estimated the costs of treating or controlling stormwater.* Table 3 summarizes the results of the three Needs Surveys.

There are several reasonable explanations for this explosion in cost estimates, the most obvious being that municipalities are competing for federal funds by overstating their "needs," and awareness of the scope of the water pollution problem is growing; indeed, more

---

* In older cities, sewers leak directly into waterways. Also, storm and sanitary sewers typically are combined, so that a storm will overwhelm the treatment works and raw sewage will be discharged. To control this, one must resewer the city, provide storage facilities to hold stormwater surges, build huge overcapacity into treatment plants — or live with the problem.

Table 3. EPA Needs Surveys ($ Billion)

Category of Expenditure	1971	1973	1974
Treatment and interceptors	18	35.2	51.4
Sewer rehabilitation	n.a.	24.9	55.9
Control stormwater	n.a.	n.a.	235.0
Totals	18	60.1	342.3

Source: Draft Staff Report, NCWQ, p. V–83, 1971 dollars; 1973 and 1974 figures are in 1973 dollars.

recent estimates of "needs" have defined them more narrowly and produced smaller numbers. But the explanations are less interesting than the implications. When it appeared that a few dozen billions of federal dollars would essentially eliminate municipal pollution, there was no need to worry much about how to manage such pollution in the long run. But when the estimate of the cost becomes hundreds of billions of dollars, the situation is qualitatively different. Now it is clear that municipal pollution is here to stay, and the real questions concern how to use limited resources efficiently, not how to force the administration to release a few billion dollars more or to streamline the grant-making machinery within EPA. If the municipal pollution control program is ever to become more than the biggest pork barrel in history, some major changes in the FWPCA are called for.

Unfortunately the 1977 amendments to the FWPCA do not move in the right direction in allocating federal construction grant funds. The rate of expenditure is increased ($24.5 billion through 1982), the federal share is increased from 75 percent to 85 percent, and more "flexibility" is granted to EPA and the states in deciding on the best technology to install. Funds are to be allocated on the basis of needs and population, rather than just needs alone, with 4 percent of the funds set aside for grants to rural states. These changes seem to be calculated to accomplish political more than environmental ends — although $24.5 billion, even inefficiently spent, should clean up a lot of municipal discharges.

Trends and Prognosis
in Water Pollution

There are no reliable data on discharges of water pollutants over the years and only limited information on water quality. EPA's 1974 National Water Quality Inventory summarized what information on national water quality trends was available and drew some conclusions. In general, it was found that water quality had improved between 1963 and 1972, in terms of the substances traditionally regarded as pollutants, such as oxygen-demanding wastes, bacteria, suspended and dissolved solids, and odors. In terms of nutrients such as phosphorus and nitrogen, which had not been thought of as pollutants and hence had not been the object of much attention from regulators, the water quality was substantially worse.

More recent (and more reliable) data on water quality trends are summarized in Table 4, taken from the 1978 CEQ Annual Report. These data indicate that most of the monitoring stations in the National Stream Quality Accounting Network (NASQAN) showed no statistically significant change in the measured water quality characteristics between 1975 and 1977. Slightly more stations showed improvement than showed deterioration for fecal coliform bacteria, dissolved oxygen, and zinc; for all other listed pollutants, the situation seems to be deteriorating.

This record is hardly one of dramatic achievement under the FWPCA; indeed, it suggests that water quality may have been improving more in the 1960s and early 1970s, before the massive subsidies and cumbersome processes of the 1972 Act were introduced. But it is still too early to expect to see the water quality benefits of much of the recent activity and investment. And anecdotal evidence about fish being caught where they have not been seen for years, and obvious

Table 4. Water Quality Changes[a] at NASQAN Stations 1975–1977

Water Quality Characteristic	Percentage of Stations		
	Improved	No Change	Deteriorated
Fecal coliform bacteria	7.3	88.9	3.8
Inorganic nitrogen	5.8	86.7	7.5
Organic nitrogen	3.8	83.4	12.8
Total phosphorus	4.3	83.2	12.5
Dissolved oxygen	4.5	92.9	2.6
Fecal streptococci bacteria	1.8	87.3	10.9
Dissolved solids	4.1	74.1	21.8
Dissolved zinc	9.1	86.5	4.4
Total zinc	12.8	85.8	1.4
Phytoplankton	2.0	93.6	4.4

Source: CEQ, Environmental Quality, 1978, p. 96.

[a] Indications of change tested for statistical significance at the 90 percent level.

improvements downstream from large new municipal sewage treatment plants, do indicate that some progress is being made.

In the next ten years continued improvement in water quality can be expected, primarily as a result of the massive federal subsidies for municipal treatment and the adoption of simple control by previously uncontrolled industrial sources. The more exotic industrial pollutants are likely to show slower improvement, as it gets more difficult to force more sophisticated and costly controls on industry, using purely regulatory processes. And nonpoint sources — runoff from farmland, city streets, construction sites, even natural areas — are hardly being controlled at all, even though in some areas they are the largest source of water pollution. Thus, the goal stated in the FWPCA of having all the water in the United States be "fishable and swimmable by 1983" is hardly in danger of being accomplished.

SOME LESSONS OF THE 1970s EXPERIENCE

The fact that the deadlines and goals in the 1970 CAA and the 1972 FWPCA have not been met does not mean that these Acts "failed." No realistic management system could have or should have accomplished these goals. In fact, the principal lessons to be learned from the experience of the 1970s are that the problems are far more difficult, will be with us far longer, and will require far more patience and continuous management than the drafters of the CAA and FWPCA imagined.

However, the pollution control laws of the 1970s can be judged to have failed in their principal regulatory innovations and in their simple-minded view of the environmental management problem. The rigid deadlines have not proven very effective in forcing action and may have been counterproductive by focusing attention on short-term, quick fixes at the expense of continuing progress in the long run. The goal of easy, total elimination of pollution, without considering questions of trade-offs and continuing management, is as unattainable today as it was implausible in 1970. And the total reliance on regulatory processes for managing an extremely complex and valuable set of resources was and is wrongheaded; probably nowhere else in American society (or elsewhere, for that matter) is such a difficult economic problem tackled with so little help from market forces.

Unfortunately, as the deadlines have come and gone, and as the complexities of the problem have become undeniable, the principal policy response has been unimaginative: the deadlines have been relaxed, and EPA has been instructed to take more things into account in making its regulatory decisions. Instead of moving toward a policy based on continuous management of valuable social resources using the kind of social institutions that have proven effective elsewhere, the trend is back toward the kind of administrative discretion and complexity that results in ineffective regulatory programs that motivated the legislation of the 1970s, only on a more massive scale. There has been some limited experimentation with economic incentives and marketlike arrangements, especially in air pollution. But even in 1980 the Chairman of the President's Council on Environmental Quality could state unequivocally that nobody in authority is thinking seriously about moving away from the pure "command and control" approach to pollution control.[14] At a time when the world is becoming increasingly complex, and when environmental values must be pursued efficiently and rationally if they are not to lose out to other social goals, this unwillingness to rethink our basic approach to pollution control is not encouraging.

NOTES

[1] Section 101(a) of NEPA, Public Law 91-190 (1970).

[2] Since NEPA is not a regulatory program, it will not be dealt with here. For a good description of how NEPA was implemented in its early years, see F. R. Anderson, Jr., "The National Environmental Policy Act," in Federal Environment Law, 1974.

[3] When asked by the court simply to explain how the annual average concentration limit of the second sulfur dioxode NAAQS related to information in the criteria document, EPA chose to withdraw this part of the standard, leaving a three-hour limitation. *Kennecott Copper* v. *EPA,* D.C. Circuit (1973).

[4] National Academy of Sciences, National Academy of Engineering, *Air Quality and Automobile Emission Control,* Vol. I. Summary Report prepared for the U.S. Senate Commission on Public Works Sec. No. 93–24 (Washington, D.C.: U.S. Government Printing Office, 1974), p. 6. Cited in 1975 CEQ Annual Report, p. 46.

[5] 1970 CAA, Section 110(a)(2)(A).

[6] *Environmental Quality,* the ninth annual report of the Council on Environmental Quality (Washington, D.C.: U.S. Government Printing Office, 1978), pp. 71–72.

[7] 40 CFR 60.4. The emission figures refer to pounds of SO_2 emitted per million Btu's of fuel burned. For coal, 1.2 lb SO_2/MMBtu is equivalent to coal containing less than 1 percent sulfur — as little as 0.5 percent sulfur for

lower-Btu western coal. Why do the NSPS allow half again as much SO_2 per heat unit for coal as for oil? Because coal is inherently dirtier. Should it work out that coal-firing is marginally cheaper than oil-firing, cost-minimizing enterprises would choose coal over oil, giving SO_2 emissions 50 percent higher than they need be with no economic advantage to society.

[8] *Portland Cement* v. *Ruckelshaus,* 5 ERC 1593 (D.C. Circuit 7AE9). See discussion in Arthur Ferguson, "Direct Federal Controls," *Ecology Law Quarterly,* 4:3 (1975), 649–650.

[9] CEQ, *Environmental Quality,* 1978, p. 4.

[10] *Ibid.,* p. 14.

[11] "National Air Quality, Monitoring, and Emissions Trends Report, 1977," U.S. EPA, December 1978.

[12] EPA memos of June 3, 1976, from *Environmental Reporter, Current Developments,* 7:6, 241–246.

[13] CEQ, *Environmental Quality,* 1978, p. 108.

[14] J. Gustave Speth, quoted in *The Energy Daily,* 8:11 (January 17, 1980).

CASE 9

State Regulation of Public Utilities and Marginal-cost Pricing

Leonard W. Weiss
University of Wisconsin, Madison

Much of the regulation that affects our everyday lives occurs at the state rather than the federal level. This case describes the industries regulated by the state commissions and the issues with which the commissions deal. The big regulatory change in the 1970s at this level was marginal cost pricing.

THE STATE COMMISSIONS

The typical state commission regulates from one to fourteen privately owned electric utilities, a similar number of gas distribution utilities, the remaining private water systems and transit lines, the local Bell system subsidiary, and dozens of independent telephone companies. (The last are usually, though not always, in small towns.) Many state commissions also regulate intrastate trucking and railroads.

State commissions consist of three to seven commissioners and staffs of several to hundreds of engineers, accountants, clerks, and — sometimes — one or two economists. On average, each such commission has a budget of about two million dollars, but some cost many times that. Commissioners' salaries vary from $13,000 to $45,000 per year (in 1972), but many of them could earn more if employed by utilities.

The leaders among the commissions are in California, New York, and Wisconsin. The first two are the largest states, and Wisconsin was the first to have a commission, and has been a consistent innovator. Before World War I, all three states were centers of the "progressive movement," which spawned a majority of the state commissions. Now they have gone farthest along the marginal-cost pricing trail, which was the major regulatory reform of the 1970s at the state level.

Commissioners in a majority of states, including all three of the leaders, are appointed by the governers, but in twelve states commissioners are elected. Most voters know little about public utility commissions and even less about individual commissioners, so an elected commissioner usually had a secure and quiet job until the 1970s. When electric and gas rates soared after 1973, however, many elected commissioners had to fight for their seats, and quite a few of them lost elections. State regulation became much more vigorous as a result.

THE CHARACTERISTICS OF PUBLIC UTILITIES

Natural Monopoly

The oldest and most widely accepted justification for regulation is "natural monopoly." This occurs where cost per unit is lower for a monopoly than it would be for several firms in competition. In many but not all cases, this comes about because cost per unit declines as output increases, at least out to the limit set by demand. In an industry where this is true, three important conclusions will follow:

1. Competition can't last, because the firm that gets ahead will have lower average costs and will be able to drive any smaller rivals out of business.
2. We wouldn't want competition if we could get it, because the average cost of two or more firms serving a market would be higher than the average cost of a single monopolist.
3. Marginal cost will be less than average cost, a mathematically necessary effect of decreasing average costs. This implication will be very important later in this chapter.

Local electric, gas, and telephone utilities certainly have decreasing average costs. Once their distribution lines are in, average cost will be lower the more electricity that consumers use. Almost everyone believes that two or more gas or electric distribution lines or tele-phone lines along the street would be wasteful. This does *not* mean that geographically larger utilities have lower average costs. Running the electric, gas, and telephone lines into new territory adds to total dis-tribution costs as well as to customers. Geographically small utilities have no higher average distribution costs than do utilities in larger cities.

Electric utilities* have large economies of scale in other parts of their business as well. This is certainly true of transmission lines, and electric generating systems appear to have decreasing average costs for all but the dozen largest systems.

Only a few of the industries regulated at the federal level have continuously decreasing average costs. Gas and oil pipeliness and inter-state electric transmission of electricity do, and long distance tele-phone, airlines, and railroads do on routes with low traffic density. But trucks, barges, trunk airlines, gas and oil production, broadcasting, and stockbrokers do not.

Capital Intensity and Storability

Another important feature of local utilities is that they are very capital intensive. Electric, gas, and telephone companies employ capital equal to 200 to 400 percent of annual revenue compared with an average of about 75 percent for manufacturers. This means that the valuation of plant and equipment and the rate of return allowed on them are very important for the utilities.

A third feature of utilities is that they generally sell services that cannot be stored.† The utilities must be able to provide service when-ever a customer throws a switch or picks up a phone. That means that they must have excess capacity most of the time. This, together with capital intensity, implies that any change that will even out demand over time can greatly reduce average cost. The technical term involved here is the "load factor" — the ratio of average demand to peak de-

---

* Most of the remainder of this chapter will deal with electric power. A few terms will be useful. A watt or a kilowatt (KW — 1,000 watts) or a megawatt (MW — a million watts or a thousand kilowatts) is a measure of capacity for a generating plant or of the energy drawn by a piece of electrical equipment. A kilowatt-hour (KWH) or a megawatt-hour (MWH) is a measure of the flow of energy from a generator or to a piece of electrical equipment over a period of an hour. A 100-watt bulb will use 0.1 KWH per hour.

† Actually, gas can be and is stored to some extent, but electric, telephone, and transportation services cannot.

mand. The higher this ratio, the lower the average cost, because of the reduced ratio of capital to total receipts.

A final feature of the local utilities is that most are growing rapidly (or at least were until recently). This, together with high capital intensity, means that utilities are making crucial decisions about investment in new plant and equipment. New additions to capacity are usually much larger than the capacity that is being retired. Moreover, at least for the electric utilities, plant and equipment prices are rising very rapidly.

PUBLIC UTILITY REGULATION

State public service commissions generally issue rules that assure monopolies to the local utilities, but then control utility rates with the purpose of preventing monopoly profits. Here is a simple statement of the objectives of these rules:

Revenue Requirement = Operating Costs + (Rate Base × Fair Return)

The revenue requirement is what the commission calculates the utility needs to cover costs while earning a fair profit. Operating costs are such things as labor, fuel, materials, and current depreciation expense. Rate base is the value that the commission feels it is appropriate to assign to capital committed to the utility service. Fair return is the rate of return that the commission judges will yield investors in the utility a reasonable but not monopolistic profit.

The process of finding the right rates for the utility is more complex than the simple equation presented above suggests. The commissions and the courts have worried through many decades of cases on every element in that equation.

Operating Costs

There are many issues involved in deciding what operating costs the utilities can reasonably ask their customers to pay for. How much can the utility legitimately be allowed for advertising to influence customers' views on the utility or the regulatory system itself? For advertising to get them to run their dishwashers at night on hot summer days? How much should the managers of the utilities earn? How can the commission make the utility bargain hard with the unions it deals with? How much depreciation should be allowed on plant and equipment each year? What prices should the utilities be allowed to collect for supplies and equipment bought from affiliated suppliers? *

These issues come up for two reasons that seldom if ever apply to unregulated businesses. First, a competitive business is expected to seek minimum-cost methods. This is not automatic if cost increases are almost automatically passed on to consumers. A second and related point is that, if the commission does keep prices below the most profitable levels for a monopolist, an increase in operating costs, and therefore in rates, not only won't hurt the utility — it may *help*, if it takes the form of higher wages and salaries (and therefore better access to talented workers), or higher payments to a parent company's affiliates. The commissions must make decisions here that no one makes in less regulated industries.

Rate Base

For the first four decades of this century the valuation of "rate base" was the main issue of regulation. We have four alternatives to choose from: (1) original cost, (2) reproduction cost, (3) replacement cost, and (4) "fair value."

Original cost is what the utility paid for its capital equipment adjusted for depreciation. It is the most widely used measure of rate base today. Its main advantage is that it is easy and definite: the utility knows what it paid for its plant and equipment, and there isn't much basis for argument about it. Its main defect is that it is wrong in a period of continuing inflation. A power plant that was built in 1970 for $100 million would cost $200 million or more to build today. Utility rates based on the $100 million figure will be too low. They are less than what society is giving up, or will give up when the plant has to be replaced, and they therefore induce consumers to use too much electricity. To make the point more emphatically, imagine what would happen if a commission set rates using original cost in a country such as Argentina where prices double every year. Five years after the plant was installed it would be valued at only 6 percent of what it would take to replace it. Electric rates would be only slightly higher than the

---

* For instance, most of the equipment used by the Bell System operating companies comes from Western Electric, which is a Bell System subsidiary.

cost of fuel. Not only would future investment in electric power plants disappear, but consumers would be induced to use far too much electricity.

The economic alternative to original cost is *replacement cost:* how much it would cost to provide the same capacity today. This is the value of plant that would yield a normal return in a purely competitive market in long-run equilibrium. If the cost of building a shoe factory is $2 million today and I own a plant that was built ten years ago for $1 million, I will make high profits as long as my plant lasts. New entrants will be attracted only if they can earn a normal return on $2 million, not $1 million. Two million dollars represents the opportunity cost of my plant, not $1 million.

The third alternative is *reproduction cost:* what it will cost to build *the same* plant and equipment now. It differs from replacement cost in that it refers to the *same* plant, no matter how obsolete it may be; replacement cost refers to the same capacity using the current least-cost techniques. Reproduction cost was required in many jurisdictions in the 1920s and 1930s. Ohio, the last state to require it, switched to original cost in 1977. Although it seems silly if taken literally, reproduction cost *is* fairly definite. It can be estimated with reasonable ease by the use of original cost and price indexes that are regularly published by a private firm. Replacement cost, on the other hand, is necessarily vague, since it refers to hypothetical best-practice plant. Reproduction cost may be a reasonable alternative to replacement cost if a percentage is deducted for obsolescence, as is done in some jurisdictions.

The fourth alternative, *fair value,* gives weight to both original cost and reproduction cost.[1] In practice in fair-value states the commission, in its wisdom, decides what weights should be given to original and reproduction cost and comes up with the indicated weighted average of the two. In 1973 eleven states used fair value.[2]

Fair Return

The effect of rate base on the rates that the utility charges its customers depends on the return allowed as well as on rate-base valuation procedures. In the years before World War II, when the courts were second-guessing the commissions' decisions, they required that the utility be allowed a "fair return on a fair value" of its rate base. It is clear that a commission can effectively confiscate much of the utility's capital if it sets a "fair return" at 2 percent. In the process, the commission would make it almost impossible for the firm to raise more capital. Or the commission could make the utility tremendously profitable by permitting a return of, say, 25 percent.

Where should the "fair return" come from? One answer used in some jurisdictions is the rate of return earned by "similar" unregulated firms. This may be roughly right if the "similar" firms are in clearly competitive markets such as textiles or lumber, but if powerful firms such as General Motors and IBM get into the list, the utility will receive quite a lot of monopoly profits. Another standard sometimes used is the return to the utility's stockholders: dividends divided by market value, plus rate of growth in the market value of the utility's stock. This criterion became much less popular in the 1970s when there was practically no growth in the market values of many utilities' stocks.

The economically correct answer is the "opportunity cost of capital" — what it would take to raise the utility's capital in capital markets today. This is what society gives up on other investment opportunities by putting capital into the utilities. It is the rate of return that would accrue to firms in purely competitive markets in long-run equilibrium.

In fact, most commissions use "imbedded cost" of debt capital plus a "fair return" on common stock. "Imbedded cost" is the interest the firm actually pays. This might be roughly right if interest rates were stable over time. But in the 1970s, a period of accelerating inflation, interest rates rose rapidly. The interest rates that the utilities actually pay on their bonds and preferred stocks issued before the 1970s were far below the opportunity costs of debt capital today.

The return allowed on capital assignable to common stock may be based on a variety of criteria, but regardless of the formal standard used, the commissions have been virtually forced to raise it in recent years. The interest rate at which a utility can borrow depends heavily on the ratio of its profits after tax to its total interest obligations on bonds outstanding. This ratio often fell sharply when utilities borrowed at the high interest rates of the 1970s. If this ratio falls, the ratings of the firm's bonds may decline, and consequently its interest costs on new debt will rise. The utility can increase its total profits by issuing more common stock, but many utilities were reluctant to do so in the 1970s because the market value of their stock was below its book value, so that new stock issues would dilute current stockholders' equity. The current stockholders would come out of a new issue with a smaller dollar claim on the utility's assets than before. In any case, the utilities preferred to solve their problem by increasing their rate of return on equity. Most commissions went along.

Risk is another relevant consideration, but commissions seldom consider it. In the unregulated sectors we expect rates of return to rise with risk. Risk is low for electric, gas, and telephone utilities, industries that have stable demands and face regulators who almost automatically raise their rates when costs go up. The natural implication is that a "fair return" would be lower than the profit rates earned by un-regulated competitive industries such as lumber or textiles.

Risks *are* high for declining regulated industries, like the few re-maining private transit lines. Here a commission could justify higher rates of return. But higher fares are not likely to be the way to increase the profitability of bus lines, since most customers have access to private cars. All the commission can do is order the bus company to charge its most profitable price, which is what it would do without regulation.

Utilities' Rates

The standard operating procedure of most state commissions is to cal-culate the "revenue requirement" of the utility by multiplying the "fair return" by the rate base and adding taxes and operating expenses. Then the utility proposes a set of rates designed to yield the revenue requirement. Ordinarily the suitability of those rates is judged by how much revenue they would yield in a "test year" — commonly the latest year for which complete results are available. The proposed rates are multiplied by the amounts of service sold in the categories to which they apply. The commission may change the proposed rates, but the criterion applied to the revised rates will also be whether they would have yielded the revenue requirement in the test year or not.

This procedure has several implications. For one thing, the com-mission is in effect assuming that the elasticity of demand is zero. If the elasticity is more than that, as it almost always will be, the new rates will not yield the revenue requirement. If rates are falling, as they were in the 1920s, 1930s, 1950s, and 1960s, actual quantities sold will exceed those in some previous test year and the utility will earn more than the revenue requirement as a result. If rates are rising, as they were in the 1970s, the opposite may happen. Higher rates may discourage consumption, so that the firm winds up with less revenue than predicted.

Another implication of the ratesetting procedure is that utilities will do badly during inflation. One reason is the use of original cost in a majority of states. Another is that rates are based on past costs and past sales. As a result, during a continuing inflation utilities will get rate increases that bring them up to the levels implied by commis-sion's policies at the end of each rate case, but in between rate cases they will fall behind. That, in turn, means that there will be many rate cases — new ones often start before the previous cases are over. The commissions find themselves in a continuous logjam today.

Fuel Adjustment Clauses

Many commissions introduced changes in attempts to straighten out the logjam. A policy change adopted widely in the 1970s was the "fuel adjustment clause." Electric utilities are permitted to pass fuel price increases directly through to their customers without rate cases. In 1977 all but six states had such clauses[3]

One effect of this is that the utility loses its incentive to bargain hard with fuel suppliers, since their prices will be automatically covered by rate increases. The situation is even worse in some states where it is fuel cost *per kilowatt hour* that is automatically passed on to the customers. With such a clause the utility has little incentive to seek more efficient generating plants. And if fuel costs are automatically passed through while plant and equipment costs are passed on only after a rate case a few years hence, the utility has some incentive to shift toward generating units that don't cost much to install but have high fuel cost. For instance, this is true of gas turbines used by many utilities in the 1970s.

The Broad Effects of Regulation

Economists put a great deal of emphasis on state regulation in the postwar years. One group emphasized the investment incentives built into regulation. A second seemed to show that regulation was ineffective. A third considered the appropriateness of marginal cost as a basis for utility ratemaking. The energy expended on these subjects had different effects on regulation.

The first argued that if profits of utilities depend on the rate base and if the "fair return" exceeded the cost of capital to the utility, it would be in the utility's interest to adopt capital-intensive methods of production (for instance, nuclear power plants, which require more investment but have lower fuel costs than fossil fuel plants) to increase their rate bases uneconomically.[4] This point and its ramifications were examined in about a hundred articles.

At the same time, a famous economist seemed to show that regulation of electric utilities was almost completely ineffective in the 1920s and 1930s in that rates and profits were no lower in states with regulatory commissions than in states without them.[5] Some subsequent studies suggested that the same was true in the 1960s.

These two lines of research had virtually no effect on actual regulation. No state regulatory commission came close to being dismantled. By contrast, marginal-cost pricing research had a great effect.

MARGINAL-COST PRICING

Regulation versus the
Unregulated Monopolist

The pricing practices of conventional price-cost-profits regulation can be given a reasonable economic rationale. This is illustrated in Figure 1, which shows the position of a monopolist with constant long-run average costs. Because cost per unit is the same regardless of the firm's size, its long-run marginal cost will also be constant and equal to long-run average cost. An unregulated monopolist with the costs and demands shown in Figure 1 would find its most profitable price to be P_1, which substantially exceeds marginal cost.

From a social point of view P_1 is too high. One more unit of output would cost only C but would be worth P_1 to consumers. P_1 repre-

Figure 1. The Relationship Between Price and Cost for a Monopolist

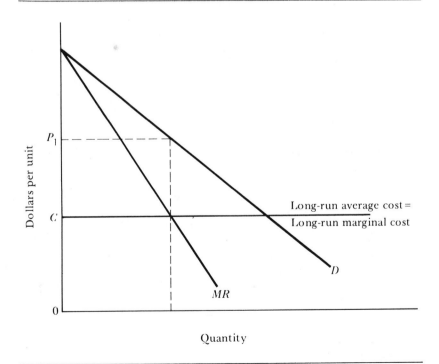

sents the value of other things consumers would give up for another unit of the monopolist's product. The long-run marginal cost is equal to the opportunity costs of resources used to produce another unit. For instance, the monopolist must pay as much for a typist or a ton of coal as they would earn in other industries. The same is true for any capital supplied by the owners of the monopoly. They will find it profitable to invest in the firm so long as it yields them at least as much as they could earn on their capital elsewhere, though they would be pleased to earn more if possible — which is what would happen if the price were in fact set at P_1.

P_1 is equal to what consumers will give up to get another kilowatt-hour of electricity. C represents the value of other goods given up to produce another kilowatt-hour. It follows that an expansion in output will increase consumer welfare, since another unit produced will cost less in terms of other goods than consumers are willing to give up of other goods. And this will continue to be true at successively lower prices until $P = C$.

Marginal-cost Pricing in Theory

Should regulatory commissions, then, set prices that just equal long-run marginal cost? If prices were set higher, society would be better off with a lower price and the resulting greater output. There would also be a misallocation of resources if price were set below C: consumers then would be willing to give up less for the last kilowatt-hour in terms of other goods than it would take to produce the last kilowatt-hour consumed. Too much electric power would be consumed and too little of other goods.

Marginal-cost pricing of this sort may not yield enough revenue to cover all costs. This will definitely be true in a decreasing-cost industry. Table 1 provides an example. On the left the cost of one more unit just equals average cost, so average cost neither rises nor falls. On the right marginal cost is less than the average, so average cost is falling. This is a mathematical necessity. Add any number less than 10 to total cost when output increases from 10 to 11 and (a) average cost will fall, and (b) marginal cost — the addition to total cost — will be less than the average.

If a commission were to set rates at long-run marginal cost for a firm with decreasing costs, it would impose losses on the utility — an action that is apt to be unconstitutional and would not be wise in any event. The utility would not be able to raise capital if it were faced by continuous losses.

One way around this problem is to pay the utility a subsidy to

Table 1. Average Cost and Marginal Cost in a Constant-cost
Industry and a Decreasing-cost Industry

	Constant Cost		Decreasing Cost	
Quantity	10	11	10	11
Total cost	100	110	100	108
Average cost	100/10 = 10	110/11 = 10	100/10 = 10	108/11 = 9.82
Marginal cost	110 − 100 = 10		108 − 100 = 8	

make up the difference between average and marginal cost, but commissions usually cannot pay subsidies to utilities, and legislatures are seldom willing to provide for them.

Price discrimination offers another solution. Figure 2 shows one household's demand for electricity and the utility's cost of providing it. The cost curve slopes downward because the cost per KWH of serving the household declines as sales grow. Marginal cost is still further below average cost because, in most areas, generating cost declines as capacity grows. If the utility sets a flat rate of P_1, the household will buy Q_1, and price will exceed marginal cost. But if the utility charges a lot for the first 100 KWH, less for the next 500 KWH, still less for the next 1,000, and so forth, it can get price down to marginal cost on the final KWH consumed by this household and still cover its costs.

Most electric utilities have declining block rates, or did until recently. In reality, different households have different demand curves. Big users may get the right signals from their tail block rates, but small customers will pay rates far above marginal costs. If small customers are also poorer, such rates redistribute income in favor of the rich. Declining block rates also give an incentive for us to use more energy, hardly our goal after 1973.

Finally, the utility might charge different rates for customers with different responsiveness to price (different elasticities of demand). They would charge high prices to those who would consume almost the same amounts regardless of price (those with inelastic demands) and charge low prices to those who would consume much more at low prices (those with more elastic demands). They could earn enough on sales to the first group to permit them to charge a price close to marginal cost for the customers whose consumption would be most affected by higher prices. In this way prices in excess of marginal cost would distort consumption decisions as little as possible. The high prices charged to consumers whose demand was unresponsive to price would not affect

Figure 2. How Price Discrimination Can "Solve" the Marginal-cost
Pricing Problem in the Case of Decreasing Long-run Average Cost

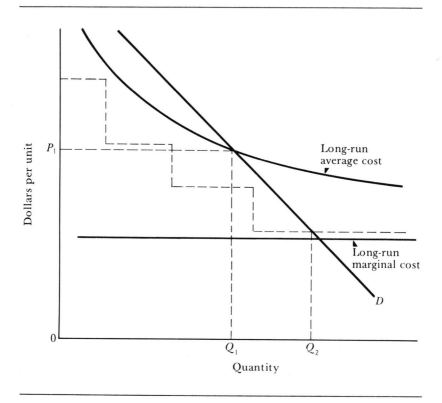

consumption much, while the price to customers with highly responsive demands would be close to marginal cost and would therefore
induce them to buy about the right amount of power. This argument
is known as the "inverse elasticity rule" — it holds that departures
from marginal-cost pricing should be inversely proportional to the
elasticity of demand.[6] In fact, most electric utilities do charge residential customers more than industrial users. The latter are more responsive to electricity rates because they have the alternatives of generating
their own electricity or moving to another part of the country. Households don't have these choices.

  An unregulated monopolist would also charge prices that exceeded
marginal cost by more the less responsive (elastic) the demand was. Does

the inverse elasticity rule wind up with the commission ordering the utilities to do just what they would do anyway? Not necessarily. The commission allows the utilities to raise their prices to customers with unresponsive demands only out to the point where total revenue just covers total cost — that is, out to the point where they have met their revenue requirement. An unregulated monopolist would raise each price above marginal cost until it was maximizing profits on its sales to each class of customer.

How Marginal-cost Pricing
Came to the Ratemakers

The discussion down to this point has been pretty much armchair economics. It is typical of the extensive literature on marginal-cost pricing that appeared in the 1930s and 1940s. Such analysis may have given some regulators some hints of what they should do or some way of rationalizing what they were doing anyway. But the economists talking about marginal-cost pricing were far removed from the actual pricing decisions of the utilities and their regulators in the United States.

That was *not* true in France, however. The French electricity industry is government-owned and is operated by an agency known as Electricité de France (EDF). In the late 1940s and early 1950s a group of economists at EDF, most notably Marcel Boiteux, set out to derive a practical pricing system for EDF wherein prices would be based on estimated marginal cost. The exercise involved measuring marginal cost, working out a method of allocating costs among peak and off-peak consumers, relating short-run to long-run marginal cost, and choosing a practical set of rates for EDF to publish. The result was the "tarif vert" — the green tariff (named for the color of its binding) — published in 1955. It applied only to customers who took electricity at high voltages, which meant mainly industrial consumers.

The British adopted marginal-cost pricing for industrial customers in the late 1950s and shifted residential customers to a form of it in the early 1960s.

In the 1970s marginal-cost pricing finally arrived in the United States. American professors had been working on it for decades by then, but it was first explicitly applied in a state rate case decided in 1974.[7] It *is* widely used in the United States today. One reason for the change was that marginal-cost pricing ordinarily emphasized current rather than original costs. With the inflation in new plant costs in the 1970s, utilities came to see the merit in that sort of pricing. In the 1950s and 1960s they were oriented toward growth, offering very low rates for customers who used a lot of energy. These promotional rates did not ordinarily fit well into marginal-cost pricing schemes. In the 1970s rapid growth was much less attractive to the utilities.

PEAK-LOAD PRICING
IN THEORY

One of the difficult issues of marginal-cost pricing is how to charge for the plant and equipment involved. In a famous article that kicked off the marginal-cost pricing debate Harold Hotelling[8] argued that use of a bridge by another car involves virtually no costs once the bridge is built, and therefore the toll should be zero. But when the bridge is used close to capacity, another car on the bridge *does* impose additional costs in the form of greater congestion. Then tolls at peak periods are appropriate. Moreover, if the congestion becomes great enough, as reflected in the peak-period tolls, more lanes or even an additional bridge would be called for.

The appropriate treatment of such capacity changes as applied to electric power was derived at EDF in the late 1940s and was expanded in the English-language journals in the 1950s and 1960s.[9]

A common assumption is that there are only two periods, perhaps day and night, and that fuel costs are the same for all plants in the system out to capacity. On these assumptions the short-run marginal-cost curves will look like a backward *L*, as in Figure 3. With existing plant the additional cost of another kilowatt-hour is just the fuel cost out to capacity, at which point marginal cost rises indefinitely with no additional output.

Figure 3 also shows peak demand (D_D for daytime demand) and off-peak demand (D_N for nighttime).

With the costs and demands shown in Figure 3, peak-load pricing would charge P_1 to the off-peak customers because the only cost to society of nighttime demand is the fuel costs. The plant is already there, and further use at night does not reduce its usefulness at other times.

Daytime customers would have to pay P_2, which is the amount that would just avoid a shortage during the peak period. Some people, especially peak-period customers, object that they are the only ones making any contribution toward the cost of the plant, such as interest, depreciation, and maintenance. The off-peak customers use the same plant. Why shouldn't they pay part of its cost?

You can see what would happen if they both paid the same price, say P_3. The daytime users would buy more power, necessitating more capacity, and nighttime users would buy less, meaning that the plant

Figure 3. Marginal-cost Pricing for Peak and Off-peak Customers

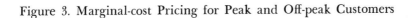

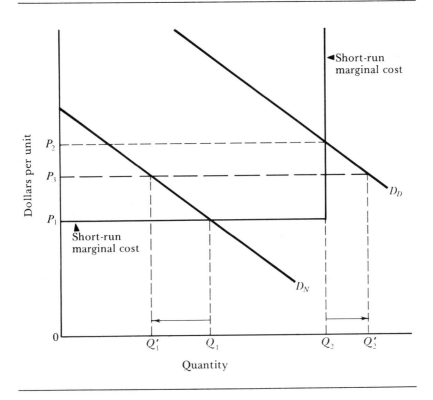

would be used even less off-peak. The load factor of the utility would clearly be lower than with full peak-load pricing. It seems clear that we would not be getting as much out of our resources with P_3 as with the P_1 off-peak and P_2 on-peak.

But the situation may be more complicated than that. Look at Figure 4. Nighttime demand is still off-peak, but if we charge night-time customers no more than P_1, *they* will become the peak consumers, and we will have to build more plant to accommodate *them*. Given existing plant, we should charge P_2 during the day and P_4 at night.

Long distance telephone charges give an example of the case shown in Figure 4. Long distance telephone has been the beneficiary of con-tinuing technical improvements, which have meant lower and lower costs over the years. For many years the FCC negotiated rate reductions

Figure 4. Increasing the Off-peak Price to Avoid Shifting the Peak

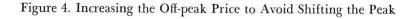

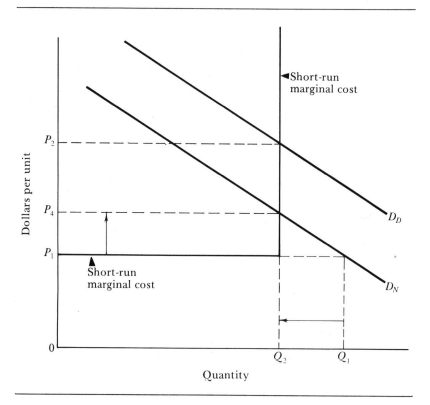

by the Bell System with the prospect of a formal rate case if Bell did not respond. In 1964 the FCC called for a rate reduction and said it ought to be off-peak. The Bell System's long lines peak period was business hours. Bell cut rates after 9 P.M. at first, bringing the cut back in several steps to after 5 P.M. It found itself unexpectedly deluged with long distance calls in the early evening. It had to put extra operators on some routes. Clearly it had shifted the peak, just as the utility in Figure 4 did when it charged night customers P_1. To deal with this situation the telephone company made a further adjustment: it still charged high rates during business hours and low rates in the middle of the night, when the main business was that of computers talking to each other, but it now charged middle-level rates from 5 to 11 P.M. Thus, after one or two false starts, Bell seems to have set rates so that it comes fairly close to using its long distance capacity fully during both business hours and evenings. These rates were *not* based explicitly on marginal costs for the various types of service, but there is no doubt that the Bell System has attained a higher load factor as a result of its new pricing system.

The Gap Between Theory and Practice

This picture is much simpler than the utilities' actual environment. For one thing, the utilities try always to have spare capacity, to avoid blackouts due to unanticipated plant outages. Customers get something for that excess capacity. When you buy an air conditioner (in the industrial states where the peak is in summer) or install electric heat (in Tennessee or Oregon where the peak is in winter) you are buying the right to use them when the weather gets really bad. If the utilities did not maintain a good deal of excess capacity most of the time, you would lose the use of your equipment just when you needed it most. Efficient pricing of electricity would require you to pay for the capacity you impose on the system by your consumption on the hottest day (or the coldest night).

In addition, the story assumes constant demands during the peak and off-peak periods. In reality there are many different periods with different levels of demand, not just two. This would be true even if the weather were completely stable. The analysis in Figures 3 and 4 can be extended conceptually to three or four or 50 or 1,000 periods, but electric meters can't handle many different periods without prohibitive cost, and consumers couldn't respond to them even if rates did differ from hour to hour and day to day. The utilities are realistically limited to a few rates — perhaps for summer, winter, spring, and fall and possibly two or three periods over the day.

In addition, differing rates per kilowatt-hour for different seasons may not serve very effectively the purpose for which they are instituted. For instance, consider your air conditioner again. The power company might set a high summer rate because summer is when its peak falls. In response to that high rate you might set the thermostat on your air conditioner up, say to 78°. As a result, you will buy less electricity during most summer days. But on the hottest day of the year your air conditioner will probably run full blast all afternoon. As a result, the utility's peak load may not fall at all, but its load factor *will* decline.

Third, in Figures 3 and 4, short-run marginal costs are assumed constant out to capacity. In fact virtually all utilities have a variety of different plants with different fuel costs. This is illustrated in Table

Table 2. Fuel Costs for the Generating Units of One Utility

Unit	Fuel costs per KWH
1	6 mills
2	8 mills
3	10 mills
4	11 mills
5	15 mills

2. The utility system has five generating units.* The lowest fuel costs per kilowatt-hour are in units 1 and 2, which are likely to be nuclear units or relatively new, large-scale coal-burning units. These are commonly referred to as "base-load plant." The utility will use them around the clock and in all seasons of the year except when they are down for scheduled maintenance during the season of least demand. Units 3 and 4 are apt to be older units that incorporate older technology. It is profitable and efficient to keep them on hand so long as their fuel cost per kilowatt-hour is less than the fuel-plus-capacity cost of new units. However, they will be used only during periods when demand exceeds base-load capacity. Finally, unit 5 might be gas turbines installed specifically to handle occasional peaks. Such peaking units are worth installing because their capital costs are much lower than those of a base-load unit. Their high fuel costs are not a serious drawback because they are run only in a few peak periods.

Figure 5 shows a schematic diagram where the five units are ranked by their fuel costs. Figure 6 shows the levels of demand during the hottest summer day in one of the northern industrial states. It is subdivided vertically into the amount of time during which the various units are running. Units 1 and 2 are run around the clock. Units 3 and 4 are in operation throughout the daylight hours including the evenings after 5 P.M. Unit 5 is run only during working hours when demand is at its peak.

This leaves us with different short-run marginal costs in different periods — 8 mills at night, 10 or 11 mills during the evenings, and 15 mills during industrial working hours. Efficient pricing would involve different energy charges as well as different capacity charges to peak and off-peak users. One more kilowatt of demand adds more to cost at midday than at midnight.

---

* A "unit" commonly consists of a fuel supply system, a burner, a boiler, and a generator. There is often more than one unit in a plant.

Figure 5. Fuel Costs for a Utility with Five Generating Units

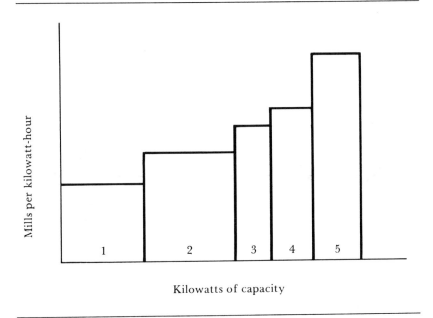

Kilowatts of capacity

There is a twist here, however. If they do succeed in filling in the nighttime "valley" in the load curve and paring the peak, the utilities will find it worthwhile to build more base-load plant and retain less peaking plant. As a result fuel costs in peak periods will be lowered, and we will use less fuel per kilowatt-hour, which is presently an American national goal.

Altogether, the pricing problems of real utilities are fairly far removed from the "solutions" in Figures 3 and 4. Some broad conclusions are useful, such that short-run marginal costs are what count off-peak and that plant costs should be allocated among customers according to their peak-period demand, but real utility managers and regulators of utilities had many unsettled issues left after they read the theoretical studies that appeared between 1949 and 1966.*

* A minor problem with Figures 3 and 4 is that they were drawn as if the peak and off-peak demands were independent of each other. In fact, they often were not. A cut in price off-peak doesn't just induce new consumption off-peak; it also leads consumers to shift their use from peak to off-peak. That is, a fall in P_N leads to a downward shift in D_D and an upward shift in D_N. For instance, when the tele-

Figure 6. Levels of Demand for a Utility with Five Generating Units.

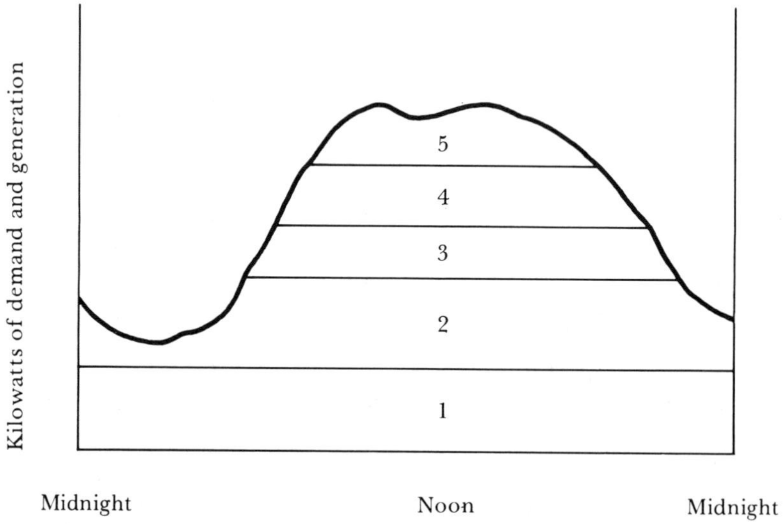

Rate Patterns under
Marginal-Cost Pricing

A practical way of pricing in peak and off-peak periods is to break down the price of service into several elements and charge for them separately. For instance, the utility might set rates as follows:

1. A fixed rate of so much per month for connecting up for electricity service. This would be set to cover meter reading and billing and for

---

phone company cut evening rates, a good deal of the increased evening business was from people who used to make their calls earlier in the day.

Taking the interperiod shifts into account would make our diagrams rather messy, but they really aren't a problem for the utilities and regulators at all. In fact, the shift of consumers away from the peaks is one of the main advantages of peak-load pricing. It means less plant and higher load factors. Moreover, if peak and off-peak prices really do reflect marginal costs of service in the two (or more) periods to which they apply, consumers will be given the right signals as to how much their consumption costs society.

the user's share of the distribution system, which must be there for him to receive any electricity at all.

2. An energy charge of so much per kilowatt-hour to cover costs that vary in proportion to output, mostly fuel. As pointed out above, the energy charge should be greater during peaks than off-peak.

3. A "demand" charge based on the maximum kilowatts of electricity used by the customer during the peak period. This would be proportional to the amount of capacity the customer required of the utility. Theoretically it would be based on the electricity purchased at the hottest moment of the hottest working day in the northern industrial states, but realistically it would be based on the customer's maximum demand during the summer (or the maximum demand that he took during the winter months in Tennessee and Oregon).

The utilities have had rates something like this for large industrial and commercial customers since early in this century. The main problem with those rates until recently was that they were based on the maximum demand of the user regardless of when it came. Actually a customer who takes a lot of power off-peak and little or none during the peak period is highly desirable. This might be true of the city street-lighting authority (whose peak is at night and comes later in summer than in winter). In recent years many utilities have shifted their "demand charges" to reflect maximum kilowatts of demand during expected peaks (e.g., during working hours of the summer). Quite a few industrial customers have changed their practices in response. For instance, many foundries now do most of their melting of metals at night during the summer.

The demand charge also solves the problem of your air conditioner. If you let it run full blast on the hottest days, you will pay a high demand charge all summer. You will therefore have an incentive to go to a movie and run your dishwasher at bedtime on really hot days. These may seem like minor adjustments for which to receive a big reward, but that's the whole point. It really doesn't take a lot to shave the peak and, therefore, to reduce the amount of capacity that the utility has to build — if the customer has the incentive to shift.

"Interruptible service" goes a step further. A customer who can be counted on not to use electricity during the peak won't have any capacity costs at all. An example might be a cold-storage plant. It can turn off the electricity completely for something like six hours without any loss. The power company can call up and tell it to do so during the few days when the peak will occur. If the peak lasts more than six hours, the interruptible-service customers can be staggered, so that the east side cold storage plant is off from 9 A.M. to 3 P.M. and the west side plant from 3 P.M. to 9 P.M. A good deal of the peak can still be avoided. For residential customers, many utilities have special low rates for off-peak water heating. They install a special meter and a switch on your water hearter that turns it off during peak hours. Again, you will continue to have hot water during the day, if you have a big enough water heater. Interruptible service has much to recommend it, but the analytical peak-load pricing literature doesn't suggest it at all.

Measuring Marginal Cost[10]

By the mid-1970s many economists and quite a lot of regulators were convinced that the electric utilities' rates should be based on marginal costs — but where do you find them? The short-run marginal costs to be charged off-peak customers are fairly straightforward, but how do you measure long-run marginal costs?* These are supposed to be the basis for peak-period prices and investment planning.

Base-load units take many years to construct, partially because they are large and complex pieces of equipment and partially because they must be approved by several agencies: the state public utility commission and EPA for all of them, the NRC for nuclear plants, and the FERC for any units that will burn gas. As a result most utilities plan new-plant expansion about ten years in advance. A typical plan is illustrated in Figure 7. Until 1985 the utility can make do with its present plant. In 1985 it brings an 800-MW unit on line. A second is planned for 1988. In 1991 it brings in a third plant, but this is partially offset by the abandonment of another smaller unit in 1990. Most old units are smaller than new ones because optimal size has risen over time. For variety, let us say that the fourth new plant is a set of gas turbines, which is installed because of anticipated growth in peak load relative to base load. It will cost less than the base-load plant to install, but it will cost more to be run.

Now consider the effect of a 100-MW *additional* load (both peak and off-peak) anticipated by 1984. What will it do to the capacity chart? Figure 8 shows its effect. The additional cost of an additional 100 MW of demand is the present value of the crosshatched areas in Figure 8 plus any additional fuel that will be used to supply the additional demand.

---

* Marginal cost is the cost of one more unit where the unit is infinitesimal — such as 1 KW of capacity or 1 KWH of output. In fact the most efficient generating units come in 800,000-KW lumps. The practical measure is "incremental costs," which would be based on the cost per additional kilowatt of capacity or kilowatt-hour of output when plant is expanded by the unit sizes actually used.

Figure 7. Planned Capacity for a Hypothetical Utility

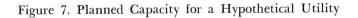

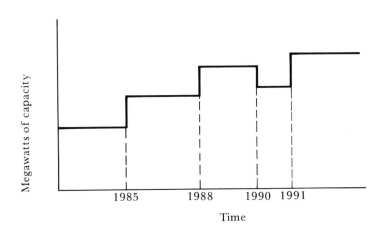

The additional cost now (1980) of the 100-MW increase in expected demand is the increase in the present value of future investments caused by building the three new units a year earlier. It is the difference between the present values of the old and new capacity plans.

The present value is calculated with the appropriate discount rate, the interest rate used in comparing present and future dollars. But what is the appropriate discount rate? Economists say it is the opportunity cost of capital — what the money invested in the new units could earn in its best alternative use. This is what society gives up in other investments by building the three additional units a year earlier.[11]

WHAT THE COMMISSIONS DID

The first state case to base rates explicitly on estimated marginal cost was the Madison Gas and Electric case before the Wisconsin Public Service Commission, decided in 1974.* The result of that decision was

* There had been peak-load rates before that, but they were based largely on ad hoc criteria with no reference to marginal costs. For instance, this was true of the long distance telephone rates adopted in the late 1960s.

Figure 8. Changes in Planned Capacity of a Utility Based on a 100-MW
Increase in Anticipated Demand

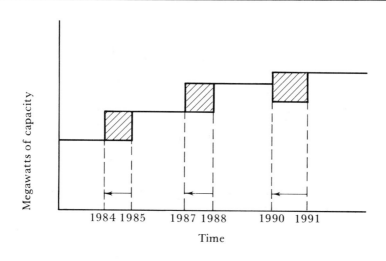

summer-winter level differences, the elimination of declining block
rates during the summer, and a call for marginal-cost-based rates
throughout Wisconsin. Over the next several years all Wisconsin utilities were ordered to base their demand charges for industrial and large
commercial users on maximum power used during daytime summer
periods rather than during the users' own peaks. This was relatively
easy to do, because those customers already had meters that recorded
their use by time of day.

In addition the declining block character of most rates — industrial, commercial, and residential — was eliminated to remove the incentive for customers to increase their loads. The Wisconsin utilities
were still in size classes where long-run average generating costs decline
with greater scale, but it was possible to eliminate discriminatory rates
without imposing financial losses on the utilities. This was because
marginal costs were forward-looking (using either current or future
plant costs), while the utilities' revenue requirements were based on
the historical cost of their plant.

By the late 1970s many of the state commissions had made some
movement toward marginal-cost pricing. Table 3 tabulates several related steps taken by the various states by October 1977. California, New
York, and Wisconsin had gone farthest toward explicit use of marginal-

cost pricing, but most states had moved some way in that direction. All but nine had made the easiest change, installing seasonal rate differences, and some that did not may not have strong seasonal peaks (e.g., Hawaii). About half (24) had required different rates at different times of day for large industrial and commercial users. Twenty-three state commissions reported that they were encouraging flat rates (elimination of decreasing block rates), and 29 actually had *some* flat rates. The last had existed for years for certain services such as street lighting.

In 1978 the federal government joined the marginal-cost pricing movement as a result of the Public Utility Regulatory Policy Act. It required that the state commissions hold hearings on rate levels and rate differences covering ten considerations related to marginal-cost pricing. The commissions could reject all or some of the "considerations," but their decisions must be based on evidence in the hearings and can be appealed by the utilities and by consumer groups.*

An attempt was made to update Table 3 in a mail survey in the spring of 1980. Only 34 usable responses were received, so only a few impressions seem appropriate. By early 1980 at least eight states were explicitly using some sort of marginal-cost or incremental-cost concepts in setting rates. These are Arizona, California, Michigan, New York, Ohio, Oregon, Vermont, and Wisconsin. In estimating incremental costs, all of these states use present or future costs to estimate the investments in plant and equipment. Most state commissions have seasonal rates for both industrial and residential customers, but some of these go back many years. A majority of states have time-of-day rates for industrial customers, and Arkansas, Michigan, Ohio, Oregon, Pennsylvania, Texas, and Wisconsin base industrial-demand charges on demand at system peak rather than at customer peak. Seventeen states have some residential time-of-day rates but most of these were experimental or optional. Some of the experiments have used sophisticated statistical techniques. The findings to date are that consumers do respond to seasonal and time-of-day rate differences, but it still is not clear that the gains are worth the cost of the more elaborate metering required.

What did all this activity accomplish? In Wisconsin, where it all started, the load factor rose steadily from 1973 to 1979, and the rate of growth in peak demand fell from 10 percent in 1972 to 6 percent per year in 1979. This last cannot be attributed entirely to marginal-cost pricing. The price of electricity was rising sharply in those years, and that should have had a negative effect on total consumption regardless of where it occurred.

---

* It also *requires* that the commissions establish "life line rates" — low rates for customers that use little electricity or for the poor. These rates have been set up as *increasing* block rates: the price *rises* as you consume more.

Table 3. Policies of State Commissions Surveyed in October 1977

State	Some Flat Rates Approved	Commission Encourages Flat Rates	Some Time-of-Day Rates in Force	Some Seasonal Rates in Force	Required Method for Measuring Time-of-Day and Seasonal Cost Differences Based on Marginal or Incremental Cost	Utilities Measure Marginal Cost by Class of Customer
Alabama	X	X		X	X	X
Alaska	X					
Arizona				X		X
Arkansas	X	X	X	X		X
California	X	X	X	X	X	X
Colorado				X		
Connecticut	X	X	X	X		
Delaware				X		
D.C.				X		
Florida	X	X	X	X		
Georgia		X	X	X		
Hawaii						X
Idaho	X			X		
Illinois	X	X	X	X		X
Indiana			X	X		X
Iowa	X	X		X		
Kansas	X			X		
Kentucky				X		X
Louisiana				X		

State						
Maine		X				
Maryland			X		X	
Massachusetts			X		X	
Michigan	X	X	X		X	
Minnesota	X	X			X	
Mississippi				X	X	
Missouri					X	
Montana	X	X	X		X	
Nevada	X	X	X		X	X
New Hampshire					X	
New Jersey	X	X	X		X	
New Mexico	X	X	X		X	
New York	X	X	X		X	X X
North Carolina	X		X	X	X	
North Dakota	X	X	X		X	
Ohio	X				X	
Oklahoma					X	
Oregon	X	X	X		X	X
Pennsylvania			X		X	
Rhode Island			X			
South Carolina	X				X	
Tennessee	X	X	X		X	
Texas	X					
Utah	X					
Vermont	X	X	X		X	
Virginia			X		X	X
Washington	X	X	X			
West Virginia	X	X	X		X	
Wisconsin	X	X	X		X	X
Wyoming	X		X		X	

Source: I. W. Stelzer, *Rate Structure Revision—A Federal or State Problem?* National Economic Research Associates, processed November 16, 1977.

Conclusions on
Marginal-cost Pricing

A purist might doubt that many of the new rates set up in the late 1970s were really based on correctly measured marginal costs. But a good deal has been accomplished even with dubious "marginal costs."

Most states have adopted peak-load pricing, at least on a seasonal basis. Quite a lot of decreasing block rates have been flattened, and some have been shifted to completely flat rates. And eight states (including the two largest) have based rates explicitly on forward-looking marginal cost. Since this basis involves estimated future plant construction valued at present or future costs, rather than undervalued historical costs, consumers are getting more realistic signals about what their consumption costs society.

These changes have almost certainly brought America a more efficient electric system. The revolution is still underway, but the progress to date has been impressive.

NOTES

[1] Before World War II all commissions were required to use it by the Supreme Court. In the original decision (*Smyth* v. *Ames,* 169 U.S. 466, 1898) they were also required to give "such weight as may be just and right" to the market value of the utility's securities. This was circular reasoning. A high valuation of a utility's rate base would yield high profits and, therefore, a high price for the firm's stock. Similarly a low value would yield low profits and a low stock price. Fortunately, this illogical phrase was ignored in subsequent decisions.

[2] FPC, *Federal and State Commission Jurisdiction & Regulation of Electricity, Gas and Telephone Utilities,* 1973, pp. 24–25.

[3] I. W. Stelzer, *Rate Structure Revision — A Federal or State Problem?* National Economic Research Associates, processed November 16, 1977.

[4] H. Averch and L. L. Johnson, "Behavior of Firms under Regulatory Constraint," *American Economic Review,* 52 (December 1962), 1052–1069.

[5] G. Stigler and C. Friedland, "What Can Regulators Regulate? The Case of Electricity," *Journal of Law and Economics,* 5 (October 1962), 1–16.

[6] W. Baumol and D. Bradford, "Optimal Departures from Marginal Cost Pricing," *American Economic Review,* 60 (June 1970), 265–283.

[7] Application of Madison Gas and Electric Company for Authority to Increase Electric and Gas Rates, by the Wisconsin Public Service Commission, 1974.

[8] H. Hotelling, "The General Welfare in Relation to Problems of Taxation and of Railroad and Utility Rates," *Econometrica,* VI (1938), 242–269.

⁹ The French Solution was by Marcel Boiteux, "La tarification des demandes en pointe: applications de la Théorie de la vente en cout marginal," *Revue Générale de l'Electricité*, 58:8 (August 1949), 321–340, translated as "Peak Load Pricing" in J. R. Nelson, *Marginal Cost Pricing in Practice* (Englewood Cliffs, N.J.: Prentice-Hall, 1964), pp. 59–89. It was developed further in France and in the English-language journals in the 1950s, most notably by H. Houthakker, "Electricity Tariffs in Theory and Practice," *Economic Journal*, March 1951, pp. 1–25, P. O. Steiner, "Peak Loads and Efficient Pricing," *Quarterly Journal of Economics*, November 1957, pp. 585–610, and O. Williamson, "Peak Load Pricing and Optimal Capacity," *American Economic Review*, September 1966, pp. 810–827.

¹⁰ This section depends primarily on R. Turvey, *Optimal Pricing and Investment in Electricity Supply* (Cambridge, Mass.: The MIT Press, 1968), and C. Cicchetti, W. Gillen, and P. Smolensky, *The Cost and Pricing of Electricity* (Cambridge, Mass.: Ballinger Publishing Co., 1977).

¹¹ This point was originally made by Marcel Boiteux in a 1960 article translated as "Electric Energy: Facts, Problems, and Prospects" in Nelson, *Marginal Cost Pricing in Practice*, pp. 7–8. The same point was developed in the English-language journals by W. Baumol.

Index